COBOL II

Other McGraw-Hill Reference Books of Interest

For more information about other McGraw-Hill materials, call 1-800-2-MCGRAW in the United States. In other countries, call your nearest McGraw-Hill office.

COBOL II

Harvey Bookman
President
Bookman Consulting, Inc.

McGraw-Hill Publishing Company

New York   St. Louis   San Francisco   Auckland   Bogotá
Caracas   Hamburg   Lisbon   London   Madrid   Mexico
Milan   Montreal   New Delhi   Oklahoma City
Paris   San Juan   São Paulo   Singapore
Sydney   Tokyo   Toronto

Library of Congress Cataloging-in-Publication Data

Bookman, Harvey
  COBOL II/Harvey Bookman

  p.   cm. — (Ranade IBM series)
  ISBN 0-07-006533-0
  1. COBOL II (Computer program language) 2. Business—Data
processing. I. Title. II. Title: COBOL two. III. Title:
COBOL 2. IV. Series: J. Ranade IBM series.
QA76.73.C252B66   1990
650'.028'55133—dc20

90-5406
CIP

   2 3 4 5 6 7 8 9 0   DOC/DOC 9 8 7 6 5 4 3 2 1 0

ISBN 0-07-006533-0

The sponsoring editor for this book was Theron Shreve, the editing
supervisor was Jim Halston, the designer was Naomi Auerbach, and
the production supervisor was Dianne Walber. It was set in Century
Schoolbook by the McGraw-Hill Publishing Company Professional &
Reference Division composition unit.

Printed and bound by R. R. Donnelley and Sons.

For information about our audio products, write us at:
Newbridge Book Clubs, 3000 Cindel Drive, Delran, NJ   08370

For more information about other McGraw-Hill materials,
call 1-800-2-MCGRAW in the United States. In other
countries, call your nearest McGraw-Hill office.

To my father, Milton, and the memory of my loving mother, Esther

Contents

Part 3   Programming Techniques   153

Preface

During the last 15 years I have seen articles stating that COBOL will become a dead language. What did these writers expect companies to do with the billions of lines of COBOL code that exist? Did they expect companies to retrain the hundreds of thousands of programmers who were using COBOL? With IBM's introduction of COBOL II in 1984, and the inclusion of COBOL as a supported language of Systems Application Architecture (SAA), it seems clear that COBOL is here to stay. Companies are spending tremendous amounts of money to convert their programs to this new standard. Eased program maintenance and features that take advantage of the most modern coding and hardware technology are the minimums expected from this new COBOL.

In recent years the emphasis has moved away from the highly technical aspects of programming toward fourth-generation languages. Within COBOL, emphasis has been placed upon coding structure. I think that a mass disservice has been done to the industry. Programmers now are motivated to learn programming style rather than the knowledge and techniques that would enable them to program and debug programs intelligently and quickly. Many think that a program with excellent style is better than a technically well-written program, and that it is an either/or situation—a program may be stylistically or technically excellent, but not both. Technically precise programs that have good style can certainly exist. Remember that style is of no value unless there is substance behind it. Once the technical aspects of a language are learned, one is ready to begin developing a style. To attempt to develop a style before would be premature.

I know a company that asks programmers applying for a job to rate the following aspects of a program from most to least important: program structure, ease of maintenance, efficiency of the program, and whether the program runs properly (produces the proper results). You would be surprised at the number of people who did not choose "producing the proper results" as the most important aspect. I wonder how many of those people would have bought a car that was well built, easy to fix, would use gas as efficiently as any other car, but did not run?

What Is COBOL II?

COBOL II is IBM's newest COBOL compiler that runs on IBM mainframes. It is based upon the VS COBOL programming language that has been used for years. It provides virtual storage constraint relief by allowing COBOL II programs, program data, the COBOL II compiler, and COBOL II library routines to run both above and below the 16-megabyte line. It also has a number of new features which make it easier to structure code and easier to perform certain functions that in the past were difficult to implement.

However, COBOL II is so different that a VS COBOL program frequently has to be converted to use it. At the end of 1988, COBOL II was enhanced with its third release. Normally, a new compiler release has many new features but does not drastically change the functionality of existing code. Release 3 has such extensive changes that it should have more correctly been called COBOL III. It requires as much time for a COBOL II Release 2 programmer to learn Release 3 as it would for a VS COBOL programmer to learn COBOL II Release 2. Release 3 has many new features and it changes the way some statements execute. Among the many changes, the new compiler allows more than one PROCEDURE DIVISION and table entries with seven levels of subscripts or indexes. The code in some COBOL II Release 3 programs may seem quite strange to a VS COBOL programmer. The program in Fig. P.1 is one example. It updates a counter corresponding to the state in which a person lives and separates a person's last name from the entire name.

Programmers now have plenty of COBOL options to deal with. The *COBOL II Application Programming Guide* for Releases 1 and 2 explained and charted the differences between VS COBOL and CO-BOL II. This eased conversions and helped programmers quickly find the new features. Beginning with Release 3, these charts were eliminated from this manual. So many changes were made between Release 2 and Release 3 that IBM now needed pages of charts to show the differences between the COBOL II releases themselves. (The charts of differences between VS COBOL and COBOL II Release 3 exist in the *IBM OS/VS COBOL to VS COBOL II Migration Guide*.)

While it is not mandatory to update a Release 2 program to run under Release 3, the Release 3 changes are extensive enough that it could lead to problems if these programs are not updated. For example,

```
000010 IDENTIFICATION DIVISION.
000020 PROGRAM-ID. PROGRAM1.
000030 DATA DIVISION.
000040 WORKING-STORAGE SECTION.
000050 01  HOLD-DATABASE              PIC X(15000000) EXTERNAL.
000060 01  FULL-NAME                  PIC X(40) GLOBAL EXTERNAL.
000070 01  LAST-NAME                  PIC X(20) GLOBAL.
000080 01  LAST-NAME-BEGIN            PIC S9(3) COMP-3 GLOBAL.
000090 01  LAST-NAME-LEN              PIC S9(3) COMP-3 GLOBAL.
000100 01  SUB1                       PIC S9(4) BINARY GLOBAL.
000110 01  HOME-STATE                 PIC XX GLOBAL EXTERNAL.
000120 01  STATE-TABLE EXTERNAL GLOBAL.
000130     05  STATE-ENTRY OCCURS 50 TIMES.
000140         10                     PIC X(5).
000150         10  STATE-ABBREV       PIC XX.
000160         10  STATE-COUNT        PIC S9(9) PACKED-DECIMAL.
000170
000180 PROCEDURE DIVISION.
000190     INITIALIZE STATE-TABLE REPLACING NUMERIC DATA BY ZERO.
000200     ...
000210     CALL 'PROGRAM2'.
000220     ...
000230     STOP RUN.
000240
000250 identification division.
000260 Program-id. Program2.
000270 Procedure division.
000280     Perform
000290         with test after
000300         varying sub1 from +1 by +1
000310         until sub1 >= 50
000320             Evaluate true
000330                 when state-abbrev (sub1) = home-state
000340                     add 1 to state-count (sub1)
000350                 when other
000360                     continue
000370             End-evaluate
000380     End-perform.
000390     Call 'program3' using by content length of state-table.
000400     Move full-name (last-name-begin:last-name-len)
000410                                    to last-name.
000420 End program program2.
000430 END PROGRAM PROGRAM1.
```

Figure P.1 Sample COBOL II code that might look unfamiliar to a VS CO-
BOL programmer.

a compiler option is required to ensure that a Release 2 program will function without modification under Release 3. A programmer may forget to use this option when a change is made to a program and the program may function improperly. Additionally, a programmer may want to use new Release features when maintaining a program but will not be able to because they are not supported under Release 2 compatibility. This book will explain the changes to Release 3 in detail so that you will be able to update your Release 2 programs.

Who This Book Is For

If you have never programmed a computer, this book is not for you. It is not intended to be an introduction to COBOL. It has the following audiences:

- Programmers who have used VS COBOL and would now like to learn COBOL II
- Programmers who have learned the basics of COBOL II and would now like to learn more about it
- Programmers who have learned COBOL II Release 2 and will eventually be using Release 3

It may be the single most useful tool for a VS COBOL programmer who has to convert a number of VS COBOL programs to COBOL II or for a COBOL II Release 2 programmer who has to upgrade programs to run under Release 3.

The Purpose of This Book

The purpose of this book is to teach enough of the important aspects of COBOL II so that programmers will be able to understand the implications of their code. This will lead to programmers with more understanding, which in turn will lead to more valuable employees. There is a great amount of pressure on programmers to produce. Unfortunately many programmers feel much more pressure than need be because of their lack of basic knowledge. The code produced by those lacking knowledge leaves subsequent programmers with the task of fixing both the major and subtle problems created by their predecessors, as well as the problems they create themselves.

What This Book Is Not

This book is not meant to replace IBM manuals. It will only deal with syntax when the syntax is specific to COBOL II or when it is different in COBOL II (as compared to VS COBOL). This should not imply to the reader that syntax is not important. Syntax is critical to writing a program. However, syntax becomes second nature through experience, not through reading.

This book will not discuss structured code or flow charts. It may seem bizarre since COBOL II is billed as the "structured" COBOL. However, I see no need for programmers to learn structure when they do not understand what they are structuring. This book will describe how, where, and why certain code should be used in a COBOL II program. It will not attempt to cover all aspects of the language but will explain the important aspects and idiosyncrasies that are often missed by even many experienced programmers. It will give VS COBOL programmers enough knowledge to program in COBOL II, explain the Release 3 differences to programmers who have used Release 2, and most of all give programmers enough understanding of the language to code faster and more efficiently, debug better, and better understand the COBOL II reference manuals.

Operating System Environment

This book has been written primarily for COBOL programmers in the MVS/XA, MVS/ESA, or MVS/SP environments using either batch processing or TSO. It is equally applicable to CMS users running under VM/SP or VM/XA.

CICS/VS and IMS/VS programmers using COBOL II will particularly benefit from the explanation of the differences required to program in COBOL II.

What Is Included

This book will discuss COBOL II updates, including those of Release 3, so that a programmer can migrate existing VS COBOL and Release 2 programs and code new programs in COBOL II. Unless otherwise noted, all discussions will be about Release 3 of COBOL II, which is the version that most companies will eventually be using. For instance, the listings shown in the book are primarily from Release 3. Changes that are mainly pertinent to CICS, IMS, and CMS will be discussed in Chap. 6, "COBOL II in Special Environments," rather than in other chapters of this book.

Rather than just explaining the differences, the book will give guidelines and recommendations on when and where to use the various COBOL verbs. After reading most reference manuals or books, a programmer is often left confused as to which statements to use. A manual with an alphabetical listing of the statements and their uses is not in the same category as a book containing explanations and comparisons of various programming techniques. This book will attempt to educate COBOL programmers about the depths of the language.

Summary

After finishing this book it is hoped that the realization will dawn that there is much more to COBOL than is generally acknowledged. The information presented should enable programmers to understand the rationale for the COBOL II commands and the functioning of the COBOL II compiler's idiosyncrasies.

Reference Manuals

COBOL II programmers should have the appropriate IBM COBOL II reference manuals available.

VS COBOL II General Information

VS COBOL II Application Programming: Language Reference

VS COBOL II Application Programming Guide

VS COBOL II Application Programming: Debugging

VS COBOL II Application Programming: Supplement for CMS Users

IBM OS/VS COBOL to COBOL II Migration Guide

Acknowledgments

I would like to especially thank Kathleen Gallagher for her preliminary editing, comments, thought provoking criticisms, and asides. Making me laugh may not have been essential for grammatical corrections, but it did help me make the book a reality. I would also like to thank Alan Friend, a Senior Data Processing Consultant with New York Life Insurance Company. His role as coordinator for COBOL and COBOL-related training for his company, and his work on COBOL II systems, enabled him to spot inconsistencies in the text and suggest clarifications of technical points.

Michael Horowitz did an extremely thorough job with the final technical editing. Despite some disagreements, his invaluable insights and opinions enabled me to clarify many topics. My sincerest thanks to the people working with McGraw-Hill: Jay Ranade, Gerry Fahey, Nancy Young, Theron Shreve, Kay Magome, and especially Jim Halston for his efforts above and beyond the call of duty.

Harvey Bookman

COBOL II Release 2

Release 1 of COBOL II was not really a language that IBM expected to be used. It was IBM's method to announce a new compiler and to get reactions from customers. Reaction was quick and strong. Its new features were applauded but the elimination of a number of features that exist in VS COBOL made company management cringe. Management knew that some day their companies would probably be converting all of their VS COBOL programs and the eliminated features would make the conversion more difficult than need be.

COBOL II Release 2 was an attempt to placate customers by returning a number of features. These features would make VS COBOL conversions much more straightforward, and they allowed COBOL II programmers more flexibility in coding. Chapter 1 discusses those elements of VS COBOL that were still eliminated in Release 2. Those elements of VS COBOL that were reinstated in Release 3 are also mentioned within Chap.1.

Chapter 2 discusses those features of Release 2 that have been updated from VS COBOL and Chap.3, those new features that have been added. Changes to the compiler options and listings are extensive and are treated separately in Chaps. 4 and 5. Chapter 6 discusses the differences from VS COBOL programming when using COBOL II programs under CICS, IMS, and CMS.

Even if you are presently coding in Release 2, do not assume that you understand COBOL II after you finish Part 1. The changes in COBOL II Release 3 are vast and affect Release 2 programs. All COBOL programmers should be aware of the Release 3 features so that their programs may be run, with minimal changes, under Release 3. Release 3 will be the standard that future releases of the COBOL II compiler will be based on.

Release 2—VS COBOL Features Eliminated and Conversions

1.1 COBOL II RELEASES

1.1.1 Release 1

When Release 1 of COBOL II was issued by IBM in 1984, many features of VS COBOL had been eliminated from the compiler. These features included READY TRACE, EXHIBIT, EXAMINE, CURRENT-DATE, TRANSFORM, ON, REMARKS, the Report Writer, exponentiation, floating-point data, complex OCCURS DEPENDING ON data items (e.g., a data item that contains the OCCURS DEPENDING ON clause and is subordinate to another data item containing the clause), the TALLY special register, and the APPLY WRITE-ONLY option. IBM's customers did not take this lightly. Converting billions of lines of code was going to cost corporations vast amounts of time and money, and IBM was asked to help make the conversions as easy as possible.

Many features eliminated in Release 1 have remained permanently eliminated. However, its new features, such as statements to more easily structure code, and options to let programs run above the 16-megabyte line in MVS/XA, allowed COBOL to take advantage of the most modern coding and hardware technology. Release 1 was the beginning of the new standard in IBM COBOL.

1.1.2 Release 2

Release 2 was made available in 1986. IBM did reinstate exponentiation, floating-point data, complex OCCURS DEPENDING ON data items, and the APPLY WRITE-ONLY option. IBM termed the reinstatement of these features "enhancements" in Release 2. They were described as "functions identified by early users as key inhibitors to conversion of applications from OS/VS COBOL to VS COBOL II." A number of other features were added to Release 2, such as a full-screen interactive debugger that functions under ISPF. However, users saw that many features were not reinstated and that these features were permanently eliminated from COBOL II.

Release 2 supports the 1974 American National Standard Programming Language (ANSI) COBOL standard except for the Report Writer, Communications Feature, and level 2 of the debug module. It also includes some of the ANSI 1985 features (e.g., EVALUATE, INITIALIZE, and the in-line PERFORM).

1.1.3   Release 3

Release 3, available at the end of 1988, was to Release 2 what COBOL II Release 2 was to VS COBOL. It had a tremendous amount of updated and new features; multiple PROCEDURE DIVISIONs could be coded in the same program, seven levels of subscripts and indexes could be used, and files and data could be EXTERNALly shared among many programs. Although IBM continued to assist in aiding the conversion of VS COBOL programs to COBOL II with the features in Release 3 [such as the NUMPROC(MIG) option which performs arithmetic of decimal fields under COBOL II in the same manner as it was done in VS COBOL, and the CONVERTING clause of the INSPECT statement to perform the function of the VS COBOL TRANSFORM], it added a number of new features that are incompatible with both VS COBOL and COBOL II Release 2 (lowercase letters now make the IF ALPHABETIC test true and a size error in an intermediate field of a MULTIPLY or DIVIDE will no longer activate an ON SIZE ERROR).

Release 3 incorporated many other changes to support the 1985 ANSI COBOL standard. Release 3 also supports Systems Application Architecture (SAA). SAA is a framework for developing applications that are portable between various IBM environments. The COBOL statements allowed in SAA are a subset of the Release 3 statements.

1.1.3.1   Release 3.1

At the beginning of 1990 COBOL II Release 3.1 became available. It removes restrictions from programs run in the VM environment, allowing programs running under VM/SP 6 to support those COBOL II functions that were only available when running under MVS.

1.2 FEATURES COMPLETELY ELIMINATED

The Indexed Sequential Access Method (ISAM) and Basic Direct Access Method (BDAM) cannot be used under COBOL II. The clauses specific to these access methods are therefore no longer allowed. The ACTUAL KEY, NOMINAL KEY, TRACK-AREA, TRACK-LIMIT, APPLY CORE-INDEX, APPLY REORG-CRITERIA, APPLY KEY, APPLY RECORD-OVERFLOW, and SEEK clauses have been eliminated from COBOL II. Programs using ISAM files should be converted to programs using KSDS VSAM files; programs using BDAM files should be converted to programs using RRDS VSAM files.

The entire Report Writer feature has been removed. It was an IBM extension to the compiler that never really gained popularity. While not commonly used, its removal does present a problem for converting those programs that do use the feature. (There are products such as the IBM Report Writer Precompiler Program to aid in the conversion.) Eliminated in the DATA DIVISION is the REPORT SECTION. Coded here was the RD entry including its PAGE, CONTROL, and CODE clauses, as well as the TYPE, LINE, NEXT GROUP, COLUMN, SOURCE, and SUM clauses. The REPORT clause in the FD can no longer be coded. The PROCEDURE DIVISION no longer allows INITIATE, GENERATE, and TERMINATE. Additionally, programs can no longer use the PAGE-COUNTER, LINE-COUNTER, and PRINT-SWITCH special registers. The LINE-COUNTER special register should not be confused with the LINAGE-COUNTER special register that existed in VS COBOL and still exists in COBOL II. LINAGE-COUNTER keeps track of the line number on the present page being output and is generated for each FD that has a LINAGE clause.

The communications feature, which was rarely used, does not exist in COBOL II. In VS COBOL it allowed the RECEIVE, SEND, DISABLE, ENABLE, and ACCEPT statements and a COMMUNICATION SECTION.

1.3 SEARCH ALL STATEMENT SYNTAX

The SEARCH ALL statement still exists in all releases of COBOL II, but its WHEN clause has added restrictions. For example, if a table contains a key named KEY-DAY-NUMBER and you wanted to code a SEARCH ALL statement to check if KEY-DAY-NUMBER was equal to WORKING-STORAGE field DAY-NUMBER, VS COBOL allowed either WHEN KEY-DAY-NUMBER (DAY-INDEX) IS EQUAL TO DAY-NUMBER or WHEN DAY-NUMBER IS EQUAL TO KEY-DAY-NUMBER (DAY-INDEX) (see Fig. 1.1). COBOL II only allows

```
000010 DATA DIVISION.
000020 WORKING-STORAGE SECTION.
000030 77   DAY-NUMBER              PIC 99.
000040 77   DAY-NAME               PIC X(9).
000050 01   DAY-TABLE.
000060      05   FILLER             PIC X(11) VALUE '01SUNDAY    '.
000070      05   FILLER             PIC X(11) VALUE '02MONDAY    '.
000080      05   FILLER             PIC X(11) VALUE '03TUESDAY   '.
000090      05   FILLER             PIC X(11) VALUE '04WEDNESDAY'.
000100      05   FILLER             PIC X(11) VALUE '05THURSDAY '.
000110      05   FILLER             PIC X(11) VALUE '06FRIDAY    '.
000120      05   FILLER             PIC X(11) VALUE '07SATURDAY '.
000130 01   FILLER REDEFINES DAY-TABLE.
000140      05   DAY-ENTRY OCCURS 7 TIMES
000150           ASCENDING KEY IS KEY-DAY-NUMBER
000160           INDEXED BY DAY-INDEX.
000170           10   KEY-DAY-NUMBER  PIC 99.
000180           10   TAB-DAY-NAME    PIC X(9).
000190
000200 PROCEDURE DIVISION.
000210      ...
000220      SEARCH ALL DAY-ENTRY
000230          WHEN DAY-NUMBER = KEY-DAY-NUMBER (DAY-INDEX)
000240              MOVE TAB-DAY-NAME (DAY-INDEX) TO DAY-NAME.
```

(a)

```
000010 DATA DIVISION.
000020 WORKING-STORAGE SECTION.
000030 77   DAY-NUMBER              PIC 99.
000040 77   DAY-NAME               PIC X(9).
000050 01   DAY-TABLE.
000060      05   FILLER             PIC X(11) VALUE '01SUNDAY    '.
000070      05   FILLER             PIC X(11) VALUE '02MONDAY    '.
000080      05   FILLER             PIC X(11) VALUE '03TUESDAY   '.
000090      05   FILLER             PIC X(11) VALUE '04WEDNESDAY'.
000100      05   FILLER             PIC X(11) VALUE '05THURSDAY '.
000110      05   FILLER             PIC X(11) VALUE '06FRIDAY    '.
000120      05   FILLER             PIC X(11) VALUE '07SATURDAY '.
000130 01   FILLER REDEFINES DAY-TABLE.
000140      05   DAY-ENTRY OCCURS 7 TIMES
000150           ASCENDING KEY IS KEY-DAY-NUMBER
000160           INDEXED BY DAY-INDEX.
000170           10   KEY-DAY-NUMBER  PIC 99.
000180           10   TAB-DAY-NAME    PIC X(9).
000190
000200 PROCEDURE DIVISION.
000210      ...
000220      SEARCH ALL DAY-ENTRY
000230          WHEN KEY-DAY-NUMBER (DAY-INDEX) = DAY-NUMBER
000240              MOVE TAB-DAY-NAME (DAY-INDEX) TO DAY-NAME.
```

(b)

Figure 1.1 Syntax of the WHEN clause of the SEARCH ALL statement in VS COBOL and COBOL II. (*a*) Code only allowed in VS
COBOL; (*b*) Code allowed in VS COBOL or COBOL II.

the first clause. The restriction is that the first field named in a WHEN condition must be a key field and the field being compared to must be a nonkey field. VS COBOL programs containing SEARCH ALL statements in which the key appears last in the WHEN clause get a severe error message and a return code of 12 when compiled under COBOL II.

The restriction in coding the WHEN clause of a binary search (SEARCH ALL) does not apply to the WHEN clause coded in a serial search (SEARCH).

1.4 READY TRACE

The READY TRACE and RESET TRACE statements were used in VS COBOL to set the trace facility on and off. The trace was produced as the program executed and listed, in the sequence executed, the name of each paragraph entered. READY TRACE and RESET TRACE do not produce a trace in COBOL II and serve no function. However, if coded in a COBOL II program, they do not cause severe compilation errors; they only produce warning messages. There are three ways to obtain a similar trace under COBOL II: (1) by using features of the improved COBOL II debugging tool (COBTEST), (2) by using a non-IBM debugger, and (3) by using the debugging facilities of the COBOL II compiler. The advantage of READY TRACE over the COBOL II methods of producing a trace is its simplicity. A programmer did not have to learn anything about COBTEST or the COBOL II debugging facilities to use READY TRACE. The trace was activated simply by putting a READY TRACE statement into the program and by ensuring that a SYSOUT DD statement appeared in the JCL.

COBTEST commands used to perform a trace will be discussed in Sec. 4.7.3. COBTEST consists of a batch and an interactive debugger. To use the COBTEST facilities, you must compile your program with the TEST option. You must then add additional statements to your run-time JCL and run your program under the debugger. One disadvantage of putting the capability of READY TRACE into the COBOL II debugger is that the IBM COBOL II debugger is a feature of the compiler that not all companies buy. Companies that use a non-IBM replacement product in place of the debugger no longer have access to a trace facility unless the replacement debugging product has one of its own. Programmers using a non-IBM debugger will have to spend additional time learning the specific debugging product used within each company they work for.

There is a way to perform the function of READY TRACE and RESET TRACE in COBOL II without using the COBOL II debugger. It involves using the debugging facilities of the COBOL II compiler, which also existed in VS COBOL. These facilities have nothing to do with the TEST compiler option or the COBTEST debug tool. The USE FOR DEBUGGING ON ALL PROCEDURES declarative is coded and the DEBUG-NAME (a field in the DEBUG-ITEM special register) is DISPLAYed (see Fig. 1.2). You would then specify DEBUG as a runtime parameter when you wish to use the trace. A 'Y' is moved to TRACE-SWITCH at the point in the program where the trace is to be activated (equivalent to READY TRACE) and an 'N' is moved to TRACE-SWITCH at the point where it is to be deactivated (equivalent to RESET TRACE). In Fig. 1.2, PARAGRAPH-1 through PARAGRAPH-20 will be traced but not PARAGRAPH-21. I do not recommend use of this method since the debugging features of the compiler are considered obsolete and will be removed from the next revision of the ANSI standard (see Sec. 7.20). It seems more prudent to learn to use COBTEST.

1.5 ON STATEMENT

The ON statement is no longer supported under COBOL II. Although it had more complex uses than the one shown in the example in Fig. 1.3, it was mainly used in place of a switch for first-time processing.

```
000010 ENVIRONMENT DIVISION.
000020 CONFIGURATION SECTION.
000030 SOURCE COMPUTER. IBM-370 WITH DEBUGGING MODE.
000040 DATA DIVISION.
000050 WORKING-STORAGE SECTION.
000060 01   TRACE-SWITCH            PIC X VALUE 'Y'.
000070
000080 PROCEDURE DIVISION.
000090 DECLARATIVES.
000100 TRACE-DEBUG SECTION.
000110     USE FOR DEBUGGING ON ALL PROCEDURES.
000120 TRACE-CHECK.
000130     IF TRACE-SWITCH IS EQUAL TO 'Y'
000140         DISPLAY DEBUG-NAME.
000150 END DECLARATIVES.
000160 MAIN-PROGRAM SECTION.
000170     MOVE 'Y' TO TRACE-SWITCH.
000180 PARAGRAPH-1.
000190     ...
000200 PARAGRAPH-20.
000210     MOVE 'N' TO TRACE-SWITCH.
000220 PARAGRAPH-21.
```

Figure 1.2 Use of the COBOL II compiler debugging feature to perform the equivalent function of the VS COBOL READY TRACE and RESET TRACE.

```
000010 DATA DIVISION.
000020 WORKING-STORAGE SECTION.
000030 PROCEDURE DIVISION.
000040     ON 1 PERFORM FIRST-TIME-PROCESSING.
000050     ...
000060 FIRST-TIME-PROCESSING.
```

(a)

```
000010 DATA DIVISION.
000020 WORKING-STORAGE SECTION.
000030 01   EACH-TIME-SW          PIC X VALUE '1'.
000040      88  FIRST-TIME-SW     VALUE '1'.
000050      88  OTHER-TIMES       VALUE '2'.
000060 PROCEDURE DIVISION.
000070     IF FIRST-TIME-SW
000080         MOVE '2' TO EACH-TIME-SW
000090         PERFORM FIRST-TIME-PROCESSING.
000100     ...
000110 FIRST-TIME-PROCESSING.
```

(b)

Figure 1.3 ON statement in a VS COBOL program and
the equivalent code in a COBOL II program. (a) Code only
allowed in VS COBOL; (b) equivalent code in COBOL II.

The IF statement or the COBOL II EVALUATE statement (discussed
in Sec. 3.4) can be used in its place, even to replace the complex forms
of the ON statement.

1.6 INSPECT, EXAMINE, AND TRANSFORM

The EXAMINE and TRANSFORM verbs do not exist in COBOL II.
The INSPECT statement in COBOL II, which previously existed in
VS COBOL, performs the function of the three verbs. EXAMINE and
INSPECT were quite similar in function and the removal of the
EXAMINE statement does not cause any major problems. An EXAM-
INE statement in VS COBOL and the equivalent INSPECT statement
that can be used in COBOL II are shown in Fig. 1.4. In many cases,
the INSPECT statement has become considerably more efficient in
COBOL II than it was in VS COBOL. The INSPECT in Fig. 1.4 took
19 object code instructions in VS COBOL to call the INSPECT run-
time library routine. COBOL II Release 2 generates only four object
code instructions to call the library routine while Release 3 generates
only a single Translate (TR) instruction and does not call any library
routine.

```
000010 DATA DIVISION.
000020 WORKING-STORAGE SECTION.
000030 01  FIELD1                PIC X(20).
000040
000050 PROCEDURE DIVISION.
000060      ...
000070      EXAMINE FIELD1 REPLACING ALL ZEROS BY SPACES.
```

(a)


```
000010 DATA DIVISION.
000020 WORKING-STORAGE SECTION.
000030 01  FIELD1                PIC X(20).
000040
000050 PROCEDURE DIVISION.
000060      ...
000070      INSPECT FIELD1 REPLACING ALL ZEROS BY SPACES.
```

(b)

Figure 1.4 EXAMINE statement that is only allowed in VS COBOL and an equivalent INSPECT statement supported in VS COBOL and COBOL II. (*a*) Code in VS COBOL; (*b*) equivalent code in VS COBOL or COBOL II.

The TALLY special register is still supported in COBOL II. Figure 1.5 shows how a VS COBOL EXAMINE statement using the TALLY-ING clause can be converted to COBOL II. Be careful when making this conversion since the EXAMINE statement overlays the contents of TALLY but INSPECT adds to the contents of TALLY. You usually must initialize TALLY to zero before an INSPECT statement using it is executed.

In COBOL II, until Release 3, there was no simple and efficient way to convert a TRANSFORM statement into an INSPECT statement. To enable the INSPECT statement to handle all of the functions of EX-AMINE and TRANSFORM, Release 3 allows an unlimited number of TALLYING and REPLACING phrases, added a CONVERTING phrase, and allows multiple BEFORE and AFTER phrases. The CON-VERTING phrase was basically added to take the place of the TRANSFORM statement and has a similar syntax as is illustrated in the code in Fig. 1.6.

1.7   EXHIBIT AND DISPLAY

EXHIBIT has been removed and its function is to be performed by the DISPLAY verb, which existed in VS COBOL as well. The EXHIBIT statement did have a number of useful features. The EXHIBIT

```
000010 DATA DIVISION.
000020 WORKING-STORAGE SECTION.
000030 01  FIELD1                    PIC X(20).
000040
000050 PROCEDURE DIVISION.
000060     ...
000070     EXAMINE FIELD1 TALLYING UNTIL FIRST '0'.
```

(a)

```
000010 DATA DIVISION.
000020 WORKING-STORAGE SECTION.
000030 01  FIELD1                    PIC X(20).
000040
000050 PROCEDURE DIVISION.
000060     ...
000070     MOVE ZERO TO TALLY.
000080     INSPECT FIELD1 TALLYING TALLY FOR CHARACTERS BEFORE '0'.
```

(b)

Figure 1.5 How an **EXAMINE** using the **TALLY** special register in VS COBOL can be converted to an **INSPECT** in COBOL II. (a) Code in VS COBOL; (b) equivalent code in COBOL II.

```
000010 DATA DIVISION.
000020 WORKING-STORAGE SECTION.
000030 01  FIELD1                    PIC X(20).
000040
000050 PROCEDURE DIVISION.
000060     ...
000070     TRANSFORM FIELD1 CHARACTERS FROM 'WXYZ' TO 'ABCD'.
```

(a)

```
000010 DATA DIVISION.
000020 WORKING-STORAGE SECTION.
000030 01  FIELD1                    PIC X(20).
000040
000050 PROCEDURE DIVISION.
000060     ...
000070     INSPECT FIELD1 CONVERTING 'WXYZ' TO 'ABCD'.
```

(b)

Figure 1.6 Example of how an **INSPECT** statement with the **CONVERTING** clause in Release 3 can be used to produce code equivalent to a VS COBOL **TRANSFORM** statement. (a) Code in VS COBOL; (b) equivalent code in COBOL II Release 3.

NAMED, EXHIBIT CHANGED NAMED, and EXHIBIT CHANGED statements have no direct translations to DISPLAY statements. You must code the field name in a literal if you want to display the name of the field. To display a field only when it has changed under COBOL II, you must save its prior value and then place the DISPLAY statement within an IF statement which compares the prior value to the present one (see Fig. 1.7). Unfortunately, this method of coding may not be as precise as the EXHIBIT statement. The EXHIBIT statement was sure to match the correct field name with the data exhibited, while you might inadvertently display the incorrect name of a field next to data you are displaying.

In Release 3, the DISPLAY statement has been updated. It now allows the WITH NO ADVANCING clause, which suppresses skipping to the next line when data is written. When data is displayed from various places in a program and the data is logically connected, this option makes it easier to read the output since the output of numerous DISPLAYs can appear on the same line.

1.7.1 LIST Command in COBOL Debugger

You might consider using the LIST command of the COBOL debugger (COBTEST) in place of the DISPLAY statement. If you are already using the debugger to TRACE program execution (enhanced replacement of

```
000010 DATA DIVISION.
000020 WORKING-STORAGE SECTION.
000030 01   FIELD1                    PIC X(20) VALUE 'ABCDE'.
000040 PROCEDURE DIVISION.
000050     EXHIBIT CHANGED NAMED FIELD1.
```

(a)

```
000010 DATA DIVISION.
000020 WORKING-STORAGE SECTION.
000030 01   FIELD1                    PIC X(20) VALUE 'ABCDE'.
000040 01   PRIOR-FIELD1              PIC X(20) VALUE HIGH-VALUES.
000050 PROCEDURE DIVISION.
000060     IF FIELD1 IS NOT EQUAL TO PRIOR-FIELD1
000070         DISPLAY 'FIELD1 = ' FIELD1
000080         MOVE FIELD1 TO PRIOR-FIELD1.
```

(b)

Figure 1.7 Sample code showing the replacement of a VS COBOL EXHIBIT statement using the DISPLAY statement which is still supported in COBOL II. (a) Code used in VS COBOL; (b) equivalent code in COBOL II.

READY TRACE) or for showing the program FLOW (replacement of the VS COBOL FLOW compiler option—see Sec. 4.7.4), it would be simple to add LIST commands to your debugging commands. The debugging commands are not entered as part of your program but are entered externally. They can only be used if your program was compiled with the TEST compiler option. (See Sec. 4.7 for a complete explanation of TEST and more information on using the debugger.) The LIST command has the following advantages over using DISPLAY:

- It can display fields in alphanumeric, hexadecimal, or in both formats (DISPLAY, HEX, BOTH).

- It can list all data items defined within a portion of your program if you simply specify the first and last data items in the range (first-data-item:last-data-item). For example, to display all fields defined between FIELD1 and FIELD100 you would code LIST FIELD1:FIELD100.

- It can list all data fields (data names, indexes, pointers, and FD areas) defined within an entire program with a single clause (LIST ALL).

1.8   ACCEPT AND MOVE OF DATE AND TIME

Special registers CURRENT-DATE and TIME-OF-DAY available as sending fields in a MOVE statement in VS COBOL do not exist in COBOL II, and the equivalent information (in a slightly different format) can be obtained using the DATE and TIME clauses of the ACCEPT statement. The ACCEPT clauses of DATE and TIME were also available in VS COBOL and if they were used, they need not be converted. The ACCEPT statement gives a more accurate time (with hundredths of seconds) than TIME-OF-DAY and gives a date in a better format for calculations than CURRENT-DATE. CURRENT-DATE was in a better format for printing. The time obtained from both TIME-OF-DAY and TIME are in 24-hour format. Figure 1.8 shows the data format of the date and time in VS COBOL and COBOL II, and the statements used to obtain the data.

   In Release 3, the ACCEPT statement has a DAY-OF-WEEK option which returns a 1-byte display numeric value from 1 to 7. A 1 represents Monday, a 2 represents Tuesday, ..., a 7 represents Sunday. To convert the numeric value to the actual word for the day, create a table of seven entries in your program. You can then use the value returned from the ACCEPT statement as a subscript to reference the table and extract the day name needed. It would have been nice if the ACCEPT command al-

```
000010 DATA DIVISION.
000020 WORKING-STORAGE SECTION.
000030*FORMAT IS MM/DD/YY
000040 01   DATE-CURRENT            PIC X(8).
000050*FORMAT IS HHMMSS
000060 01   TIME-DAY                PIC X(6).
000070
000080 PROCEDURE DIVISION.
000090     MOVE TIME-OF-DAY TO TIME-DAY.
000100     MOVE CURRENT-DATE TO DATE-CURRENT.
```

(a)

```
000010 DATA DIVISION.
000020 WORKING-STORAGE SECTION.
000030 01   DATE-ACCEPT.
000040     05   DATE-ACCEPT-YY       PIC XX.
000050     05   DATE-ACCEPT-MM       PIC XX.
000060     05   DATE-ACCEPT-DD       PIC XX.
000070 01   DATE-CURRENT.
000080     05   DATE-CURRENT-MM      PIC XX.
000090     05   FILLER              PIC X VALUE '/'.
000100     05   DATE-CURRENT-DD      PIC XX.
000110     05   FILLER              PIC X VALUE '/'.
000120     05   DATE-CURRENT-YY      PIC XX.
000130*FORMAT IS HHMMSSHH
000140*(HOURS, MINUTES, SECONDS, HUNDREDTHS OF SECONDS)
000150 01   TIME-ACCEPT             PIC X(8).
000160
000170 PROCEDURE DIVISION.
000180     ACCEPT TIME-ACCEPT FROM TIME.
000190     ACCEPT DATE-ACCEPT FROM DATE.
000200     MOVE DATE-ACCEPT-YY TO DATE-CURRENT-YY.
000210     MOVE DATE-ACCEPT-MM TO DATE-CURRENT-MM.
000220     MOVE DATE-ACCEPT-DD TO DATE-CURRENT-DD.
```

(b)

Figure 1.8 How the date and time can be obtained in a VS COBOL program and a COBOL II program. The COBOL II program reformats the date obtained from ACCEPT into the format of CURRENT-DATE in VS COBOL. (a) VS COBOL code; (b) code in VS COBOL or COBOL II.

lowed you to obtain the day of the week for any date. It presently only returns the day of the week for the current date.

The ACCEPT statement is quite inefficient. If you frequently need the DATE or DAY-OF-WEEK in a program, only issue the ACCEPT statement to obtain the information the first time it is required. Then move the information whenever it is needed later in the program.

1.9   REMARKS AND NOTE

The REMARKS paragraph and NOTE statement have been eliminated. Standard comments [containing an asterisk (*) or a slash (/) in
column 7] are used instead. It seems that statements that only served
as documentation could have remained, not adding to the burden programmers face when converting their programs to COBOL II. IBM
states that REMARKS and NOTE were removed because they were
not in the ANSI 74 COBOL standard.

1.10   QUALIFICATION OF INDEX NAMES

Qualification of data names and paragraph names is still supported in
COBOL II. However, qualification of index names is not. Figure 1.9 is
an example of code that compiled properly under VS COBOL but gets
a severe compilation error under COBOL II.

```
000010 DATA DIVISION.
000020 WORKING-STORAGE SECTION.
000030 01  TABLE1.
000040     05  ENTRYX OCCURS 10 TIMES
000050             INDEXED BY INDEX1    PIC X.
000060 01  TABLE2.
000070     05  ENTRYX OCCURS 10 TIMES
000080             INDEXED BY INDEX1    PIC X.
000090 01  FIELD1                       PIC X.
000100
000110 PROCEDURE DIVISION.
000120     MOVE ENTRYX (INDEX1 OF TABLE1) TO FIELD1.
```

Figure 1.9 Qualification of index names is not supported under COBOL II.

1.11   RESERVED WORDS

While not actually an eliminated feature, there are new *reserved
words* in COBOL II. These can cause errors in programs that would
have compiled correctly. For instance, if a program used a paragraph
name of INITIALIZE or a DATA DIVISION field name of EVALU-
ATE, these names will cause compilation errors since they are now
COBOL II reserved words. The entire list of reserved words that have
been added to COBOL II appears in Fig. 1.10. The ones that only apply to Release 3 are so indicated.

ALPHABET*	END-REWRITE
ALPHABETIC-LOWER*	END-SEARCH
ALPHABETIC-UPPER*	END-START
ALPHANUMERIC	END-STRING
ALPHANUMERIC-EDITED	END-SUBTRACT
ANY	END-UNSTRING
BINARY*	END-WRITE
CLASS*	EVALUATE
COBOL	EXTERNAL*
COM-REG	FALSE
COMMON*	GLOBAL*
CONTENT	INITIALIZE
CONTINUE	KANJI
CONVERTING*	NULL
DAY-OF-WEEK*	NULLS
DBCS*	NUMERIC-EDITED
DISPLAY-1	ORDER*
EGCS	OTHER
END-ADD	PACKED-DECIMAL*
END-CALL	PADDING*
END-COMPUTE	PURGE*
END-DELETE	REFERENCE
END-DIVIDE	REPLACE*
END-EVALUATE	SHIFT-IN
END-IF	SHIFT-OUT
END-MULTIPLY	SORT-CONTROL
END-PERFORM	STANDARD-2*
END-READ	TEST
END-RECEIVE*	TITLE
END-RETURN	TRUE

* Words reserved in Release 3 only.

Figure 1.10 Reserved words in COBOL II that were not reserved words in VS COBOL.

1.12 INCONSISTENCIES BETWEEN VS COBOL AND COBOL II

Most of the changes between VS COBOL and COBOL II Release 2 are highlighted in charts in the following IBM manuals: *VS COBOL II General Information*, *VS COBOL II Application Programming Language Reference*, and *VS COBOL II Application Programming Guide*. However, the differences between VS COBOL and COBOL II that are not clearly defined in these charts may cause the greatest problems. Some differences are obvious when seen in a compilation. VS COBOL was more lenient in some areas in which Releases 1 and 2 of COBOL II have decided to strictly enforce the rules. For instance if the file name in an FD statement began in column 11 rather than column 12, it was accepted and no warning was given (see Fig. 1.11). The same statement will cause an E level error (condition code 8) in COBOL II Release 2. Also, if a data name

```
000010 DATA DIVISION.
000020 FILE SECTION.
000030*THE FILE AND RECORD NAMES BEGIN IN COLUMN 11.
000040*THEY DID NOT CAUSE AN ERROR IN VS COBOL.
000050 FD INPUT-FILE
000060     BLOCK CONTAINS 0 RECORDS
000070     LABEL RECORDS ARE STANDARD.
000080 01 INPUT-RECORD           PIC X(80).
000090
000100 WORKING-STORAGE SECTION.
000110 01   CITY-CODE            PIC XX.
000120*VALUE BELOW COMPILES WITHOUT ERRORS IN VS COBOL
000130*BUT WITH ERRORS IN COBOL II
000140     88  VALID-CITIES      VALUE 10 20 30.
```

Figure 1.11 Code that compiled cleanly in VS COBOL but gets errors when compiled under COBOL II.

began in column 11 after an 01 level in column 8, it was only given a warning message in VS COBOL but produces an error message in COBOL II Release 2. IBM has realized these inconsistencies. When the same code is used in Release 3, it compiles cleanly without any type of message being issued. Although the change in Release 2 was documented in the text of the manuals, it was omitted from the charts of differences. You either have to read the entire language reference manual to realize minor changes such as this or accept the fact that you will only find certain differences when they appear as compilation errors.

In VS COBOL if you failed to place a period after a paragraph name, you got a warning message. (Old releases of VS COBOL did not produce any message at all.) In COBOL II the situation produces an error message. Another example of enforcing restrictions in COBOL II is in values given to an 88 level for an alphanumeric field. Figure 1.11 shows code that compiled cleanly in VS COBOL (until recent maintenance levels—it was probably changed in VS COBOL for compatibility with COBOL II) but cannot be used in COBOL II. When numeric values were given to an alphanumeric field in VS COBOL, they did not have to be enclosed in quotes. The COBOL II compiler enforces the rule that the values in an alphanumeric field must be defined within quotes or apostrophes. The code that previously compiled with no errors now gets an S level (condition code 12) error. (The error level severities have changed from VS COBOL and will be discussed in Sec. 2.7.)

1.12.1 Unexpected and Concealed COBOL II Differences

Some inconsistencies (such as those in the values for 88 levels) are documented in the manual for the IBM Conversion Aid, a program written to help convert VS COBOL programs into programs that will compile and execute under COBOL II. Others are clearly pointed out only in the Release 3 *IBM OS/VS COBOL to VS COBOL II Migration Guide*. (There is also the IBM *VS COBOL II Migration Guide* for Release 2 that was published as a technical bulletin by the IBM Dallas Systems Center.) However, many programmers may not know of the existence of these manuals or do not have them available. If conversion software is unavailable, they will need to convert programs manually. Their basic choices for finding out the differences between VS COBOL and COBOL II is to either examine the charts of differences listed in the appendix of the IBM programmers guide as an aid (thinking that it is complete), or read the entire set of COBOL II manuals hoping to spot differences. Both of these methods are problematic. Several inconsistencies (such as those just mentioned) are unclear in the manuals or do not appear in them. It would have been nice if IBM had done things properly and created a complete list programming differences.

While the differences just discussed are annoying, they are found during compilation. Even more problematic are those differences that may not be found until an appropriate condition occurs during execution. If the differences in execution are not found during regression testing, they can occur in production. They can cause a program to ABEND or produce incorrect results. For example, if a field defined as PIC 99 was moved to a field defined as PIC S99, VS COBOL moved the field and then inserted a positive sign in the receiving field. This may have prevented an 0C7 program exception that would have occurred later in the program. Depending on options used in a compilation, COBOL II may only execute a straight Move Character (MVC) instruction, which is faster but may generate different results. Until Release 3, none of the compiler options instructed COBOL II to create code that exactly matches display and packed decimal numeric processing in VS COBOL.

Some of the concealed differences are in the positive direction. Take the code in Fig. 1.12 for instance. The results normally expected were not received in VS COBOL but are properly received in COBOL II. In VS COBOL the results are "01 01, 02 01, 03 01" while in COBOL II they are "01 01, 02 02, 03 03."

1.13 CONVERSION

While the eliminated features do not cause any real restrictions for new programmers, they do cause considerable problems in converting VS COBOL programs to COBOL II. While the changes are not difficult, they are tedious and not preferred work by most programmers. Changes to COBOL programs that run under CICS include all standard changes plus those specific to CICS.

```
000010 DATA DIVISION.
000020 WORKING-STORAGE SECTION.
000030 01   TABLE1                          VALUE '010203'.
000040      05   ENTRY1 OCCURS 3 TIMES      PIC XX.
000050 01   SUB1                            PIC S99.
000060 01   SUB2 REDEFINES SUB1             PIC S99.
000070
000080 PROCEDURE DIVISION.
000090      MOVE +1 TO SUB1.
000100      DISPLAY ENTRY1 (SUB1) ' ' ENTRY1 (SUB2).
000110      ADD +1 TO SUB1.
000120      DISPLAY ENTRY1 (SUB1) ' ' ENTRY1 (SUB2).
000130      ADD +1 TO SUB1.
000140      DISPLAY ENTRY1 (SUB1) ' ' ENTRY1 (SUB2).
```

Figure 1.12 Code that functions quite differently under VS COBOL and COBOL II. Redefined subscripts are not always handled properly under VS COBOL.

There are, however, a number of conversion software products available for CICS and batch COBOL programs. IBM has its own COBOL and CICS/VS Command Level Conversion Aid. There are other conversion programs available [e.g., CA-Optimizer/CMO (COBOL Migration Option) from Computer Associates and MHtran-2 from Prince Software Products]. Both of these programs convert CICS as well as batch programs. Any conversion aid should also handle any software-specific statements your company uses such as DB2 and IDMS code and should run with software products you have such as VM, Panvalet, or Librarian. Additionally, it should clearly flag any code that it is unsure how to convert and should ensure that any program not fully converted will compile with errors. This will prevent inadvertent runs of a partially converted program.

Companies exist that specialize in VS COBOL to COBOL II conversions, such as Scientific Developments, Inc. They use software to begin the changes and then supply the staff to manually convert those areas of programs that the conversion software has spotted as problem areas. Additionally, they will then fix any errors that the conversion software was unable to locate. These services are much more expensive than just buying a conversion product. You have to do a cost comparison and determine whether the cost of using your own staff will be cheaper than hiring consultants that specialize in this type of work. On the positive side, hiring outsiders to do a conversion may boost morale, since conversion can be a boring task. On the negative side, your programmers may have missed a valuable opportunity to learn the differences between VS COBOL and COBOL II and build a foundation for their COBOL II training.

Chapter

2

Updated Features from VS COBOL to Release 2

The next area of changes to be discussed will be the COBOL features that have been updated. Many features can function differently in COBOL II Release 2 than they did in VS COBOL. This is because additional functions are available when using specific features or because the actual processing of a feature has changed. Use of the new functions, such as additional clauses in the CALL statement or the ability to use in-line PERFORM statements, leaves more options open to the subjective coding style of the individual.

The features in COBOL II that process differently from VS COBOL must be fully understood. For instance, a VS COBOL program using floating-point fields that requires no coding changes to be run under COBOL II may yield different results when it is executed (these differences will be discussed later). You do not want to write code you are accustomed to using (or run a program that had already been in production using VS COBOL) only to find out later that it no longer executes the way you thought it would.

WRITE...AFTER POSITIONING is not supported under COBOL II since WRITE...AFTER ADVANCING can be used instead. The UNSTRING statement can no longer have a numeric edited field as a receiving field. VS COBOL allowed the DISP, LEAVE, REREAD, and REVERSED clauses in the OPEN statement; they are not supported in COBOL II. In the FILE CONTROL section, RESERVE NO ALTERNATE AREA(S) is not allowed and RESERVE x ALTERNATE AREA(S) must be coded as RESERVE x AREAS (where x is an integer).

2.1 EXTENDED FILE STATUS CODES

The FILE STATUS has been expanded with an extended VSAM feedback area. In addition to the 2-byte file status that was previously used, an additional 6-byte VSAM status is available. When a programmer wants to get the extended file status information, the SELECT statement must be coded with two data items after the FILE STATUS clause (see Fig. 2.1). The first data item is the standard 2-byte file status (that was available in VS COBOL) and the second data item is the 6-byte extended status. The second data item may only be coded for a VSAM file and an error message is produced if it is coded for a non-VSAM file.

The extended file status information consists of three 2-byte binary fields and is only filled in when the standard file status is not zero. The first 2 bytes contain the VSAM return code (the values of the return code placed into register 15 by VSAM are shown in Fig. 2.2). When the return code is not zero, the two fields that follow it are filled in. (When the return code is zero, the two fields may be filled in but their contents will not always be accurate.) They contain the VSAM

```
000010 INPUT-OUTPUT SECTION.
000020 FILE-CONTROL.
000030     SELECT INPUT-FILE ASSIGN TO AS-INFILE
000040         FILE STATUS IS STANDARD-STATUS-INFO
000050                        EXTENDED-STATUS-INFO.
000060 DATA DIVISION.
000070 ...
000080 WORKING-STORAGE SECTION.
000090 01  STANDARD-STATUS-INFO       PIC XX.
000100
000110*ADDITIONAL SIX BYTE VSAM STATUS IS AVAILABLE
000120*IT IS ONLY FILLED IN WHEN THE STATUS IS NOT ZERO
000130 01  EXTENDED-STATUS-INFO.
000140*VSAM RETURN CODE (REGISTER 15)
000150     05  VSAM-RET-CODE          PIC S9(4) COMP.
000160*WHEN RETURN CODE IS NOT ZERO,
000170*THE VSAM FUNCTION CODE AND FEEDBACK CODE ARE RETURNED
000180     05  VSAM-FUNCTION-CODE     PIC S9(4) COMP.
000190     05  VSAM-FEEDBACK-CODE     PIC S9(4) COMP.
000200
000210 PROCEDURE DIVISION.
000220     READ VSAM-FILE
000230         AT END GO TO FILE-END-ROUTINE.
000240     IF STANDARD-STATUS-INFO IS NOT EQUAL TO ZERO
000250         DISPLAY 'VSAM ERROR, STATUS = ' STANDARD-STATUS-INFO
000260         IF VSAM-RET-CODE NOT = ZERO
000270             DISPLAY 'RETURN CODE = ' VSAM-RET-CODE
000280                 ', FUNCTION CODE = ' VSAM-FUNCTION-CODE
000290                 ', FEEDBACK CODE = ' VSAM-FEEDBACK-CODE
000300             GO TO VSAM-ERROR-ROUTINE
000310         ELSE GO TO VSAM-ERROR-ROUTINE.
```

Figure 2.1 Sample of how a program is coded when one wants to use the extended VSAM status information.

Return code	Meaning
0	The VSAM request successfully completed.
4	For an OPEN request, the OPEN was successful but a warning message was issued; for a CLOSE request, the CLOSE failed.
8	A logical error occurred. The feedback code in the fifth and sixth bytes of the extended file status describe the specific error. Refer to the logical error feedback codes in Fig. 2.4.
12	A physical error occurred. The feedback code in the fifth and sixth bytes of the extended file status describe the specific error. Refer to the physical error feedback codes in Fig. 2.4.

Figure 2.2 The VSAM return code (shown in decimal) is now available in the extended FILE STATUS.

function code and the feedback code. The function codes are listed in Fig. 2.3. Unfortunately, COBOL programmers often do not have access to, nor do many know where to find the explanation of the VSAM feedback codes. Every programming department should have a copy of either the *VSAM Administration: Macro Instruction Reference* or *VSAM Administration Guide* available; they contain the VSAM feedback codes and their explanations. A partial list of the feedback codes returned from OPEN, CLOSE, and other I/O requests is shown in Fig. 2.4.

These extended file status codes will precisely pinpoint a VSAM error and may save many hours of debugging time. It is certainly better to receive a feedback code of 108 indicating a time stamp problem for a data set than to receive a file status of 90 only indicating a logic error. For this reason, I strongly recommend that every program using VSAM files request the additional file status information. (When converting programs from VS COBOL to COBOL II, it is a good idea to

Function code	Meaning
0	Access of the base cluster was attempted. The upgrade set (the set of alternate indexes that are automatically updated and kept in synchronization when the base cluster to which they belong is updated) status is correct.
1	Access of the base cluster was attempted. The upgrade set status may be incorrect.
2	Access of the alternate index over a base cluster was attempted. The upgrade set status is correct.
3	Access of the alternate index over a base cluster was attempted. The upgrade set status may be incorrect.
4	Upgrade processing was attempted. The upgrade set status is correct.
5	Upgrade processing was attempted. The upgrade set status may be incorrect.

Figure 2.3 VSAM function codes and their meanings.

·Feedback code	Meaning
	Feedback codes from OPEN
0	The file is already open or the DDNAME is invalid.
100	Warning—An empty alternate index which is part of an upgrade set was encountered.
104	Warning—The time stamp in the data set does not match its time stamp in the catalog.
108	The time stamp in a data component and an index component do not match.
116	The data set had not been properly closed. An implicit VERIFY was unsuccessful.
118	The data set had not been properly closed. An implicit VERIFY was successful.
128	A DD statement for the file is missing.
136	Not enough virtual storage is available in the address space for work areas, control blocks, or buffers.
144	An uncorrectable I/O error occurred when VSAM was reading or writing a catalog record.
168	The data set could not be opened for the type of processing requested, or another program had the data set open.
180	A VSAM catalog specified in the JCL does not exist or is not open. The data set to be opened could not be found in any other catalog.
184	An uncorrectable I/O error occurred when VSAM was completing an I/O request.
196	An attempt was made to access data via an empty path.
232	Reset was specified for a non-reusable data set that was not empty.
	Feedback codes from CLOSE
4	The data set is already closed.
136	Not enough virtual storage was available in the program's address space.
144	An uncorrectable I/O error occurred when VSAM was reading or writing a catalog record.
148	An error occurred when VSAM was searching the catalog.
184	An uncorrectable I/O error occurred during VSAM's completion of outstanding I/O.
	Logical error feedback codes from all other I/O requests
4	Either an end-of-file condition was reached during sequential or skip-sequential processing, or the key in use is greater than the highest key in the data set.
8	Either an attempt was made to store a record with a duplicate key, or there is a duplicate record in for an alternate index that has the unique key option.
12	A key sequence error occurred during KSDS or RRDS processing.
16	A record was not found.
20	A control interval required by the program was already in use by another program.

Figure 2.4 Selected VSAM feedback codes (in decimal) and their meanings.

	Logical error feedback codes from all other I/O requests
28	An out-of-space condition has occurred. Either space does not exist for a secondary allocation, or an attempt was made to increase the size of a data set processed with SHROPT=4 and DISP=SHR.
36	The key specified is not a valid key for the data set. This can only occur if specific key ranges are defined for the data set.
40	Not enough virtual storage was available in the address space to complete the request.
68	Processing was attempted that was not allowed when the data set was opened (e.g., writing to a data set that was opened as input).
72	Keyed access was requested on an entry sequenced data set.
80	An attempt was made to delete a record from an ESDS file.
92	A REWRITE or DELETE was requested without a previous READ.
96	An attempt was made to update the prime key of a KSDS file.
108	An attempt was made to process with an invalid record length.
112	The key length specified is either too large or equal to zero.
116	A request other than a WRITE was issued to a data set opened in OUTPUT mode.
144	An invalid pointer exists in an alternate index. There is no associated base record.
148	The maximum number of pointers in the alternate index has been exceeded.
152	Not enough buffers (when shared resources are used) were available to process the request.
156	An invalid control interval was detected during keyed processing.
192	An invalid relative record number was used.
	Physical error feedback codes from all other I/O requests
4	A read error occurred for a data set.
8	A read error occurred for an index set.
12	A read error occurred for a sequence set.
16	A write error occurred for a data set.
20	A write error occurred for an index set.
24	A write error occurred for a sequence set.

Figure 2.4   *(Continued)*

add code to request the extended file status information.) This information is available elsewhere even when the extended file status information is not requested, but many COBOL programmers do not know how to find it. (See Chap. 14 describing the TGT so that you will be able to locate the information should it ever be necessary to do so in a dump.)

2.2   OCCURS DEPENDING ON

The internal processing of the OCCURS DEPENDING ON clause has been changed from the way it was done in VS COBOL. While VS COBOL code using the clause will produce the same results when run

under Release 2, depending on the coding technique used in a VS CO-
BOL program, the program may be either more efficient or less efficient. COBOL II will perform the length computation of a data item
defined with the OCCURS DEPENDING ON clause when the data
item containing the clause is referenced [only on line 000180 in Fig.
2.5(b)]. In VS COBOL, when the value of the object field of the clause
(e.g, VAR-NUM in Fig. 2.5) was updated, the length of the data item
was computed [only on line 000190 in Fig. 2.5(a)] whether or not the
variable length data item was used. This meant that if you were keeping track of the number of occurrences in a table by continuously adding to the object field of an OCCURS DEPENDING ON clause, the table length would be computed each time.

If a VS COBOL program ran under CICS or used a database to read
a record whose description contained an OCCURS DEPENDING ON
clause, COBOL usually would not set the length of the record properly. This was because there was no code produced that specifically
moved a value to the object field of the clause. A program often had to
contain an enigmatic statement that moved the object field to itself
(e.g., MOVE VAR-NUM TO VAR-NUM). This informed COBOL of
the length of the variable length data item.

The VS COBOL length computation would be considerably more efficient if a variable length table was created once each time the program ran and was then repeatedly used. The new method is more efficient when the table length is constantly changing. It should be
mentioned that while there is no way to increase the efficiency of the
COBOL II method, the VS COBOL method could have been programmed very efficiently by incrementing a data item that was not
the object of the OCCURS DEPENDING ON clause and then moving
this item to the object [see Fig. 2.5(a)]. In this case, the length computation would only be made when the move to the object field was
made, not when the incrementing took place.

The object code generated in VS COBOL for modifying the object
field of an OCCURS DEPENDING ON was not only less efficient than
it is in COBOL II, but it was quite difficult to follow in a Procedure
Map. For line 000190 in Fig. 2.5(a), VS COBOL created code that
branched to a generated routine that was placed at the end of the program. This generated routine is not created if the same statement appears in a COBOL II program. However, COBOL II (but not VS CO-
BOL) branches to a generated routine for statement 000180 in the
code in Fig. 2.5(b).

2.3 FLOATING-POINT NUMBERS

Floating-point numbers are only used by COBOL when at least one
number in an arithmetic expression is defined as floating-point or is a

```
000010 DATA DIVISION.
000020 WORKING-STORAGE SECTION.
000030 01   HOLD-VAR-NUM              PIC S9(4) COMP VALUE ZERO.
000040 01   VAR-NUM                   PIC S9(4) COMP.
000050 01   VARIABLE-TABLE.
000060      05   VAR-ENTRY OCCURS 1 TO 100 TIMES
000070           DEPENDING ON VAR-NUM  PIC X(80).
000080 01   HOLD-VARIABLE-TABLE       PIC X(8000).
000090
000100 PROCEDURE DIVISION.
000110 READ-REC1.
000120      READ IN-FILE1
000130        AT END GO TO PROCESSING-BEGIN.
000140      ADD +1 TO HOLD-VAR-NUM.
000150      MOVE IN-REC1 TO VAR-ENTRY (HOLD-VAR-NUM).
000160      GO TO READ-REC1.
000170
000180 PROCESSING-BEGIN.
000190      MOVE HOLD-VAR-NUM TO VAR-NUM.
000200      MOVE VARIABLE-TABLE TO HOLD-VARIABLE-TABLE.
```

(a)

```
000010 DATA DIVISION.
000020 WORKING-STORAGE SECTION.
000030 01   VAR-NUM                   PIC S9(4) COMP VALUE ZERO.
000040 01   VARIABLE-TABLE.
000050      05   VAR-ENTRY OCCURS 1 TO 100 TIMES
000060           DEPENDING ON VAR-NUM  PIC X(80).
000070 01   HOLD-VARIABLE-TABLE       PIC X(8000).
000080
000090 PROCEDURE DIVISION.
000100 READ-REC1.
000110      READ IN-FILE1
000120        AT END GO TO PROCESSING-BEGIN.
000130      ADD +1 TO VAR-NUM.
000140      MOVE IN-REC1 TO VAR-ENTRY (VAR-NUM).
000150      GO TO READ-REC1.
000160
000170 PROCESSING-BEGIN.
000180      MOVE VARIABLE-TABLE TO HOLD-VARIABLE-TABLE.
```

(b)

Figure 2.5   Two different methods of filling a variable length table. Efficiency differs depending upon whether a program is run under VS COBOL or COBOL II. (*a*) Efficient code recommended for VS COBOL; (*b*) equivalent code recommended for COBOL II.

floating-point constant. Internal conversions of floating-point numbers (between decimal and hexadecimal) have been enhanced to be more precise in COBOL II. Results of operations using floating-point numbers are now more accurate and may actually differ from VS COBOL. (On line 000110 in Fig. 2.6 FIELD3 is set to 6.999994 when run using VS COBOL and 7.000000 when using COBOL II.) This may make it difficult to use automated procedures to do regression testing to verify that the VS COBOL and COBOL II versions of a program produce the "same" results. The results from floating-point operations in COBOL II are now more compatible with floating-point results produced in VS FORTRAN programs.

2.3.1 Exponentiation

Floating-point exponentiation under COBOL II can yield more accurate results than fixed-point exponentiation. In addition, both VS COBOL and COBOL II do computations of fixed-point data items with large exponents faster in floating-point. It does not make sense to me that floating-point computations should even be more accurate than fixed-point computations and that a programmer should have to worry about forcing an exponentiation to use floating-point to get the added accuracy. Nevertheless, Fig. 2.7 illustrates the standard coding method, followed by the recommended method of coding fixed-point exponentiation with large exponents. The mixture of floating-point and fixed-point fields on line 000110 causes the compiler to do floating-point arithmetic.

In Fig. 2.7, the COBOL II compiler produces the same precise results of 13422659310152401 for both lines 000080 and 000110. This occurs even though the fixed-point exponentiation on line 000080 is done by the COBOL II library routine IGZCXPR and the floating-point double precision library routine IGZCFPW is called to do the

```
000010 DATA DIVISION.
000020 WORKING-STORAGE SECTION.
000030 01   FIELD1                    COMP-1.
000040 01   FIELD2                    COMP-1.
000050 01   FIELD3                    PIC 9(5)V9(6) COMP-3.
000060 PROCEDURE DIVISION.
000070      MOVE 777.777 TO FIELD1.
000080      MOVE 111.111 TO FIELD2.
000090      MULTIPLY 100.E+00 BY FIELD1.
000100      MULTIPLY 100.E+00 BY FIELD2.
000110      DIVIDE FIELD1 BY FIELD2 GIVING FIELD3.
```

Figure 2.6 Program that yields different results in FIELD3 when run using VS COBOL and run using COBOL II.

```
000010 DATA DIVISION.
000020 WORKING-STORAGE SECTION.
000030 01  FIELD1                   PIC S9(18) COMP-3 VALUE +41.
000040 01  FIELD2                   PIC S9(18) COMP-3.
000050
000060 PROCEDURE DIVISION.
000070*FIXED-POINT EXPONENTIATION
000080     COMPUTE FIELD2 = FIELD1 ** 10.
000090
000100*FLOATING-POINT EXPONENTIATION
000110     COMPUTE FIELD2 = FIELD1 ** 10.E+00.
```

Figure 2.7 Code showing how a program can force the COBOL II compiler to do either fixed-point or floating-point exponentiation of a fixed-point number.

calculation for line 000110. VS COBOL produces the same results as COBOL II for the fixed-point exponentiation on line 000080 but produces less accurate results (13422659310152343—the last three digits differ) for the floating-point exponentiation on line 000110.

2.4 VALUE CLAUSES

It was rather annoying that VS COBOL expected the VALUE of a numeric field to contain a sign when the PICTURE of the field was signed. In Fig. 2.8, FIELD1 will compile without any problem in either VS COBOL or COBOL II. The VALUE clause of FIELD2 will cause a warning message to be produced in VS COBOL because the sign is missing (the value is processed as if it was coded with a positive sign). The COBOL II compiler is more reasonable in assuming that unsigned fields are positive. The VALUE clause of FIELD2 compiles without producing a warning message. It is still true that if a VALUE clause of a numeric field is signed, the PICTURE clause must also be signed. (If the VALUE clause is signed and the PICTURE clause is unsigned, the VS COBOL compiler produces a warning message while COBOL II produces a severe error message.)

2.5 CALL STATEMENTS

All parameters in a CALL statement were implicitly passed by reference in VS COBOL. This meant that when one program called an-

```
000010 DATA DIVISION.
000020 WORKING-STORAGE SECTION.
000030 01  FIELD1                   PIC S9(5) COMP-3 VALUE +123.
000040 01  FIELD2                   PIC S9(5) COMP-3 VALUE 123.
```

Figure 2.8 Numeric VALUE clauses without a sign specified in them are allowed in COBOL II for signed numeric fields.

other using a parameter, only the address of the parameter was passed. The data was not copied; when the called program referenced the passed data, it was using exactly the same data area that was used in the calling program. In COBOL II conventional parameters passed in a CALL are considered passed BY REFERENCE (the default). As an example, if you wish to pass TABLE1 to PROGRAM2, in COBOL II you may code the call with either USING TABLE1 (the syntax used in VS COBOL) or USING BY REFERENCE TABLE1.

The CALL statement in COBOL II permits the use of the BY CONTENT phrase to allow constants to be passed to another program and the BY CONTENT LENGTH OF phrase to allow the length of a data item to be passed to another program. Lengths are fullword binary fields and have implicit definitions of S9(9) COMP. Release 3 allows the BY CONTENT phrase to be used with data items as well as constants. If any data item passed in the BY CONTENT phrase gets modified in the called program, its value is not affected in the calling program; COBOL II makes a copy of the data to be passed and passes the address of the copied data to the called program.

As an example, suppose that PROGRAM1 calls PROGRAM2, passing BY CONTENT PARM1, and that PROGRAM2 calls PROGRAM3, passing BY REFERENCE PARM1. If PROGRAM2 modifies PARM1, it will not affect the PARM1 used in PROGRAM1. However, if the modification is done before PROGRAM3 is called, PROGRAM3 will receive the modified copy. Additionally, if PROGRAM3 modifies PARM1, it is affecting the PARM1 used in PROGRAM2.

The USING clause in the called program is coded the same way whether or not the BY REFERENCE or BY CONTENT phrases were used in the calling program. Figure 2.9 shows the use of these phrases in CALL statements. Note that when a data item is passed without specifying BY REFERENCE or BY CONTENT directly before it, the phrase last coded above it applies. In the first call in Fig. 2.9 EMPLOYEE-NAME is passed BY REFERENCE, in the second call BY CONTENT.

Be careful with the length of literals passed BY CONTENT. If a called program has STATE-CODE defined as 14 bytes long, it is fine to code USING BY CONTENT 'NORTH CAROLINA' or USING BY CONTENT 'OHIO   ' in the calling program. However, if you code USING BY CONTENT 'OHIO', problems may arise. The statement IF STATE-CODE IS EQUAL TO 'OHIO' may not result in an equal condition in the called program. Literals passed BY CONTENT that are shorter in the calling program than their definitions in the called program can also cause protection exceptions (0C4s).

COBOL II programs can pass the DCB of a non-VSAM file to an assembler program if the file name is coded as a BY REFERENCE

```
000010 IDENTIFICATION DIVISION.
000020 PROGRAM-ID. PROGRAM1.
000030 DATA DIVISION.
000040 WORKING-STORAGE SECTION.
000050 01  MONTH-TABLE.
000060     05  FILLER              PIC X(11) VALUE '01JANUARY  '.
000070     05  FILLER              PIC X(11) VALUE '02FEBRUARY '.
000080     05  FILLER              PIC X(11) VALUE '03MARCH    '.
000090     05  FILLER              PIC X(11) VALUE '04APRIL    '.
000100     05  FILLER              PIC X(11) VALUE '05MAY      '.
000110     05  FILLER              PIC X(11) VALUE '06JUNE     '.
000120     05  FILLER              PIC X(11) VALUE '07JULY     '.
000130     05  FILLER              PIC X(11) VALUE '08AUGUST   '.
000140     05  FILLER              PIC X(11) VALUE '09SEPTEMBER'.
000150     05  FILLER              PIC X(11) VALUE '10OCTOBER  '.
000160     05  FILLER              PIC X(11) VALUE '11NOVEMBER '.
000170     05  FILLER              PIC X(11) VALUE '12DECEMBER '.
000180 01  FILLER REDEFINES MONTH-TABLE.
000190     05  MONTH-ENTRY OCCURS 12 TIMES
000200           ASCENDING KEY IS MONTH-TAB-NUMBER
000210           INDEXED BY MONTH-INDEX.
000220         10 MONTH-TAB-NUMBER PIC 99.
000230         10 MONTH-TAB-NAME   PIC X(9).
000240 01  EMPLOYEE-NAME           PIC X(40).
000250
000260 PROCEDURE DIVISION.
000270     CALL 'PROGRAM2' USING
000280               BY REFERENCE MONTH-TABLE
000290                            EMPLOYEE-NAME
000300           BY CONTENT '063089'
000310           BY CONTENT LENGTH OF MONTH-TABLE.
000320
000330*RELEASE 3 ALLOWS 'BY CONTENT' TO BE USED WITH DATA ITEMS
000340     CALL 'PROGRAM2' USING
000350           BY CONTENT MONTH-TABLE
000360                      EMPLOYEE-NAME
000370           BY CONTENT '010190'
000380           BY CONTENT LENGTH OF MONTH-TABLE.
```

(a)

```
000010 IDENTIFICATION DIVISION.
000020 PROGRAM-ID. PROGRAM2.
000030 DATA DIVISION.
000040 LINKAGE SECTION.
000050 01  MONTH-TABLE.
000060     05  MONTH-ENTRY OCCURS 12 TIMES
000070           ASCENDING KEY IS MONTH-TAB-NUMBER
000080           INDEXED BY MONTH-INDEX.
000090         10 MONTH-TAB-NUMBER PIC 99.
000100         10 MONTH-TAB-NAME   PIC X(9).
000110 01  DATE-MMDDYY             PIC 9(6).
000120 01  MONTH-TABLE-LENGTH      PIC S9(9) COMP.
000130 01  EMPLOYEE-NAME           PIC X(40).
000140 PROCEDURE DIVISION USING
000150                      MONTH-TABLE
000160                      EMPLOYEE-NAME
000170                      DATE-MMDDYY
000180                      MONTH-TABLE-LENGTH.
```

(b)

Figure 2.9 CALL from PROGRAM1 to PROGRAM2 using new options of the CALL statement supported by COBOL II. (a) Calling and (b) called programs.

parameter. This was allowed in VS COBOL as well. VS COBOL also allowed a CALL statement that passed a paragraph name to an assembler program, but this is no longer supported in COBOL II.

A CALL BY CONTENT using a data item is less efficient than a CALL BY REFERENCE using the same data item. The BY CONTENT phrase instructs COBOL to use extra storage for a copy of the parameter and then requires the overhead of moving the parameter to the new area. For these reasons, using large data items as parameters in the BY CONTENT phrase should certainly be avoided. When the BY CONTENT phrase is used, the passed fields are placed in the TEMPORARY STORAGE-2 fields within the TGT. (Refer to Sec. 14.6.4 for a more complete explanation of temporary storage.)

I see little advantage in using the BY CONTENT phrase with data items, but there are cases when its use can enable the IBM optimizer to produce more efficient code. When data is processed in WORKING-STORAGE, the IBM optimizer checks to see if the data never changes. If the data is passed to another program by REFERENCE, the optimizer assumes that it might be changed and is not a constant. When data is passed BY CONTENT, the optimizer is sure that it will not be modified and may be able to produce more efficient code. However, it is rare if ever that this optimization will outweigh the inefficiency of using BY CONTENT in the first place.

Passing data BY CONTENT does prevent the called program from changing the parameter data in the calling program, but this is simple enough to do through coding in the called program. BY CONTENT might be useful in cases where the protection of data in a calling program is essential for security and you have no control over the code in the called programs. For instance, if you write software which calls some programs of your clients you might code BY CONTENT in your calls to ensure that their programs do not alter the critical data in your program.

2.6 PERFORMS

2.6.1 Traditional Out-of-Line PERFORMs

The PERFORM statement has often confused programmers because conditions in the UNTIL clause were examined before the PERFORM was executed, not after it. COBOL II allows you to specify whether the UNTIL condition is evaluated before or after a paragraph is performed; code either WITH TEST BEFORE (the default if not coded, compatible with VS COBOL) or WITH TEST AFTER (which is easier to follow and will probably be used by the next generation of programmers). Figure 2.10 illustrates three types of PERFORMs. A

```
000010 PROCEDURE DIVISION.
000020     PERFORM INIT-TABLE THRU INIT-END
000030         VARYING SUB1 FROM +1 BY +1
000040         UNTIL SUB1 IS GREATER THAN +3.
000050     ...
000060 INIT-TABLE.
000070     MOVE ZERO TO TABLE-ENTRY (SUB1).
000080 INIT-END. EXIT.
```

(a)

```
000010 PROCEDURE DIVISION.
000020     PERFORM INIT-TABLE THRU INIT-END
000030         WITH TEST BEFORE
000040         VARYING SUB1 FROM +1 BY +1
000050         UNTIL SUB1 IS GREATER THAN +3.
000060
000070     PERFORM INIT-TABLE THRU INIT-END
000080         WITH TEST AFTER
000090         VARYING SUB1 FROM +1 BY +1
000100         UNTIL SUB1 IS EQUAL TO +3.
000110     ...
000120 INIT-TABLE.
000130     MOVE ZERO TO TABLE-ENTRY (SUB1).
000140 INIT-END. EXIT.
```

(b)

Figure 2.10 Three out-of-line PERFORMs that all produce the same results. (a) Code allowed under VS COBOL or COBOL II; (b) PERFORMs only allowed under COBOL II.

PERFORM WITH TEST AFTER will always execute a paragraph at least once while a PERFORM WITH TEST BEFORE may not.

2.6.2 In-line PERFORMs

The COBOL II PERFORM statement also allows the performed procedure to be coded in-line (see Fig. 2.11). In an in-line PERFORM, the code to be performed is put directly after the PERFORM statement and the paragraph name to be performed is not coded. An END-

```
000010 PROCEDURE DIVISION.
000020     PERFORM
000030         VARYING SUB1 FROM +1 BY +1
000040         UNTIL SUB1 IS GREATER THAN 3
000050             MOVE ZERO TO TABLE-ENTRY (SUB1)
000060     END-PERFORM.
```

Figure 2.11 Example of a COBOL II in-line PERFORM.

PERFORM statement is required at the end of an in-line PERFORM (but may not be coded with an out-of-line PERFORM). END-PERFORM is a COBOL II scope terminator, which is discussed later in this section and more fully in Sec. 3.1.

The WITH TEST BEFORE and WITH TEST AFTER clauses are supported for in-line PERFORMs but the AFTER portion of the VARYING clause is not. However, you can accomplish the same results as using AFTER by nesting in-line PERFORMs. The out-of-line PERFORM and the nested in-line PERFORMs in Fig. 2.12 are equivalent. The example shows how a nested in-line PERFORM can be used to produce the equivalent function of an out-of-line PERFORM that contains AFTER in its VARYING clause.

Scope terminators explicitly mark where the scope of one statement ends and the next statement begins. The use of the COBOL II scope

```
000010 PROCEDURE DIVISION.
000020     PERFORM INIT-TABLE THRU INIT-END
000030        VARYING SUB1 FROM +1 BY +1
000040           UNTIL SUB1 > 5
000050        AFTER SUB2 FROM +1 BY +1
000060           UNTIL SUB2 > 7
000070        AFTER SUB3 FROM +1 BY +1
000080           UNTIL SUB3 > 9.
000090
000100 INIT-TABLE.
000110     MOVE ZERO TO TABLE-ENTRY (SUB1, SUB2, SUB3).
000120 INIT-END. EXIT.
```

(a)

```
000010 PROCEDURE DIVISION.
000020     PERFORM
000030      VARYING SUB1 FROM +1 BY +1
000040      UNTIL SUB1 > 5
000050        PERFORM
000060         VARYING SUB2 FROM +1 BY +1
000070         UNTIL SUB2 > 7
000080           PERFORM
000090            VARYING SUB3 FROM +1 BY +1
000100            UNTIL SUB3 > 9
000110             MOVE ZERO TO TABLE-ENTRY (SUB1, SUB2, SUB3)
000120           END-PERFORM
000130        END-PERFORM
000140     END-PERFORM.
```

(b)

Figure 2.12 How in-line PERFORMs can be coded to function equivalently to an out-of-line PERFORM with the AFTER clause. (*a*) Out-of-line PERFORM; (*b*) equivalent in-line PERFORMs.

```
000010 PROCEDURE DIVISION.
000020      PERFORM UNTIL FILE-END IS EQUAL TO 'Y'
000030         IF READ-RECORD = 'Y'
000040            READ IN-FILE
000050               AT END MOVE 'Y' TO FILE-END
000060            END-READ
000070         ELSE PERFORM B500-WRITE-RECORD
000080         END-IF
000090      END-PERFORM.
```

Figure 2.13 Use of scope terminators within an in-line PERFORM.

terminators can be used to turn conditional statements into imperative statements as seen Fig. 2.13. When coding in-line PERFORMs, remember that all statements contained in them must be imperative statements, not conditional ones.

Confronted with the choice of using the in-line PERFORM or the conventional out-of-line PERFORM, which should you use? It is more efficient to code an in-line PERFORM since the linkage required to branch out-of-line and then to return is not required. More importantly, the code is easier to read when an in-line PERFORM is used. You no longer have to hold your finger on the page containing the PERFORM statement while you flip through the listing to another page containing the performed paragraph, or split a screen into two to follow a program.

The advantage of an out-of-line PERFORM is that if a procedure is performed from many different places in a program, it is easier to code and less error prone to place the code only in one location in the program. By not duplicating a procedure throughout a program, the code will be easier to maintain. The program will also require less storage. However, this last statement is only sometimes true since the IBM optimizer copies some out-of-line performs into the place from which they are performed, making them more efficient in-line performs. In some cases this can actually require more storage than coding in-line PERFORMs because the original performed procedure is left out-of-line even when copies are placed in-line. More specific details on optimization are discussed in Sec. 12.5.5.

2.7 ERROR PROCESSING

Some error processing done by COBOL II has become considerably more user friendly than the error processing in VS COBOL. For example, when you have an erroneous GO TO in a program, you might fall through the code beyond the last line in the program. In VS COBOL this produced a 519 User ABEND without any message indicating the cause of the problem. When the same condition occurs in COBOL II, a 1037 User ABEND occurs. However, the major difference is that in COBOL II a message is produced informing the programmer that the execution preceded beyond the last line of the program. A full list of the run-time messages, debug tool messages, and the common ABENDs can be found in the appendix of the *VS COBOL II Application Programming: Debugging* manual.

Not only have the error messages produced by the compiler changed, but the letter that indicates the severity has changed as well. The errors in VS COBOL were, from least to most severe, W (Warning, return code of 4), C (Caution, RC = 8), E (Error, RC = 12), and D (Disaster, RC = 16). The severity levels in COBOL II are I (Informational, RC = 0), W (Warning, RC = 4), E (Error, RC = 8), S (Severe, RC = 12), and U (Unrecoverable, also called terminating, RC = 16). Notice particularly that the meaning of the term "error message" has changed. In VS COBOL it meant a severe error and in COBOL II it applies to what used to be called a cautionary error.

Information messages did not exist in VS COBOL. In COBOL II they are used to inform the programmer of coding inefficiencies or other conditions that the programmer has the option to change. For example, if your program contains an internal sort that might run faster when the FASTSRT compiler option is used, the compiler issues an informational message.

2.8 COMPILER LIMITS

A nice advantage of COBOL II is that a number of compiler limits have been expanded. A 77 or 01 level data item may now be up to 16 megabytes long. Elementary fields, previously limited to 32K, now also can be up to 16 megabytes. Table entries may have a maximum length of 8 megabytes (see Fig. 2.14). Do not be surprised if you see quite large BL cell numbers in a program with a large WORKING-STORAGE SECTION. One BL cell is required for each 4096 bytes. VS COBOL had a WORKING-STORAGE limit of 1 megabyte while CO-BOL II allows up to 128 megabytes. The LINKAGE SECTION which

```
000010 DATA DIVISION.
000020 WORKING-STORAGE SECTION.
000030 01  BIG-FIELD                  PIC X(15000000).
000040 01  LARGE-TABLE.
000050     05  LARGE-ENTRY OCCURS 2 TIMES PIC X(8000000).
```

Figure 2.14 Large fields allowed under COBOL II's relaxed limits. While the fields may look excessive, they are supported under COBOL II.

supported up to 255 BLL cells in VS COBOL has no fixed upper limit in COBOL II.

2.9 LEVEL NUMBERS

Data items with a 77 level were not aligned in VS COBOL and therefore required less storage than equivalent 01 level data items. (Equivalent 77 and 01 level data items required the same amount of storage if their length was a multiple of 8.) There is no longer any advantage to code a 77 level rather than an 01 level since they are both doubleword aligned. The storage required for either is rounded up to the next multiple of 8 bytes. Data items coded with other level numbers are not aligned in VS COBOL or COBOL II unless they contain the SYNCHRONIZED clause. In this case the data item becomes halfword, fullword, or doubleword aligned.

COBOL II allows nonstandard level numbers. This means that level numbers at the same level do not have to be equal. In Fig. 2.15, the standard coding of the 07 level would be a 10 level and the 02 level would be an 05 level. Nonstandard level numbers are confusing and I recommend that they not be used. However, if they are used, they will not cause compilation errors.

There is a time when nonstandard level numbers are helpful. Suppose that in Fig. 2.15, PART1 and its subfields were contained in one copy member and PART2 in another. It is sometimes difficult to fit copy members into code when the level numbers within the copy members do not seem to correspond with each other. This problem can sometimes be resolved by using COPY statements with somewhat complex REPLACING phrases to dynamically change the level numbers in the copy member. Nonstandard level numbers might be useful in this case to be able to use the COPY members without dynamic changes. (The example just described assumes that you do not want to update copy members. This may be the case when they contain the proper level numbers for use in some programs but not others.)

```
000010 DATA DIVISION.
000020 WORKING STORAGE SECTION.
000030 01   GROUP1.
000040      05   PART1.
000050           10   PART1-SUBA     PIC X.
000060           07   PART1-SUBB     PIC X.
000070      02   PART2              PIC X(5).
```

Figure 2.15 Example of nonstandard level numbers allowed under COBOL II.

2.10   COPY STATEMENT

COPY statement processing has been enhanced in COBOL II to allow
nested COPYs, i.e., a copy member may contain COPY statements.
This is allowed in many other languages and is a welcome addition to
COBOL. There is, however, a restriction on nested COPY statements.
A COPY statement that contains a REPLACING clause cannot use a
copy member that contains a nested COPY, and a nested COPY statement cannot contain the REPLACING clause. Be careful not to allow
a COPY statement to COPY, directly or indirectly, the copy member
that copied it. This is a recursive COPY statement. It is not supported
by COBOL II and will cause a severe error message.

COPY statement processing has somewhat changed in Release 3. In
Release 2 lowercase letters in a COPY member were processed as
equivalent to uppercase letters; in Release 3 they are not. Additionally, Release 3 allows COPY members to contain characters that are
not in the standard COBOL II character set.

2.11   SECTIONS

The segmentation feature implemented by coding SECTIONs is supported by the COBOL II compiler. A segment of code in a VS COBOL
or COBOL II program may be made into a section by specifying a section name (in the same manner as specifying a paragraph name) and
following the name with the word SECTION. A priority number may
be coded on each section. However, all sections with a priority number
of 0 through 99 are considered fixed permanent segments. In VS
COBOL segment numbers up to 49 were considered fixed permanent
segments. The SEGMENT-LIMIT clause, which allowed this limit to
be changed to a smaller number, is not supported under COBOL II. VS
COBOL originally used the priority number to determine whether a
segment was a fixed permanent segment, a fixed overlayable segment,
or an independent segment. Virtual storage eliminated the need for
overlayable segments and Release 2 of VS COBOL began to phase out
part of the segment concept. Overlays no longer existed. In COBOL II
all segments are treated like fixed permanent segments and the use of
storage is not affected by segment numbers.

The priority numbers can affect program optimization. Paragraphs
performed from sections that have a different priority number than
the priority number of the performed paragraph's section cannot be
optimized by being converted to in-line performs (see Sec. 10.6.1.).
When section names are used for a part of a COBOL II program but
the entire program is not broken into sections, the compiler issues a

warning message that some paragraphs prior to the first section were not contained within sections.

When the SORT statement was issued in VS COBOL, a section name was expected as the INPUT PROCEDURE or the OUTPUT PROCEDURE. The compiler accepted a paragraph name instead but issued a warning message. In COBOL II Release 2, a paragraph name is accepted but the compiler issues an error message. The Release 3 compiler allows either a section name or a paragraph name for the procedures in a SORT and no warning or error message is issued if a paragraph name is used.

2.12 WHEN-COMPILED SPECIAL REGISTER

The WHEN-COMPILED special register can be used as the sending field in a move statement to obtain the compilation date and time. It is used in the same manner in COBOL II as it was in VS COBOL. However, the format of the information it contains has changed. The format is now consistent with the format in DOS/VS COBOL. In VS COBOL, WHEN-COMPILED had the format "hh.mm.ssMMM DD, YYYY" where hh was the hour (in 24-hour format), mm the minutes, ss the seconds, MMM the first three letters of the month name, DD the day, and YYYY the full year. In COBOL II the format is "MM/DD/YYhh.mm.ss" where MM is the numeric month, DD is the day, YY is the last two digits of the year, and the time is in the same format as was used in VS COBOL.

3

New Features in Release 2

3.1 EXPLICIT SCOPE TERMINATORS

In VS COBOL, as well as in COBOL II, the period is an implicit scope terminator that ends the scope of any statements that have not yet terminated. For example, the scope of an AT END, ON OVERFLOW, or ON SIZE ERROR clause in a VS COBOL program remains in effect until a period is reached. This prevents statements containing these clauses from being nested.

Figure 3.1 shows the explicit scope terminators which have been added to the COBOL II compiler. Explicit scope terminators allow sections of code to be written without the periods that may have been required in a VS COBOL program. What they basically do is show the end of a particular statement in the PROCEDURE DIVISION. While they are often used to improve program structure, they are valuable to turn conditional statements into imperative statements, allowing the statement to be nested. Figure 3.2 shows how a READ statement with an AT END clause can appear in the middle of nested IF statements, something that was not possible in VS COBOL. An explicit scope ter-

```
END-ADD                    END-READ
END-CALL                   END-RETURN
END-COMPUTE                END-REWRITE
END-DELETE                 END-SEARCH
END-DIVIDE                 END-START
END-EVALUATE               END-STRING
END-IF                     END-SUBTRACT
END-MULTIPLY               END-UNSTRING
END-PERFORM                END-WRITE
```

Figure 3.1 Listing of the explicit scope terminators.

```
000010 DATA DIVISION.
000020 WORKING-STORAGE SECTION.
000030 01  WS-RECORDS-READ        PIC S9(5) COMP-3 VALUE ZERO.
000040 01  WS-GET-REC             PIC X.
000050
000060 PROCEDURE DIVISION.
000070     ...
000080     IF WS-GET-REC = 'Y'
000090         READ FILE1 AT END
000100             IF WS-RECORDS-READ = ZERO
000110                 PERFORM NO-RECORDS
000120             ELSE PERFORM SOME-RECORDS
000130             END-IF
000140         END-READ
000150     ELSE PERFORM DONT-READ-FILE
000160     END-IF.
```

Figure 3.2 Use of explicit scope terminators in a COBOL II program.

minator ends the last occurrence of its associated statement. The END-IF on line 000130 in Fig. 3.2 ends the IF statement on line 000100, not the IF statement on line 000080, which is terminated by the END-IF on line 000160.

Note that the END-PERFORM statement is required to be used with an in-line PERFORM and cannot be coded on a standard out-of-line PERFORM. It is the only scope terminator required for a statement that is not nested.

3.2 CONTINUE STATEMENT

The CONTINUE statement is a null statement that does not generate executable code. It can be used wherever the compiler syntax allows an imperative or conditional statement. Examples of its use are in an IF statement instead of a NEXT SENTENCE, or in an EVALUATE statement (discussed in Sec. 3.4) since it does not allow a NEXT SENTENCE. While CONTINUE may be used instead of NEXT SENTENCE in an IF statement, they are not always equivalent. When NEXT SENTENCE is processed in an IF statement, execution continues from after the next period; when CONTINUE is processed in an IF statement, execution continues from after the next END-IF. In Fig. 3.3, PERFORM BIG-STATE is executed after the CONTINUE statement is processed. If NEXT SENTENCE was coded instead of CONTINUE, PERFORM BIG-STATE would not have been executed.

3.3 INITIALIZE STATEMENT

The INITIALIZE statement allows the initialization of all fields within a group data item (or of an elementary data item) with a single

```
000010 DATA DIVISION.
000020 WORKING-STORAGE SECTION.
000030 01   STATE-CODE              PIC XX.
000040 01   CITY-CODE               PIC XX.
000050
000060 PROCEDURE DIVISION.
000070      IF STATE-CODE = '07'
000080          IF CITY-CODE = '02'
000090              PERFORM BIG-CITY
000100          ELSE CONTINUE
000110          END-IF
000120          PERFORM BIG-STATE
000130      END-IF.
```

Figure 3.3 CONTINUE and NEXT SEN-
TENCE are not equivalent. The code will
produce different results if CONTINUE is
replaced with NEXT SENTENCE.

statement. It does not require that each individual elementary field
within a group be listed. Each alphabetic, alphanumeric, or
alphanumeric-edited field is cleared to spaces while numeric,
numeric-edited, and floating-point items are cleared to zeros. The
statement also allows specific values (if other than spaces and zeros
are desired) to be used, as well as allowing only certain types of data
(numeric, alphanumeric, etc.) to be initialized. This is requested with
the REPLACING clause.

The format of the INITIALIZE statement is as follows:

```
INITIALIZE item-1 [item-2 item-3 ... item-n]
    [REPLACING] [ALPHABETIC DATA BY object-1]
                [ALPHANUMERIC DATA BY object-2]
                [NUMERIC DATA BY object-3]
                [ALPHANUMERIC-EDITED DATA BY object-4]
                [NUMERIC-EDITED DATA BY object-5]
                [DBCS DATA BY object-6]
                [EGCS DATA BY object-7]
```

where *item* is a data item in the program and *object* is either a data
item or a literal. The bracketed data is optional.

3.3.1 REPLACING Clause

When the REPLACING clause is not used, alphabetic, alphanumeric,
and alphanumeric-edited fields are filled with spaces, while numeric
and numeric-edited fields are filled with zeros. When the REPLAC-
ING clause is used on a group data item, only those fields that exactly
match the category of data specified in the REPLACING clause are
initialized. Be very careful when specifying data categories in the RE-

```
000010 DATA DIVISION.
000020 WORKING-STORAGE SECTION.
000030 01  FIELD3                      PIC ZZ9.
000040
000050 PROCEDURE DIVISION.
000060     INITIALIZE FIELD3.
000070     INITIALIZE FIELD3
000080            REPLACING NUMERIC DATA BY 0.
```

Figure 3.4 Use of the INITIALIZE statement
with an elementary field.

PLACING phrase or you will get unwanted results. For instance,
while line 000060 in Fig. 3.4 will initialize FIELD3 to 0, lines 000070
and 000080 will not move any data. This is because FIELD3 does not
contain NUMERIC data but does contain NUMERIC-EDITED data.

Lines 000070 and 000080 generate an interesting line in the Procedure Map. The statement is shown but no code is shown next to it
since none was produced. Be careful when coding statements like this
since while Release 2 gives it an error (return code = 8), Release 3
only produces a warning message for the code.

There are a number of specifics about the INITIALIZE statement
that must be understood. In Release 2 only one REPLACING phrase is
allowed in an INITIALIZE statement while multiple REPLACING
phrases are allowed in Release 3. (The word "REPLACING" only appears once but multiple clauses specifying data to be initialized can be
coded, e.g., REPLACING ALPHANUMERIC DATA BY HIGH-
VALUES NUMERIC DATA BY 5.) Fields that contain the OC-
CURS DEPENDING ON clause, or have subordinate fields containing
the clause, may not be acted upon with the INITIALIZE statement.

3.3.2 Group Items

When a group item (or a group item within a group item) is initialized, the specific rules of the INITIALIZE statement determine which
of the elementary fields are affected. The fields that are initialized
will either be set to the default value or the value specified in the
REPLACING phrase except as follows:

- Elementary FILLER fields are not initialized.

- Explicit and implicit index data items are not initialized.

- Pointer fields are not initialized. (Pointer fields are described in Sec.
  6.1.3.)

- Data items containing the REDEFINES clause and data items subordinate to the REDEFINES clause are initialized as per their nonredefined definitions.

Figure 3.5 shows how the INITIALIZE statement, with and without the REPLACING option, works with group fields. Line 000120 will initialize all fields within TABLE-INIT except for the FILLER. When line 000130 is executed, only TI-FIELD2, TI-FIELD4, and TI-FIELD5 will be initialized because they are the only named fields that are defined as numeric. Notice that TI-FIELD3 is not initialized because it is a numeric-edited field, not a numeric field. The FILLER was not initialized even though it was defined as numeric and TI-FIELD1 was not initialized because it is an alphanumeric field.

Be aware that it makes no difference to the INITIALIZE statement whether or not a VALUE clause appears for a data item. In Fig. 3.6, the INITIALIZE statement will initialize all data items except for the FILLER fields on lines 000040 and 000060. This means that the value 'PRESIDENT' in TI-TITLE will be set to spaces but the 'NAME: ' and 'TITLE: ' values will remain unchanged. It makes sense that the INITIALIZE statement does not clear elementary FILLER fields (named data items below group FILLER fields, such as those on lines 000090 and 000100, are initialized), since this gives you the ability to define headings that will not be wiped out when the INITIALIZE statement is executed.

The INITIALIZE statement yields a nice advantage when compared to MOVE statements used to initialize data fields. If a DATA DIVISION copy member or a record description is modified with new or deleted fields, the INITIALIZE statement usually does not have to be updated. When the program is recompiled, the new or deleted field will be recognized by the compiler. The only negative aspect of the

```
000010 DATA DIVISION.
000020 WORKING-STORAGE SECTION.
000030 01   TABLE-INIT.
000040      05   TI-FIELD1          PIC X(7).
000050      05   TI-FIELD2          PIC S9(3) COMP-3.
000060      05   TI-FIELD3          PIC ZZ9.
000070      05   FILLER             PIC.9(5).
000080      05   TI-FIELD4          PIC S9(4) COMP.
000090      05   TI-FIELD5          PIC 9(2).
000100
000110 PROCEDURE DIVISION.
000120      INITIALIZE TABLE-INIT.
000130      INITIALIZE TABLE-INIT
000140            REPLACING NUMERIC DATA BY +999.
```

Figure 3.5 Use of the INITIALIZE statement with a group data item.

```
000010 DATA DIVISION.
000020 WORKING-STORAGE SECTION.
000030 01   TABLE-INIT.
000040      05   FILLER                    PIC X(6) VALUE 'NAME: '.
000050      05   TI-NAME                   PIC X(20).
000060      05   FILLER                    PIC X(7) VALUE 'TITLE: '.
000070      05   TI-TITLE                  PIC X(10) VALUE 'PRESIDENT'.
000080      05   FILLER.
000090           10   TI-ADDRESS-LINE1     PIC X(40).
000100           10   TI-ADDRESS-LINE2     PIC X(40).
000110
000120 PROCEDURE DIVISION.
000130      INITIALIZE TABLE-INIT.
```

Figure 3.6 Use of the INITIALIZE statement with data items that contain VALUE clauses.

statement is that it clears each field with an individual move instruction. A programmer can code a more efficient initialization routine (efficient methods to clear a table are discussed in Sec. 11.4.). However, the added efficiency would be at the expense of ease of maintenance.

3.4   EVALUATE STATEMENT

The EVALUATE statement allows enhanced condition testing to simplify decision logic. In structured programming a *case* structure is used to refer to the situation in which a choice between many paths is based on a set of conditions. EVALUATE is an easy way for a COBOL programmer to code a *case* structure. Its format is as follows (the bracketed data is optional):

```
EVALUATE x [ALSO x] ...
    WHEN y | [NOT] z [THROUGH | THRU  z] ...
    [ALSO y | [NOT] z] [THROUGH | THRU  z] ...
        imperative statement
    [WHEN OTHER imperative statement]
    [END-EVALUATE]
```

where x is either an identifier, a literal, an expression, or TRUE or FALSE; y is either ANY, TRUE, or FALSE; and z is either an identifier, a literal, or an arithmetic expression.

3.4.1   Comparison of EVALUATE and IF Statements

In its simplest form, the EVALUATE statement can be used instead of an IF statement (see Fig. 3.7). Note that IF statements may not

```
000010 DATA DIVISION.
000020 WORKING-STORAGE SECTION.
000030 01  CITY-CODE              PIC X(2).
000040     88  CITY-NY            VALUE '01'.
000050     88  CITY-ALBANY        VALUE '02'.
000060     88  CITY-BUFFALO       VALUE '03'.
000070 01  CITY-NAME             PIC X(8).
000080
000090 PROCEDURE DIVISION.
000100     ...
000110     IF CITY-NY
000120         MOVE 'NEW YORK' TO CITY-NAME
000130     ELSE
000140      IF CITY-ALBANY
000150          MOVE 'ALBANY' TO CITY-NAME
000160      ELSE
000170       IF CITY-BUFFALO
000180           MOVE 'BUFFALO' TO CITY-NAME
000190       ELSE
000200           MOVE 'UNKNOWN' TO CITY-NAME.
```

(a)

```
000010 DATA DIVISION.
000020 WORKING-STORAGE SECTION.
000030 01  CITY-CODE              PIC X(2).
000040     88  CITY-NY            VALUE '01'.
000050     88  CITY-ALBANY        VALUE '02'.
000060     88  CITY-BUFFALO       VALUE '03'.
000070 01  CITY-NAME             PIC X(8).
000080
000090 PROCEDURE DIVISION.
000100     ...
000110     EVALUATE CITY-CODE
000120         WHEN '01'
000130         MOVE 'NEW YORK' TO CITY-NAME
000140         WHEN '02'
000150         MOVE 'ALBANY' TO CITY-NAME
000160         WHEN '03'
000170         MOVE 'BUFFALO' TO CITY-NAME
000180         WHEN OTHER
000190         MOVE 'UNKNOWN' TO CITY-NAME
000200     END-EVALUATE.
```

(b)

Figure 3.7 Use of the (a) IF statement and (b, c) two EVALUATE statements to check for the values of a field. They all produce the same results.

```
000010 DATA DIVISION.
000020 WORKING-STORAGE SECTION.
000030 01  CITY-CODE              PIC X(2).
000040      88  CITY-NY           VALUE '01'.
000050      88  CITY-ALBANY       VALUE '02'.
000060      88  CITY-BUFFALO      VALUE '03'.
000070 01  CITY-NAME              PIC X(8).
000080
000090 PROCEDURE DIVISION.
000100     ...
000110     EVALUATE TRUE
000120       WHEN CITY-NY
000130         MOVE 'NEW YORK' TO CITY-NAME
000140       WHEN CITY-ALBANY
000150         MOVE 'ALBANY' TO CITY-NAME
000160       WHEN CITY-BUFFALO
000170         MOVE 'BUFFALO' TO CITY-NAME
000180       WHEN OTHER
000190         MOVE 'UNKNOWN' TO CITY-NAME
000200     END-EVALUATE.
```

(c)

Figure 3.7 (*Continued*)

```
000010 DATA DIVISION.
000020 WORKING-STORAGE SECTION.
000030 01  CITY-CODE              PIC X(2).
000040      88  CITY-NY           VALUE '01'.
000050      88  CITY-ALBANY       VALUE '02'.
000060      88  CITY-BUFFALO      VALUE '03'.
000070 01  CITY-NAME              PIC X(8).
000080
000090 PROCEDURE DIVISION.
000100     ...
000110     EVALUATE CITY-CODE
000120       WHEN CITY-NY
000130         MOVE 'NEW YORK' TO CITY-NAME
000140       WHEN CITY-ALBANY
000150         MOVE 'ALBANY' TO CITY-NAME
000160       WHEN CITY-BUFFALO
000170         MOVE 'BUFFALO' TO CITY-NAME
000180       WHEN OTHER
000190         MOVE 'UNKNOWN' TO CITY-NAME
000200     END-EVALUATE.
```

Figure 3.8 The EVALUATE statement will produce a compilation error because a condition name must correspond to TRUE or FALSE, not to a data item.

contain the OTHERWISE clause in COBOL II; ELSE must be used instead.

One of the problems with the EVALUATE statement is the flexibility of its coding syntax. A number of restrictions apply to the agreement between what is coded in the EVALUATE portion and what is coded in the WHEN portion. Determining whether the conditions should be coded in the EVALUATE or WHEN clause of the statement may seem confusing at first. For example, conditional expressions, and TRUE or FALSE, must be used in conjunction with each other to specify whether you are checking a condition for true or false. However, the condition may be coded in the EVALUATE portion, and the TRUE or FALSE in the WHEN portion, or vice versa.

An 88 level condition name cannot be used in an EVALUATE statement to match its corresponding data item. For example, the code in Fig. 3.8 will produce a compilation error and should have been coded as in Fig. 3.7.

In many cases the EVALUATE statement can replace nested IF statements containing AND operators (see Fig. 3.9). EVALUATE statements can have from zero to many ALSO clauses to specify multiple conditions to be checked. The EVALUATE statement in Fig. 3.9 is checking the condition of when GENDER = 'MALE' and ALSO the condition of when AGE > 25.

3.4.2 Placing Expressions in the EVALUATE or WHEN Portions

The EVALUATE statement allows expressions within the WHEN phrase rather than within the EVALUATE phrase (see Fig. 3.10). This method of coding is not as efficient as the code in Fig. 3.9 that has the expressions at the beginning of the EVALUATE statement, and the TRUE and FALSE clauses within the WHEN portions. The reason it is less efficient is that the expressions are reevaluated each time they are used. For instance, the GENDER and AGE compares may be executed three times in Fig. 3.10 but only once in Fig. 3.9.

A more important reason for coding as in Fig. 3.9 rather than Fig. 3.10 is that the code produced will be shorter and easier to follow in the case of an ABEND. In Fig. 3.9, a problem such as a decimal data exception (0C7) will come at the beginning portion of the EVALUATE statement, before any WHEN conditions are executed. The code in Fig. 3.10 can get a decimal data exception at three different places.

If WHEN ANY is coded, the corresponding expression is always considered true. The WHEN OTHER phrase is used to specify the statement to be executed when all of the other WHEN phrases are false. The WHEN OTHER phrase, when used, must be coded last. If all

```
000010 DATA DIVISION.
000020 WORKING-STORAGE SECTION.
000030 01  GENDER                    PIC X(6).
000040 01  AGE                       PIC S9(3) COMP-3.
000050
000060 PROCEDURE DIVISION.
000070     ...
000080     IF GENDER = 'MALE' AND AGE > 25
000090        PERFORM RATE-1
000100     ELSE IF GENDER = 'MALE' AND AGE NOT > 25
000110         PERFORM RATE-2
000120        ELSE IF GENDER NOT = 'MALE' AND AGE > 25
000130             PERFORM RATE-3
000140             ELSE PERFORM RATE-4.
```

(a)

```
000010 DATA DIVISION.
000020 WORKING-STORAGE SECTION.
000030 01  GENDER                    PIC X(6).
000040 01  AGE                       PIC S9(3) COMP-3.
000050
000060 PROCEDURE DIVISION.
000070     ...
000080     EVALUATE GENDER = 'MALE' ALSO AGE > 25
000090       WHEN TRUE ALSO TRUE
000100         PERFORM RATE-1
000110       WHEN TRUE ALSO FALSE
000120         PERFORM RATE-2
000130       WHEN FALSE ALSO TRUE
000140         PERFORM RATE-3
000150       WHEN OTHER
000160         PERFORM RATE-4
000170     END-EVALUATE.
```

(b)

Figure 3.9 Use of the (a) IF and (b) EVALUATE statements compared when checking a compound condition.

WHEN phrases are false and no WHEN OTHER phase is coded, program execution continues with the next program statement.

Arithmetic expressions can be coded in either the EVALUATE or the WHEN clause. In Fig. 3.11 the expressions appear within the WHEN portion rather than in the EVALUATE portion since this is clearer than if they were coded within the EVALUATE portion.

3.4.3 Using the THRU Clause

Another option in the EVALUATE statement is to use the THRU (or THROUGH) clause to check for ranges of a data item. Figure 3.12 shows an example of how it can be used in this manner.

```
000010 DATA DIVISION.
000020 WORKING-STORAGE SECTION.
000030 01  GENDER                    PIC X(6).
000040 01  AGE                       PIC S9(3) COMP-3.
000050 PROCEDURE DIVISION.
000060     ...
000070     EVALUATE TRUE ALSO TRUE
000080        WHEN GENDER = 'MALE  ' ALSO AGE > 25
000090           PERFORM RATE-1
000100        WHEN GENDER = 'MALE  ' ALSO AGE NOT > 25
000110           PERFORM RATE-2
000120        WHEN GENDER = 'FEMALE' ALSO AGE > 25
000130           PERFORM RATE-3
000140        WHEN OTHER
000150           PERFORM RATE-4
000160     END-EVALUATE.
```

Figure 3.10 EVALUATE statement with the condition in the WHEN rather than the EVALUATE portion of the statement.

```
000010 DATA DIVISION.
000020 WORKING-STORAGE SECTION.
000030 01  RATE                      PIC S9V9(4) COMP-3.
000040 01  PRINCIPAL                 PIC S9(7)V99 COMP-3.
000050 01  INTEREST                  PIC S9(7)V99 COMP-3.
000060
000070 PROCEDURE DIVISION.
000080     ...
000090     EVALUATE TRUE ALSO TRUE
000100        WHEN PRINCIPAL + INTEREST > 50000 ALSO RATE > .095
000110           ADD .0075 TO RATE
000120        WHEN PRINCIPAL + INTEREST > 10000 ALSO RATE > .09
000130           ADD .005 TO RATE
000140     END-EVALUATE.
```

Figure 3.11 Arithmetic expressions used in an EVALUATE statement.

```
000010 DATA DIVISION.
000020 WORKING-STORAGE SECTION.
000030 01  AGE                       PIC S9(3) COMP-3.
000040 01  WEIGHT                    PIC S9(3) COMP-3.
000050 01  PREMIUM                   PIC S9(7)V99 COMP-3.
000060
000070 PROCEDURE DIVISION.
000080     ...
000090     EVALUATE AGE ALSO WEIGHT
000100        WHEN 21 THRU 30 ALSO 140 THRU 200
000110           MOVE 200 TO PREMIUM
000120        WHEN 31 THRU 40 ALSO 150 THRU 225
000130           MOVE 250 TO PREMIUM
000140     END-EVALUATE.
```

Figure 3.12 Use of the THRU clause in an EVALUATE statement.

The WHEN phrases in an EVALUATE statement are evaluated in the order they are coded. For efficiency, the most probable WHEN conditions should be coded closest to the beginning of the EVALUATE statement and the least probable conditions closest to the end.

3.5   SET STATEMENT

The SET statement in COBOL II allows, in addition to its function of manipulating indexes (that was allowed in VS COBOL), a number of new functions. You now can SET addresses and POINTER data items. While addresses and pointers may be used in a batch program, they are more applicable to CICS and will be discussed in CICS Secs. 6.1.3, 6.1.4, and 6.1.5.

In VS COBOL you were able to update a data item by referring to the data item name, not by referring to a corresponding condition name (88 level). COBOL II allows the use of the SET verb with a condition name to update a data item (see Fig. 3.13). Realize that only a condition name, not a data name, can be set to TRUE. If line 000070 in Fig. 3.13 was coded as follows, a compilation error would occur:

```
000070    SET CITY-CODE TO TRUE.
```

Setting a condition name to TRUE instructs the COBOL II compiler to generate code equivalent to moving a literal to a data item, making the conditional expression true. When multiple values appear in an 88 level used in the SET...TO TRUE statement, the first value in the 88 level is used to set the associated data item to true. In Fig. 3.13, the code on line 000070 will set CITY-CODE to a value of '02'.

Note that there is a difference in the SET...TO TRUE statement between COBOL II Release 2 and Release 3. Release 2 sets the condition to true based upon the rules of the MOVE statement while Release 3 sets the condition to true based upon the rules of the VALUE clause. This can be a very subtle difference as illustrated in Fig. 3.14. The VALUE clause on EDIT-NUM initializes it to '089' regardless of whether the Release 2 or Release 3 compiler is used. In Release 2, the

```
000010 DATA DIVISION.
000020 WORKING-STORAGE SECTION.
000030 01   CITY-CODE              PIC XX.
000040      88 VALID-CITIES        VALUE '02' '05' '07'.
000050
000060 PROCEDURE DIVISION.
000070      SET VALID-CITIES TO TRUE.
```

Figure 3.13 Example of using the SET statement to set a condition to TRUE.

```
000010 DATA DIVISION.
000020 WORKING-STORAGE SECTION.
000030 01  EDIT-NUM                PIC ZZ9 VALUE '089'.
000040     88 EDIT-OK              VALUE '089'.
000050
000060 PROCEDURE DIVISION.
000070     SET EDIT-OK TO TRUE.
000080     ...
000090     MOVE '089' TO EDIT-NUM.
```

Figure 3.14 The SET statement places a different value into EDIT-NUM depending upon whether the Release 2 or Release 3 compiler is used.

code on lines 000070 and 000090 both set EDIT-NUM to ' 89'; in Release 3 line 000090 sets EDIT-NUM to ' 89', but the SET on line 000070 sets it to '089'.

3.6   TITLE STATEMENT

In the top line of each page in a COBOL II listing, the right side of the line contains the program name specified in the PROGRAM-ID of the outermost program (nested programs are discussed in Sec. 8.2), the page number, and the compilation date and time (e.g., PROGRAM1 Date 08/15/89 Time 15:53:13   Page 2). The left side of the title line contains the COBOL II compiler identification, the release number, and the date of the release (e.g., PP 5668-958 IBM VS COBOL II Release 3.0 09/13/88).

The TITLE statement allows you to change the information appearing on the left side of the title line on each page. It can be used to give a descriptive name to each part of a program (e.g., TITLE 'ACCOUNTING PROCEDURE - MONTHLY UPDATES.'). I recommend its use since titles can quickly show what part of a program you are looking at as you flip through a hard-copy listing.

The TITLE statement may appear anywhere within a program and will always force the listing to begin a new page. More than one TITLE statement can appear in a program and each new TITLE statement nullifies the previous one.

3.7   DOUBLE BYTE CHARACTER SET (DBCS)

The COBOL II compiler supports the Double Byte Character Set (DBCS). Double byte characters are characters that each occupy 2 bytes. They are used by programs that require a larger character set than is normally supported by COBOL. Applications that can make use of DBCS characters are those that use the Japanese Kanji character set or applications that use texts of chemical abstracts.

Double byte characters can be used as data or as code in a COBOL II program. When used as code, they can be used for most words, including data names, file names, and paragraph names. They cannot be used as COBOL II reserved words, level numbers, operators, or names that refer to an external item (e.g., the name of a copy member). DBCS characters used in code must contain a value from '41' to 'FE' for each byte. Additionally, a hexadecimal '4040' is a space and double byte EBCDIC characters can be represented with a hexadecimal '42' in the first byte of a pair of characters.

For a DATA DIVISION field to be defined as a DBCS data item it must contain a USAGE IS DISPLAY-1. The PICTURE clause on DBCS fields contains a G to signify each 2-byte character position. A G is also used to indicate a DBCS literal by placing it before the literal in the VALUE clause in the DATA DIVISION or before a literal in the PROCEDURE DIVISION (see Fig. 3.15). DBCS literals must contain an even number of bytes since each DBCS character is 2 bytes long. A DBCS literal (whether used in a VALUE clause or in the PROCEDURE DIVISION) consists of DBCS characters where each byte contains any hexadecimal value from '00' to 'FF'. SPACES can be used as a DBCS literal while HIGH-VALUES, LOW-VALUES, ZERO, and QUOTE cannot.

```
000010 DATA DIVISION.
000020 WORKING-STORAGE SECTION.
000030 01  DBCS-ITEM1.
000040     05  SO-CHAR1          PIC X VALUE X'0E'.
000050     05  DBCS-INFO1        PIC G(7) DISPLAY-1
000060                           VALUE G'< *dbcs-info** >'.
000070     05  SI-CHAR1          PIC X VALUE X'0F'.
000080 01  DBCS-ITEM2.
000090     05  SO-CHAR2          PIC X.
000100     05  DBCS-INFO2        PIC G(7) DISPLAY-1.
000110     05  SI-CHAR2          PIC X.
000120 01  MIXED-DBCS            PIC X(37).
000130
000140 PROCEDURE DIVISION.
000150     MOVE SHIFT-OUT TO SO-CHAR2.
000160     MOVE G'< *dbcs-info** >' TO DBCS-INFO2.
000170     MOVE SHIFT-IN TO SI-CHAR2.
000180     MOVE ' EBCDIC-data   < *dbcs-info** >   EBCDIC-data'
000190         TO MIXED-DBCS.
```

Figure 3.15 Use of SHIFT-IN and SHIFT-OUT special registers and literals with DBCS character strings. (The values for SO-CHAR1 and SI-CHAR1 are given in hexadecimal, a new feature allowed in Release 3.)

When double byte characters are used within a character string, the shift-out (hexadecimal '0E') and shift-in (hexadecimal '0F') characters have to appear around the string. For instance, in Fig. 3.15 the symbols < and > represent where shift-out and shift-in characters must appear. SHIFT-IN and SHIFT-OUT are special registers that contain shift-in and shift-out values, respectively, and may be used as the sending field in a MOVE statement. You can mix EBCDIC and DBCS characters in a character string by using the shift-out and shift-in characters before and after the DBCS portion of the string. The shift-in and shift-out characters count in the length of DBCS character strings used as code and in nonnumeric character strings that contain DBCS characters. A COBOL II word (which can be 30 characters long) can be up to 14 DBCS characters (28 bytes) plus a shift-in character and a shift-out character. However, the shift characters do not count within the length of a DBCS literal (DBCS-INFO1 in Fig. 3.15 contains seven DBCS characters plus the shift characters).

3.7.1 DBCS Class Test

A field may be checked to see whether or not it contains valid DBCS characters. The statement IF FIELD1 IS DBCS (similar to the statement IF FIELD1 IS NUMERIC) will be true if each byte of a DBCS character contains a value of hexadecimal '41' through 'FE' or both bytes are spaces. The class test of KANJI (IF FIELD1 IS KANJI) checks for a subset of DBCS characters. For the test to be true, the DBCS character must either be a space or have its first byte between hexadecimal '41' and '7F' and its second byte between hexadecimal '41' and 'FE'.

3.7.2 Service Routines for DBCS Manipulation

Certain COBOL II verbs that support byte-oriented data, such as the INSPECT, STRING, and UNSTRING commands, will yield unpredictable results if they use a character string that contains a mixture of EBCDIC and DBCS characters. Release 3 has two service routines to help in the manipulation of nonnumeric data items that contain DBCS data. These routines can be helpful when you have a mixture of DBCS and non-DBCS characters in a character string and wish to convert the entire string to a single character type.

Service routine IGZCA2D converts mixed data to pure DBCS data. It basically puts a hexadecimal '42' before each EBCDIC character in the string, converting the EBCDIC character to a DBCS character. The space character, however, is converted into hexadecimal '4040'.

To convert a pure DBCS character string into a string containing

EBCDIC and DBCS characters, service routine IGZCD2A can be called. It reverses the process that IGZCA2D performs. A programmer wanting to use an INSPECT statement on a mixed nonnumeric character string can call IGZCA2D before the INSPECT is executed, execute the INSPECT, and convert the data back to its original format by calling IGZCD2A. Note that the two service routines are not affected by the DBCS compiler option added to Release 3. (The DBCS compiler option is discussed in Sec. 8.6.5.)

Refer to the *COBOL II Application Programming Guide* for the exact parameters that must be passed to the DBCS service routines.

Updates to
Compiler Options

COBOL II compiler options have changed considerably from VS COBOL. The COUNT, STATE, and FLOW compiler options no longer exist in COBOL II since their functions are performed by the debugger (discussed in Sec. 4.7). The OSDECK option was used with a VS COBOL program compiled under CMS to produce a text deck compatible with a batch operating system (MVS, DOS/VSE) rather than with CMS. Text decks are automatically compatible under COBOL II, so OSDECK has been removed from the compiler options.

The LISTER feature that included the LSTONLY and LSTCOMP options is no longer part of the compiler. Although the listing produced by this feature was quite nice, the feature was not widely used. Additionally, the COBOL II compilation listing is improved over VS COBOL and contains some of the details produced by the LISTER feature.

4.1 COMPILER OPTION NAME CHANGES

I find it extremely annoying that, for no apparent reason, the names of a number of the COBOL II compiler options have been changed from their VS COBOL names. For example, PMAP (which produces a Procedure Map in VS COBOL) and CLIST (which produces a Condensed Listing) now have the less meaningful names of LIST and OFFSET. To further confuse the issue, the SXREF option is now XREF, and the VS COBOL XREF option (that produced a nonsorted cross-reference) is no longer supported. Figure 4.1 lists the main options that have had

```
VS COBOL Compiler Option     Equivalent COBOL II Compiler Option
CLIST                        OFFSET
CSYNTAX                      NOCOMPILE(S)
SYNTAX                       NOCOMPILE
DMAP                         MAP
FLAGE                        FLAG(E)
FLAGW                        FLAG(W)
LOAD                         OBJECT
PMAP                         LIST
SXREF                        XREF
```

Figure 4.1   Some VS COBOL compiler options that have been renamed in COBOL II.

their names changed (Appendix B contains a full list of changes to compiler option names).

4.2 FLAG OPTION

A number of new compiler options have been added to the COBOL II compiler, the most important of which are FLAG, SSRANGE, RENT, NUMPROC (called PFDSGN in Release 2), and FASTSRT. FLAG (x,y) is an enhancement of the FLAGW and FLAGE options of the VS CO-BOL compiler. The FLAGW and FLAGE options, respectively, inform the compiler to only list error messages with a warning level (W) or higher, or with an error level (E) or higher. The x in the COBOL II FLAG option serves a similar function and tells the compiler to only list error messages with a severity greater than or equal to the value substituted for x. The y value is a new feature that requests errors with a severity greater than or equal to y (y cannot be less than x) to be placed in the listing at the point at which they are detected (see Fig. 4.2). This is usually the point at which they occur but due to compilation logic may be somewhat later. The error messages are also placed at the end of the listing when this option is used. I find that embedded error messages make it much easier to fix compilation errors and strongly recommend their use.

4.3 SSRANGE OPTION

The SSRANGE option, which should have been included in COBOL years ago, checks references to subscripted areas, indexed areas, and OCCURS DEPENDING ON areas to ensure that the subscript, index, or DEPENDING ON value does not exceed the storage size allotted to the data areas by the compiler. Invalid values can cause storage overlays and/or protection exceptions (0C4s). For example, the program in Fig. 4.3 contains a one-dimensional table with 10 entries. Line 000090 attempts to move data to the fifteenth entry of the table. If the pro-

```
000001        000010 IDENTIFICATION DIVISION.
000002        000020 PROGRAM-ID. PROGRAM1.
000003        000030 ENVIRONMENT DIVISION.
000004        000040 DATA DIVISION.
000005        000050 WORKING-STORAGE SECTION.
000006        000060 01  FIELD1              PIC X(4).
000007        000070 01  FIELD2              PIX 9(4).
```

==000007==> IGYDS1089-S "PIX" was invalid. Skipped to the next area "A"
item, level-number, or the start of the next clause.

==000007==> IGYDS1159-E A "PICTURE" clause was not found for elementary
item "FIELD2". "PICTURE X(1)" was assumed.

```
000008        000080 01  FIELD3              PIC S9(3) COMP-3 VALUE +5.
000009        000090 01  FIELD4              PIC X.
000010        000100 PROCEDURE DIVISION.
000011        000110     MOVE FIELD1 TO FIELD5.
```

==000011==> IGYPS2121-S "FIELD5" was not defined as a data-name. The
statement was discarded.

```
000012        000120     GOBACK.
```

Figure 4.2   Example of a listing from a COBOL II program compiled with
the FLAG(I,E) option.

```
000010 DATA DIVISION.
000020 WORKING-STORAGE SECTION.
000030 01  TABLE1.
000040     05  ENTRY1 OCCURS 10 TIMES  PIC X(5).
000050 01  SUB1                        PIC S9(3) COMP-3.
000060
000070 PROCEDURE DIVISION.
000080     MOVE 15 TO SUB1.
000090     MOVE 'ABCDE' TO ENTRY1 (SUB1).
```

Figure 4.3   If the program is compiled with the SSRANGE
option, it is terminated when line 000090 is reached.

gram was compiled with the SSRANGE option, when line 000090 is
reached during program execution, an error message is displayed and
the program is terminated. The data movement to the fifteenth entry
will not occur and therefore a storage overlay will be prevented. It
makes no difference whether a range error occurs when a field is only
being examined or actually being moved to; the error is still caught
when the option is in effect.

SSRANGE also instructs the compiler to ensure valid values in a
reference modification statement. Reference modification is a new feature that was added in Release 3 (for more information refer to

Sec. 8.4). SSRANGE ensures that the starting position of a reference modification falls within the data item, that it is between 1 (the first position) and the length of the data item. It also makes sure that the length is at least 1 and that the reference modification (starting position plus length of the reference) does not go beyond the end of the data item.

SSRANGE checking occurs at execution time. However, the compiler can check constant (literal) subscripts at compilation time. If a constant subscript greater than the maximum value allowed for a table was coded in VS COBOL, no warning or error message was produced during program compilation. In COBOL II an error message (level E) will be produced during compilation if this condition occurs, whether or not the SSRANGE option is used. If the object code is run, the maximum value for the subscript is used. COBOL II also produces an error message for constant subscripts that are zero or negative; a constant 0 subscript is changed to a 1 and constant negative subscripts are given their absolute value. The changing of invalid subscripts to valid subscripts by the compiler can be very dangerous; severe error messages would have been more appropriate.

The implementation of the SSRANGE option is somewhat bizarre. If it makes no sense to you, you are in excellent company. When the SSRANGE option is used in a compilation, each use of a subscripted data name generates a call to a COBOL library routine (an incredibly inefficient method). The Release 2 compiler even calls the library routine when constant subscripts are used (the Release 3 compiler no longer does any run-time checking of constant subscripts). Furthermore, if a subscript is referenced on multiple statements within a paragraph and is not changed, the COBOL library routine will be called to revalidate the subscript for each reference.

If it still makes sense to you, realize that the full extent of the absurdity of the SSRANGE option is yet to be described. When the INITIALIZE statement is used to clear a table, the code generated by the compiler frequently calls the subscript range check routine to ensure that it is not outside of the table's limits.

Also realize that each subscript of a multisubscripted table element is not checked for validity, only the resulting address. For instance, if a three-dimensional table has a maximum subscript of (12, 10, 3) and you incorrectly use a subscript that generates a value (1, 1, 6), the code will compile and execute without producing any error message. Although one of the subscripts is outside its proper range, the address computed using all three subscripts will fall well inside the table limits.

While the SSRANGE option is useful, the machine code added by the compiler makes the program run considerably more slowly. Each time a subscript is used, even if it has not been changed, a COBOL library routine is used to check it. While useful in development of programs, the SSRANGE option should be avoided in the production environment; its inefficiency outweighs its advantages.

There is a run-time compiler option (also called SSRANGE) that can be used to turn off subscript checking even after the SSRANGE option has been used to compile a program. The program will process more efficiently when SSRANGE checking is turned off. However, a program processes most efficiently when the option is not used during compilation. (Refer to Sec. 12.6.1 for more information on the SSRANGE run-time option.)

4.4   RENT AND DATA OPTIONS

The RENT option makes a program reentrant. This allows one copy of a program to be shared by many users, such as is the case with CICS programs. For batch programs, it allows them to be put in the Link Pack Area (LPA) where one copy of a program can be shared by many batch jobs. The system implements the RENT option by copying the areas of the COBOL program that can be modified (e.g., the TGT and WORKING-STORAGE SECTION) into a GETMAINed area. In MVS and CMS it is put into subpool 0 storage, while in CICS it is put into CICS managed storage. A program compiled with the RENT option will take up more storage when it runs than a program compiled with the NORENT option (which makes a program non-reentrant). This is because besides the copy of the TGT and WORKING-STORAGE that are actually used by a program compiled with the RENT option, the program load module in storage also contains a copy of the TGT and WORKING-STORAGE. The copy in the load module is used by COBOL to initialize the GETMAINed area.

The following programs must be compiled with the RENT option:

- CICS programs.
- Programs that will be preloaded by IMS/VS.
- Programs that will be executed above the 16-megabyte line. [Prior to Extended Architecture (XA) and Enterprise Systems Architecture (ESA) all programs ran in up to 16 megabytes of virtual memory (below the 16-megabyte line). Addresses up to 16 megabytes can be represented with 24 bits. Programs that were written to only run in up to 16 megabytes of memory run in 24-bit addressing mode. Programs written to run in XA or ESA can address up to 2

gigabytes (2 billion bytes) of virtual memory. To do so they run in 31-bit addressing mode, allowing them to run either above or below the 16-megabyte line.]

- Programs that will be LOADed and DELETEd by programs that are not written in COBOL.

Programs compiled with the RENT option can run above or below the 16-megabyte line; programs compiled with NORENT can only run below the line. When the RENT option is used in conjunction with the DATA option, you may specify that program storage (e.g., WORKING-STORAGE and file areas) be acquired from unrestricted storage (i.e., storage located either above or below the 16-megabyte line). To do so you must run in XA or ESA and make sure that DATA(31) (the default) is used as a compilation option. By requesting the COBOL II compiler to allow a program and its data to reside above the 16-megabyte line you have helped achieve virtual storage constraint relief, allowing more storage for programs and data that must reside below the line. DATA(24) instructs the compiler that the data areas are to be allocated below the 16-megabyte line. This allows called programs running in 24-bit addressing mode to address data when it is passed as a parameter. When a program is compiled to run in 24-bit addressing mode (i.e., when a program is compiled with NORENT), the DATA option has no effect on the compilation.

When RENT is used, the RESIDENT option (discussed in Sec. 12.5.3) is required and is automatically put into effect by the COBOL II compiler. An additional requirement must be ensured by the programmer—if a program is compiled with the RENT option and is to run with other programs, all of the programs must be compiled with the RESIDENT option. If they are not, error message IGZ005I occurs at run-time and User ABEND U1005 follows.

4.4.1 AMODE and RMODE

Programs that run under MVS have an AMODE (addressing mode) and an RMODE (residency mode). AMODE(24) specifies that a program uses only 24-bit addressing mode, AMODE(31) specifies that a program uses only 31-bit addressing mode, and AMODE(ANY) specifies that a program can run in either 24-bit or 31-bit addressing mode. RMODE(24) indicates that a program will run below the 16-megabyte line and RMODE(ANY) means that it can run above or below the 16-megabyte line.

The compiler assigns AMODE and RMODE values for a COBOL II program based upon the compilation options. Programs compiled with the RENT option are given AMODE(ANY) and RMODE(ANY). When a program is compiled with the NORENT option, the AMODE and RMODE defaults are determined by the RESIDENT option. When RESIDENT is in effect, AMODE(ANY) and RMODE(24) are the defaults; otherwise AMODE(24) and RMODE(24) are used.

The AMODE and RMODE defaults of ANY can be overridden to 24 or 31 in the PARM of the linkage-editor. There are cases when you will have to request the linkage-editor to override the AMODE and RMODE assigned by the COBOL II compiler. For instance, if VS COBOL and COBOL II programs statically call each other and are link-edited into a single load module, the load module must be marked as AMODE(24) and RMODE(24).

4.5 NUMPROC OPTION

NUMPROC(PFD) (this option was called PFDSGN in Release 2) is a new option that can make a program run more efficiently. It affects packed decimal and external decimal numeric fields only. It instructs the compiler that (1) your numeric fields have valid signs, (2) the signs are F for unsigned fields and C or D for signed fields, and (3) signed fields containing a zero have a C as a sign. Programmers often do not realize that on IBM 370 hardware A, C, E, and F are positive signs while B and D are negative signs. None of these values will cause data exceptions (0C7s). However, when packed decimal calculations are performed on an IBM mainframe, the preferred signs of C and D are placed into the results.

The NUMPROC(NOPFD) option (this option was called NOPFDSGN in Release 2) tells the compiler that signed numeric fields in a program can have a sign of F, C, and D [not only C and D allowed by NUMPROC(PFD)]. Additionally, if the NUMCLS(ALT) installation option rather than the NUMCLS(PRIM) installation option was chosen for the compiler (the NUMCLS option is not changeable other than when the compiler is installed), the NUMPROC(NOPFD) option allows the values of A, B, and E for numeric signed fields.

The NUMPROC(PFD) and NUMPROC(NOPFD) options may not seem to be problematic until you realize that neither a program compiled with NUMPROC(PFD) nor NUMPROC(NOPFD) will always generate executable code that produces the same results as a program compiled and run using VS COBOL. For this reason, in addition to the other NUMPROC options, a new option was added to Release 3. As a migration aid, NUMPROC(MIG) requests COBOL II to perform similar sign processing to VS COBOL. Although NUMPROC(MIG) allows the same signs that are allowed by NUMPROC(NOPFD), the object code produced to process the fields differs. Among its differences, the NUMPROC(MIG) option instructs the compiler to produce Compare

Packed (CP) instructions when comparing numeric packed decimal fields. This is how VS COBOL worked. For the other two NUMPROC options, in many cases the COBOL II compiler will produce a Compare Logical Character (CLC) instruction instead. The CLC instruction is faster than the CP instruction and never causes a decimal data exception (0C7). The IF statement in Fig. 4.4 can only cause an 0C7 if the program was compiled with the NUMPROC(MIG) option. This has its pluses and minuses since many would prefer to ABEND rather than process with bad data and then have to determine why incorrect results were received.

Remember that the NUMPROC(MIG) option only affects packed decimal and display decimal fields. It does not affect the processing of floating-point or binary numeric fields. Binary fields may produce different results when processed under VS COBOL and under COBOL II. The TRUNC option, rather than the NUMPROC option, affects binary fields. Its proper use is discussed in Secs. 8.6.2 and 12.5.1.

The NUMPROC(MIG) and NUMPROC(NOPFD) options may both repair signs (place a valid sign) in fields that have an invalid sign. The compiler may either repair a sign explicitly (based upon its PICTURE) or implicitly (if it has to convert a numeric field from one format to another, e.g., from packed decimal to binary because a computation is being done with a binary data item). NUMPROC(MIG) will not do any explicit sign repair on fields input to an operation (although it may do implicit sign repair); it does not repair the sign of fields used in an arithmetic operation or in a comparison. The signs on input fields are repaired when NUMPROC(NOPFD) is used. If the program in Fig. 4.4 was compiled with NUMPROC(NOPFD), FIELD1 and FIELD2 are given positive signs before the IF is executed; if compiled with NUMPROC(MIG), the actual signs of the fields are used.

NUMPROC(MIG) produces preferred signs only on the output of MOVE statements and arithmetic computations. [NUMPROC(PFD) does not fix any signs; NUMPROC(NOPFD) ensures proper signs on both the receiving and sending fields.] When display or packed deci-

```
000010 DATA DIVISION.
000020 WORKING-STORAGE SECTION.
000030 01  FIELD1                    PIC 9(3).
000040 01  FIELD2                    PIC 9(3).
000050
000060 PROCEDURE DIVISION.
000070      IF FIELD1 > FIELD2
000080      ...
```

Figure 4.4 Code that may produce different results depending on the NUMPROC option used during compilation.

```
000010 DATA DIVISION.
000020 LINKAGE SECTION.
000030 01  FIELD1                        PIC S9(3) COMP-3.
000040 PROCEDURE DIVISION USING FIELD1.
000050     IF FIELD1 IS NUMERIC
000060         DISPLAY '****FIELD1 IS NUMERIC****'.
```

Figure 4.5 The NUMPROC option may affect the results of an IF...NUMERIC test.

mal data is moved, when computations are performed, or when invalid numeric data is used after it is moved, code produced from the NUMPROC(PFD) option yields the greatest chance of a decimal data exception. NUMPROC(NOPFD) yields code with the least chance of an 0C7.

Even though the NUMPROC(PFD) option leads to more efficient code being produced (the code is usually shorter and runs faster than when the other NUMPROC options are used), there are times when the other NUMPROC options should be used instead. For fields that are not in the format that NUMPROC(PFD) expects, the IF...IS NUMERIC test may produce different results when the NUMPROC(PFD) option is used rather than the other NUMPROC options. Line 000050 in Fig. 4.5 checks a packed decimal field for NUMERIC. Assume that FIELD1 has a hexadecimal value of '000F'. If the program is compiled with the NUMPROC(NOPFD) or NUMPROC(MIG) options, FIELD1 will be considered numeric. However, if compiled with the NUMPROC(PFD) option, the NUMERIC test will fail. FIELD1 does not have the preferred sign of C in a packed decimal field containing zero. To ensure that signed numeric data is properly processed when numbers are passed to or from a non-COBOL II program (such as when a COBOL II program calls or is called by a FORTRAN or PL/I program), IBM recommends that the NUMPROC(NOPFD) or the NUMPROC(MIG) option be used rather than the NUMPROC(PFD) option. I recommend NUMPROC(PFD) be used for all programs unless a program is sharing data with another program that is not passing data with preferred signs.

4.6 FASTSRT OPTION

The FASTSRT option allows a program to process a sort faster. This is accomplished by having the sort I/O run external to the program rather than having every record funnel through the COBOL I/O routines. It therefore only works when a SORT statement contains either a USING or a GIVING clause. An added restriction when using FASTSRT is that the USING and GIVING clauses may each contain only one file name (the GIVING clause only allowed one file name until Release 3). Figure 4.6 shows which SORT statements in a program would be affected by the FASTSRT compiler option.

If a program contains SORT statements that are not affected by the FASTSRT option, FASTSRT does not cause an error if it is used as a compilation option. However, during compilation you receive an informational message that a fast sort is not being performed. If the FASTSRT option was not used and SORT statements in the program exist for which the option would improve performance, informational messages inform you of this fact.

You may wonder why the FASTSRT option is not automatically implemented wherever it would improve performance. This is because of a number of very specific instances in which the sort not only runs faster but processes with other differences that may not be suitable for the needs of certain programs. For instance, if a FILE STATUS clause is defined for the sort file, it is ignored when FASTSRT is in effect. This is because the I/O is done external to COBOL II, and therefore the file status information is not available to the COBOL II program. FASTSRT cannot be used when the same VSAM file is used in both the USING and GIVING clauses of a SORT statement; it can only process a QSAM file used in both clauses if each clause refers to a separate file name and two different DD statements exist for the file in the JCL. Unless these or one of the other very specific restrictions is in conflict with your program (the full list of restrictions can be

```
000010 PROCEDURE DIVISION.
000020*IN SORT BELOW, FASTSRT OPTION HAS NO EFFECT.
000030     SORT SORT-FILE
000040         ON ASCENDING KEY SORT-KEY
000050         INPUT PROCEDURE PROC-IN
000060         OUTPUT PROCEDURE PROC-OUT.
000070
000080*IN SORT BELOW, FASTSRT OPTION SPEEDS OUTPUT PROCESSING
000090     SORT SORT-FILE
000100         ON ASCENDING KEY SORT-KEY
000110         INPUT PROCEDURE PROC-IN
000120         GIVING OUT-FILE.
000130
000140*IN SORT BELOW, FASTSRT OPTION SPEEDS INPUT AND
000150*                              OUTPUT PROCESSING
000160     SORT SORT-FILE
000170         ON ASCENDING KEY SORT-KEY
000180         USING IN-FILE
000190         GIVING OUT-FILE.
```

Figure 4.6 Different forms of the SORT statement and how they affect sort performance when the FASTSRT compiler option is specified.

found in *VS COBOL II Application Programming Guide*), I strongly
recommend that you always use the FASTSRT option.

The SyncSort/COBOL Accelerator is a non-IBM product that
Syncsort benchmark tests show reduces COBOL internal sort task
and elapsed times by approximately 70 percent and reduces I/O by an
even greater percentage when compared to a standard COBOL internal sort. It does internal sort processing as if the FASTSRT compiler
option had been used for every COBOL II program in an installation.
It not only works for all COBOL II programs (even if they had not
been compiled with the FASTSRT option) but works for all VS CO-
BOL programs as well (for which the FASTSRT compiler option does
not exist). In programs in which a fast sort cannot be used because of
restrictions (e.g., the same VSAM file is used in both the USING and
GIVING clauses of a sort), the sort reverts to a standard COBOL internal sort. However, obeying restrictions (such as the program not
having the file status of the sort files available to it when FASTSRT is
in effect) is the responsibility of the programmer. If the
SyncSort/COBOL Accelerator is installed at a company, programmers
should code all programs realizing that restrictions applying to
FASTSRT are always in effect.

4.7 TEST OPTION

In both VS COBOL and COBOL II the TEST compiler option allows
interactive debugging. The interactive debugger in VS COBOL is invoked through the TESTCOB command; the COBTEST command is
used to run the COBOL II debugger. VS COBOL only allowed interactive debugging in line mode; input and output were sequentially
processed one line at a time. The interactive debugger has been considerably updated in COBOL II, allowing it also to be run in full-
screen mode, placing the entire screen under control of the debugger.

When the TEST option is used in COBOL II, a program can also process noninteractively with the batch mode debugger. The batch mode
debugger is a new feature that allows a predefined list of debugging
commands to be used in MVS, CICS, or CMS. Each of the debugging
modes (line mode, full-screen mode, and batch mode) has advantages
and disadvantages which will be discussed later. Be aware that programs compiled with the TEST option will have their performance degraded. If a program compiled with the option is to be put into production, it is recommended that it be recompiled without the option to
improve performance.

While COBTEST performs all of the functions that were available
under TESTCOB, a few of the debugging commands have changed.
The function of the VS COBOL END command (used to terminate a

debugging session) is supplied by QUIT under the COBOL II debugger, the functions of the LIST and LISTFILE commands are now both performed by the LIST command, the HELP command is available in CMS and TSO (it was only available under TSO in the VS COBOL interactive debugger), and the SOURCE command that was available under TESTCOB is only available in full-screen mode in COBTEST.

The COBOL II debugger can only be used to debug COBOL II programs; the VS COBOL interactive debugger can only be used to debug VS COBOL programs. You can debug a mixture of VS COBOL and COBOL II programs that call each other. When you run the VS COBOL interactive debugger, the debugging commands will not affect COBOL II programs (these programs will execute as if they were VS COBOL programs compiled without the TEST option); when you run the COBOL II debugger, the debug commands will not affect VS COBOL programs. The COBOL II run-time option of NOSTAE (passed as a parameter) must be used when the VS COBOL interactive debugger is run using the COBOL II run-time libraries, and the run-time option of STAE (the default) must be used when the COBOL II interactive debugger is used.

IBM has made it quite difficult to debug VS COBOL and COBOL II programs at the same time. For this reason many companies have decided to use non-IBM debugging products that allow debugging in a mixed environment. XPEDITER (Centura Software) fills this need. It works in interactive and/or batch mode depending on which software it is used with (TSO, ISPF, DB2, SQL/DS, IMS/DB, IMS/DC, CICS, or CMS). There are other products that work only in interactive mode and/or under CICS.

4.7.1 The Interactive Debugger

The IBM interactive debugger runs in full-screen or line mode under TSO or CMS. When used in full-screen mode, ISPF is required. Full-screen mode processes a screen of information at a time. Line mode is an interactive request/response session with the requests and responses appearing sequentially as if processed on a typewriter.

When a program is executed using the interactive debugger, program execution always stops at the first verb in the program. It is as if you set a break point at the first line of code (a break point is a place in a program where you have asked the debugger to temporarily halt execution). From this point on, you are able to enter whatever commands seem appropriate until you end the debugging session with the QUIT command.

The beauty of interactive debugging is that you can stop a program at any point. This allows you to examine fields, change fields, or alter the path of execution. Additionally, you can suddenly decide to stop a program during execution if unexpected circumstances arise, such as an infinite program loop. A program is stopped with an attention interrupt. Entering the attention interrupt varies depending upon which system you are using. When ISPF is not used, the PA1 key is hit once under TSO or twice under CMS. Under ISPF, the PA1 key is hit once under TSO, while the Reset and then the Enter key must be hit instead of PA1 when running under CMS.

4.7.1.1 Full-screen mode

If your company does not have ISPF (required for full-screen mode), or if you work on a typewriter type terminal, you must use line mode. The full-screen mode is the most powerful version of the debugger. It has a number of commands that are not available when batch mode or line mode is used. They enable you to customize the screen panel, highlight areas and change their colors, move the cursor between areas on the screen, and use other functions particular to using a full screen. In addition to the standard debugging features, if you work in a company that has PDF, you can use a split screen. This enables you to view or edit the program in one screen and debug in the other. Additionally, under TSO you can recompile a program from one of the screens.

A nice feature of the full-screen debugger is the ability to restart a debugging session. Suppose that you spend quite a long time debugging and have not isolated the problem. If you have to stop your debugging session because another more urgent problem has arisen, you can stop without losing your place. You can pick up from the exact point at which you left off. To use this feature, a log must have been created during your original run. When you begin the next run, the log file from the original file is specified as the restart file. The log file is automatically updated with interactive line mode debug commands and terminal output as you proceed through your debugging session. (Commands only available in full-screen mode and ISPF commands are not written to the log.) When a restart is done, each command that was originally processed is executed except for the QUIT command.

You may even edit the log file (a fixed-length sequential file of 80-byte records) between the end of the original run and the restart. This method can be used to restart to a point prior to where you originally left off. Each command written to the log file by the debugger begins with an asterisk and a space. If you do edit the log file, you must follow the same syntax and begin each added command with an asterisk and a space. Be aware that most editors have an option to add sequence numbers at the end of each line. This editor option should be turned off since the sequence numbers will be considered as part of the debug command and will cause errors.

Creation of the log file during a run is activated by entering YES
after LOG on the full-screen invocation panel and entering the log file
name after LOG FILE ID. In all modes of the debug facility, the
RECORD command can be used to begin logging and the NORECORD
command to halt it. However, the log file created by specifying YES on
the full-screen invocation panel is independent from the log file created with the RECORD command. Using the RECORD command for
logging gives you more flexibility than using the full-screen log facility since you can activate and deactivate logging during a debugging
session.

4.7.2 Batch Mode Debugger

There are certain advantages to using the batch mode rather than the
interactive debugger. The batch mode debugger uses fewer resources
than the interactive debugger. It also enables you to do other work
while the debugger is running. You can send a program to a batch machine to run with the batch debugger while you do other work. Finally, certain debugging options lend themselves to batch rather than
interactive mode. For instance, if you wanted output equivalent to
that produced by the VS COBOL COUNT compiler option (discussed
in Sec. 4.7.5), you would use the LISTFREQ debug command.
LISTFREQ output is generally meant to be a report, not information
that would normally be examined in an interactive environment.

Before running a program with the batch mode debugger, a sequential file of 80-byte records must be created that contains the debug
commands used during program execution. They are placed in the
JCL using the SYSDBIN DD statement. In CICS/VS the commands
are placed into temporary storage queue CSCOxxxx, where xxxx represents the terminal upon which the debugging will be done. Note
that the batch debugger can also be used under CMS and CICS/CMS.
In CMS, FILEDEFs are used instead of the DD statements in JCL
[e.g., FILEDEF SYSDBIN DISK SYSDBOUT FILE A (LRECL 80
RECFM F)].

Realize that although input records are limited to 80 bytes, they can
be continued. A plus sign (+), minus sign (-), or comma (,) as the last
nonblank character on a line indicates continuation. The maximum
length of a command, including its continuation, is 32,763 bytes. A
command that exceeds this limit would be interesting to see.

The input file must begin with the COBTEST command, which contains as a parameter the name of the main load module that is being
executed. This command must be followed by either a QUALIFY,
RECORD, or NORECORD command. The QUALIFY command is required in batch mode and contains the PROGRAM-ID of the program

to be debugged. Other debugging commands that you wish to use during program execution are then sequentially placed into the input file. Additional QUALIFY commands followed by other debugging commands tell the batch debugger what to do with each called program. Remember that debug commands do not affect programs compiled without the TEST option.

Batch debugger output goes to DD statement SYSDBOUT in MVS, the file defined with a SYSDBOUT FILEDEF in CMS, and to temporary storage queue CEBR*xxxx* in CICS. The batch debugger ends processing when either your program ends execution or the QUIT statement is encountered as a batch debug command.

Refer to Fig. 4.7 for the standard JCL to execute the batch debugger. When running under CMS or CICS/CMS, the batch debugger is invoked through the "COBTEST pgmname BATCH" command, where "pgmname" is the name of the program you are executing.

There are a number of fine points that must be understood when using the batch mode debugger. A poor understanding will lead to useless runs. The most important point is that timing is critical. All commands are read and processed before your program begins executing. You must also realize that some commands execute immediately (e.g., LIST, LISTFREQ), while others are delayed (e.g., AT, WHEN). Misunderstandings can lead to unwanted results. For instance, if you request a TRACE (the equivalent of the VS COBOL READY TRACE) and then request QUIT, since TRACE is delayed (the IBM debug manual states that TRACE is an immediate command with additional further action rather than considering it a delayed command) and QUIT is immediate, the debug session will terminate without producing any results.

```
//BATCH    JOB    ,MSGLEVEL=(1,1)
//DEBUG    EXEC   PGM=COBDBG
//STEPLIB  DD     DSN=USERLIB,DISP=SHR
//         DD     DSN=SYS1.COB2LIB,DISP=SHR
//SYSDBOUT DD     SYSOUT=A
//SYSOUT   DD     SYSOUT=A
//SYSUDUMP DD     SYSOUT=A
//SYSDBIN  DD     *
COBTEST PROGRAM1
QUALIFY PROGRAM1
TRACE NAME
/*
//
```

Figure 4.7 Example of JCL used to execute the batch debugger (COBDBG). USERLIB is the library that contains the program you are running. (The library or libraries required are installation dependent.)

Most commands in batch mode debugging work essentially the same as in interactive mode. One difference between the two modes is that in batch mode there is an implied GO (continue execution command) whenever the interactive debugger would normally expect input from the user at the terminal.

If syntax errors are encountered while processing the input commands to the batch mode debugger, the debugger ignores the line but continues processing. This is a problem since the program will then run without executing the debug command you desired. You may waste an entire run. There is no easy solution to this problem since syntactical checking is not done unless the debugger is actually used. Very severe errors, such as not being able to find the program to execute, will, however, terminate the debugger.

4.7.3 Replacement of VS COBOL READY TRACE

The VS COBOL interactive debugger was not used extensively. COBOL II has the full-screen interactive debugger, which may get more use because of its added flexibility. Additionally, the COBOL II batch mode debugger should get considerable use. This is because it can perform functions similar to some verbs and compiler options that existed in VS COBOL but were removed from COBOL II. For instance, counterparts to READY TRACE and the COUNT and FLOW compiler options in VS COBOL exist, with improvements, under the COBOL II debugger. The debug TRACE command allows the PARA, ENTRY, NAME, OFF, and PRINT options. The TRACE command is an improvement over READY TRACE because not only can it list paragraph names but it also shows finer program flow by listing which path was followed within an IF or EVALUATE statement.

When PARA (the default) is used, the line number of each paragraph (not the paragraph name) is displayed when the paragraph is executed. Additionally, as mentioned above, line numbers where program flow is conditional, will also be shown. The NAME option is more similar to the VS COBOL READY TRACE, displaying paragraph names as each paragraph is executed. As with PARA, line numbers of IF or EVALUATE statements that are conditionally executed will be shown. The ENTRY option of the TRACE command requests that each program name be displayed when the program is entered.

The OFF option of TRACE stops the trace and is equivalent to the VS COBOL RESET TRACE. The TRACE command is more powerful than READY TRACE since, when it is on, it applies to all COBOL II programs being debugged, not simply the one presently in execution.

TRACE output goes to the terminal when used in interactive mode or to the SYSDBOUT DD statement in batch mode. The PRINT option of the TRACE command allows the output to be sent to the SYSDBOUT DD statement rather than to a terminal. The output can also be sent to a DD statement other than SYSDBOUT. In this case the alternate DD statement is specified using the PRINTDD debug command (e.g., PRINTDD OUTFILE2).

If you wish to trace execution of all programs from the beginning to the end by using the TRACE command in batch mode, timing is not critical. This is because batch debug commands are processed before the program runs and the TRACE will stay in effect until explicitly shut off. To set the trace on at one point and/or set it off at another point, the TRACE command should be used in the command list of an AT debug command. AT sets a break point and allows you the option of specifying a command to be executed when the break point is reached [e.g., AT 50 (TRACE OFF) would set off a trace when statement number 50 is reached in the current program being debugged].

4.7.4 Replacement of VS COBOL FLOW

The FLOW command of the debugger lists the sequence of program statements executed prior to a given point in the program. FLOW ON instructs COBOL II to save within a table the statement numbers of the last 255 verbs executed, starting from the point that FLOW is set on and continuing until FLOW OFF is issued. FLOW is similar to the VS COBOL FLOW compiler option but has one major difference. In VS COBOL, if the FLOW compiler option was used, a flow listing would automatically be produced if an ABEND occurred. In the COBOL II debugger, to get the flow listing you must request it with the FLOW PRINT command. To execute a command only when an ABEND has occurred, the debugger has the ONABEND command. Like the AT command, ONABEND works with a command list. The command "ONABEND (FLOW PRINT)" will print the flow only if the program ABENDs.

When a FLOW PRINT command is issued, the print options work similarly to the print options of the TRACE command. Output is printed to either the SYSDBOUT or an alternate DD statement specified with the PRINTDD command. The FLOW debug command is more flexible than the VS COBOL FLOW compiler option. The FLOW command allows any amount, up to the maximum of 255 entries of the flow table, to be displayed on a terminal or printed at any time [e.g., FLOW (100) PRINT], not only when an ABEND occurs.

Timing is critical when the FLOW command is used in batch mode. If you simply issue a FLOW ON command and then a FLOW PRINT command, no information will be output since the FLOW PRINT will execute before the program executes. The FLOW PRINT should be used in a command list of an AT command whenever you want the flow listing produced, or used in a command list of an ONABEND command.

4.7.5 Replacement of VS COBOL COUNT

FREQ is a debug command that produces output similar to the VS COBOL COUNT compiler option. The COUNT option listed each verb in a VS COBOL program, its line number, and a count of the number of times the verb was executed. In COBOL II verb counting can be set on in a program-by-program basis and can be reset during a program's execution. Setting FREQ on does not print any information; it merely tells the debugger to count verb execution. The LISTFREQ command is used to print the totals. It allows you to print verb counts in all programs (LISTFREQ ALL) or in a single program, and it has the nice feature LISTFREQ ZEROFREQ that only prints verbs that have never been executed. The timing of the LISTFREQ command when using the batch debugger is similar to the FLOW PRINT command.

Figure 4.8 shows the batch debug commands and the output generated when a verb frequency listing and a program flow listing are requested when statement 15 is reached in PROGRAM1. When command LISTFREQ ALL is processed, the statement "FREQUENCY OF VERB EXECUTIONS IN pgmname" is listed, where "pgmname" is the name of the program for which verb counts are being shown. Following this line appears each statement number and verb number separated by a period (e.g., 10.1 signifies the first verb on line 10 in the code). This is followed by an equal sign and the number of times the verb was executed. For PROGRAM1 in Fig. 4.8, the first verb on lines 9, 11, and 13 was executed once and the first verb on line 17 was executed five times.

The output from FLOW PRINT in Fig. 4.8 begins with:

```
PGM=PROGRAM1 STTMNT & VERB=000015.01
```

This indicates that the first verb on line 15 in PROGRAM1 was executed. The following four lines in the figure show that statements 13 and 11 in PROGRAM1 were executed, followed by statement 10 in PROGRAM2 and statement 17 in PROGRAM1.

4.7.6 WHEN Command

Although not a new command, the WHEN debug command is worth discussion. It is among the most powerful of the debug commands but prob-

```
COBTEST PROGRAM1
QUALIFY PROGRAM1
FLOW ON
FREQ ALL
AT 15 (LISTFREQ ALL; FLOW PRINT)
```

(a)

```
IGZ100I PP - 5668-958 VS COBOL II DEBUG FACILITY -- REL 2.0
IGZ100I (C) COPYRIGHT IBM CORPORATION 1986
IGZ105I AT PROGRAM1.000015.1
FREQUENCY OF VERB EXECUTIONS IN PROGRAM2
000010.1=5
TOTAL VERBS=1      TOTAL VERBS EXECUTED=1      PERCENT EXECUTED=101
FREQUENCY OF VERB EXECUTIONS IN PROGRAM1
000009.1=1        000011.1=1        000013.1=1        000017.1=5
TOTAL VERBS=6      TOTAL VERBS EXECUTED=4      PERCENT EXECUTED=67
IGZ102I PROGRAM1.000015.1
PGM=PROGRAM1 STTMNT & VERB=000015.01
PGM=PROGRAM1 STTMNT & VERB=000013.01
PGM=PROGRAM1 STTMNT & VERB=000011.01
PGM=PROGRAM2 STTMNT & VERB=000010.01
PGM=PROGRAM1 STTMNT & VERB=000017.01
PGM=PROGRAM2 STTMNT & VERB=000010.01
PGM=PROGRAM1 STTMNT & VERB=000017.01
PGM=PROGRAM2 STTMNT & VERB=000010.01
PGM=PROGRAM1 STTMNT & VERB=000017.01
PGM=PROGRAM2 STTMNT & VERB=000010.01
PGM=PROGRAM1 STTMNT & VERB=000017.01
PGM=PROGRAM2 STTMNT & VERB=000010.01
PGM=PROGRAM1 STTMNT & VERB=000017.01
PGM=PROGRAM1 STTMNT & VERB=000009.01 REPEATED 0000000 TIMES
END OF FLOW
IGZ129I PROGRAM UNDER COBTEST ENDED NORMALLY
IGZ350I ******** END OF COBTEST ********
```

(b)

Figure 4.8 Input to batch debugger and output generated of program flow and verb frequency information. (a) Batch debug command input file; (b) output from batch debugger.

ably the least efficient. It allows you to check for a specific condition (such as when a field is set to a particular value). It can literally save hours or days of debugging time. However, it is implemented through checking the condition before each verb in the program executes. This can make a program run many times its normal processing time. While extremely helpful in a short-running program, within a long-running program it should only be used in an isolated area of code.

4.7.7 COBOL Compiler Options Assumed
by Debug

When literals requiring a quote or apostrophe are required, the debugger allows you to enter either (regardless of whether the APOST or QUOTE compiler option was used). For instance, if you were using the SET command that allows you to change the value of a DATA DIVISION field, both SET CITY = 'BOSTON' and SET CITY = "BOSTON" are allowed.

The debugger always uses the compiler options of NUMPROC(NOPFD) and TRUNC(STD) for the data it processes, such as when the SET command is executed. This does not mean that the debugger overrides the options you used in the compilation if they were not these two. It can, however, mislead you into thinking a program will produce the same results when run without the debugger that were produced when the debugger was used. Suppose you use the debugger to set a data item to a value and then continue program execution. After completion of your debugging session, you may put a MOVE statement into the program which sets the data item to the same value and recompile the program with your standard options. The results received during execution without the debugger may not be the same. The NUMPROC(NOPFD) and TRUNC(STD) compiler options are quite complex. Refer to Secs. 4.5 and 12.5.1 for a complete explanation.

Another problem with using the SET debug command is that it does not allow you the full flexibility of placing invalid values into a field. The data entered must conform to the PICTURE of the data item being set. This is unfortunate since it nullifies one of the major advantages that is normally associated with using a debugger, to test error conditions that rarely arise.

5

Updates to Compiler Listings and Procedures

I will only discuss the compiler listing produced in COBOL II Release 3 since the listing produced by Release 2 is a subset of it. The Data Division Map and the Procedure Division Map are only briefly mentioned in this paragraph and are fully discussed in Chap. 13, in the debugging section of the book. The compiler listing of the assembler language expansion of the source code in COBOL II shows fields by their real names, not names like DNM = 1-245 that VS COBOL used. You therefore no longer have to cross reference the generated field names in the Procedure Map to the Data Division Map in order to find the actual field names. The error messages produced during compilation also include actual field names rather than the generated names. This makes it considerably easier to fix errors while working on a terminal without a listing.

5.1 PROGRAM AND STATEMENT NESTING LEVELS

The Release 3 compiler produces a statement nesting level (SL) of source code. The source nesting levels given by the compiler to a short segment of code can be seen in Fig. 5.1. The first column in the listing (LineID) shows the sequential sequence number assigned to the code by the compiler, and the other line number shown (after the source level number) is the sequence number coded in columns 1 through 6 of the source code. While the statement nesting level was never shown before, the concept of nested statements always existed in COBOL (e.g., a nested IF statement). Program statements that are not nested have a space in the SL column. Nested statements get a numeric value in the SL column beginning at 1 and incrementing by 1 as the nesting level increases.

If your first impression is that the nesting level will only apply to IF and EVALUATE statements, you are incorrect. Features in COBOL II such as in-line PERFORMs and explicit scope terminators allow nesting within a PERFORM, even to the point of a nested READ statement with an AT END clause coded within a PERFORM.

The source nesting level can come in useful when you want to check your listing to make sure your code is doing what you intended. You can check that an IF statement corresponds to an ELSE and an END-IF since the three verbs will all contain the same nesting level. This method works as long as each COBOL verb is on a separate line like the IF, ELSE, and END-IF with sequence numbers of 000140, 000160, and 000180 in Fig. 5.1. However, if you have code like line 000100 that contains an ELSE and a MOVE statement, this method does not work. The ELSE is not nested and its nesting level would be blank. The MOVE is at nesting level 1. When verbs at different nesting levels appear on the same line, the lowest numbered nesting level number (other than a space) is shown in the listing, in this case 1.

Release 3 allows nested programs (multiple programs all within a single source code file, each program containing a separate PROCEDURE DIVISION), which will be discussed in detail in Sec. 8.2. The program listing now includes the program nesting level (PL) to go

```
LineID  PL SL   ----+-*A-1-B--+----2----+----3----+----4----+----5

000019           000060 PROCEDURE DIVISION.
000020           000070    . . .
000021           000080    IF WS-RECORDS-READ = 9999
000022    1      000090       MOVE 'N' TO WS-GET-REC
000023    1      000100    ELSE MOVE 'Y' TO WS-GET-REC.
000024           000110
000025           000120    IF WS-GET-REC = 'Y'
000026    1      000130       READ FILE1 AT END
000027    2      000140          IF WS-RECORDS-READ = ZERO
000028    3      000150             PERFORM NO-RECORDS
000029    2      000160          ELSE
000030    3      000170             PERFORM SOME-RECORDS
000031    2      000180          END-IF
000032    1      000190       END-READ
000033           000200    ELSE
000034    1      000210       PERFORM DONT-READ-FILE
000035           000220    END-IF.
```

Figure 5.1   Release 3 listing showing source code nesting levels.

along with this new feature. The program nesting level in the listing is discussed in Sec. 8.7.

5.2 CROSS-REFERENCES

The cross-references (obtained when the XREF compiler option is specified) have been considerably enhanced in Release 3 when compared to Release 2. In addition to the Data Name and the Procedure Name cross-references that were previously available, two new cross-references have been added. One is an imbedded cross-reference, somewhat of a subset of a combination of the Data Name and Procedure Name Cross-References. Additionally, a Program Cross-Reference is given when cross-references are requested.

There are a number of new features in the COBOL II cross-references which are applicable for both Release 2 and Release 3. There have also been some minor changes to the referencing methodology. For instance, a file name in VS COBOL was considered to be defined in the SELECT statement and the file name used in the FD did not appear in the cross-reference. In COBOL II the file is regarded as defined in the FD, and the SELECT statement is considered a reference. The cross-references have also been enhanced to show a reference from one data item to another (e.g., when a REDEFINES is used), not just a PROCEDURE DIVISION reference to a data item. For instance, if the statement TABLE1-REDEF REDEFINES TABLE1 appears in a program, the statement is a reference to TABLE1. This was not true in VS COBOL. Another difference in the COBOL II Data Cross-Reference is that group data items used in a MOVE CORRESPONDING are shown, not just the elementary fields moved.

5.2.1 Imbedded Cross-Reference

When cross-references are requested, an imbedded cross-reference appears in the right-most column of the source listing (see Fig. 5.2) in addition to the standard cross-references which appear later in the listing. When cross-references are not requested at compilation time, the heading "Cross Reference" still appears in the right-most column of every page of the source listing but the column is left blank next to each source statement.

The cross-reference listing imbedded within the source code only shows the statement number where a data item or procedure name is defined in the program. It does not specify all references to the data item or procedure name that appear within the program. These refer-

```
----+-*A-1-B--+----2----+----3----+----4----+----5----+----6----+----7-]   Cross Reference
000001 IDENTIFICATION DIVISION.
000002 PROGRAM-ID. PROGRAM1.
000003 DATA DIVISION.
000004 WORKING-STORAGE SECTION.
000005 01   NAME                       PIC X(20) VALUE SPACES.            IMP
000006 01   FILLER REDEFINES NAME.                                       5
000007     05   NAME-LET OCCURS 20 TIMES
000008             INDEXED BY NAME-INDEX   PIC X.
000009 01   ERROR-COUNT                PIC S9(7) COMP-3 EXTERNAL.
000010 01   TOTAL-DOLLARS              PIC S9(5)V99 COMP-3 VALUE ZERO.    IMP
000011 01   SUB1                       PIC S9(4) COMP.
000012 01   TAB-LENGTH                 PIC S9(4) COMP.
000013 01   TABLE1.
000014     05   ENTRY-X OCCURS 5 TO 50 TIMES
000015             DEPENDING ON TAB-LENGTH PIC X.                        12
000016 01   TABLE2.
000017     05   ENTRY-X OCCURS 5 TO 50 TIMES
000018             DEPENDING ON TAB-LENGTH PIC X.                        12
000019
000020 PROCEDURE DIVISION.
000021     ...
000022     ADD +1 TO ERROR-COUNT.                                       9
000023     CALL 'PROGRAM2' USING NAME.                                  * 5
000024     MOVE 'Y' TO ENTRY-X (SUB1).                                  DUP 11
000025     MOVE SPACE TO NAME-LET (NAME-INDEX).                         IMP 7 8
000026     PERFORM ADDUP-DOLLARS THRU ADDUP-END.                        28 32
000027     ...
000028 ADDUP-DOLLARS.
000029     IF SUB1 = 5                                                  11
000030         GO TO ADDUP-END.                                         32
000031     ADD 20 TO TOTAL-DOLLARS.                                     10
000032 ADDUP-END.
```

Figure 5.2   Example of an imbedded cross-reference in a Release 3 program.

ences only appear in the full cross-references that appear later in the listing.

In addition to the line numbers normally used to reference fields, the imbedded cross-reference uses the following symbols:

UND   The data item or procedure name is undefined in the program. A compilation error has occurred.

DUP   The data item or procedure name is defined more than once in the program and has caused a compilation error. The DUP appears next to the line that caused the error, not the line where the items were defined. This makes sense since an item may be defined in the DATA DIVISION more than once as long as it is qualified when it is used. A paragraph name also will not cause any error if it is defined more than once as long as the paragraph name is qualified within a section or not referenced at all.

IMP   The data item is implicitly defined. This applies to figurative constants (SPACES, ZEROS, HIGH-VALUES, LOW-VALUES, QUOTES, NULLS) and special registers (e.g., RETURN CODE, LENGTH OF, ADDRESS OF, SORT-MESSAGE).

EXT   Appears when a program name referenced is external, such as a call to another program. This should not be confused with the EXTERNAL attribute, a new feature in Release 3 (see Sec. 8.1).

*   Has the same meaning as EXT. The asterisk (*) rather than EXT is shown in a compilation when no object code was produced because the NOCOMPILE option (described in Sec. 12.2.1) was coded and is in effect.

5.2.2 Cross-Reference of Data-Names

The Cross-Reference of Data-Names is improved over the VS COBOL data name reference (see Fig. 5.3). It now shows whether each use of a data field caused a modification of the field or is just a reference to the field. An M appears before each reference that modifies a field. This is a nice help when debugging. Suppose that a data field contained an

```
PP 5668-958 IBM VS COBOL II Release 3.0 09/13/88
An "M" preceding a data-name reference indicates that the data-name is
modified by this reference.

Defined    Cross-reference of data names    References

   107     AMOUNT-INDEX . . . . . . . . .   M332 333 335 M495 496
    19     IN-REC-FIELD-1
    21     IN-REC-FIELD-2 . . . . . . . .   156 160
    12     INPUT-FILE . . . . . . . . . .   7 141 149 150
    18     INPUT-RECORD
   114     LINK-FIELD-1 . . . . . . . . .   413
   115     LINK-FIELD-2 . . . . . . . . .   413
   113     LINK-FIELDS. . . . . . . . . .   416
    85     MONTH-INDEX. . . . . . . . . .   M225 228 229 312
    34     OUT-REC-FIELD-1. . . . . . . .   M442
    35     OUT-REC-FIELD-2. . . . . . . .   M441
    27     OUTPUT-FILE. . . . . . . . . .   8 142 149 150
    33     OUTPUT-RECORD. . . . . . . . .   M445
   107     WS-AMOUNT-ENTRY. . . . . . . .   M335 M337 M345 M348 M351
    45     WS-COMPARE-VALUE . . . . . . .   238 M239 241 M242 244
    53     WS-COMP3-DECIMAL . . . . . . .   320
    52     WS-COMP3-NO-DECIMAL. . . . . .   321 M531 M532
    47     WS-CONSTANT-N
    86     WS-EACH-MONTH. . . . . . . . .   228
    87     WS-EACH-MONTH-NAME . . . . . .   229 311 312 313 314 315
    43     WS-FILE-SWITCH1. . . . . . . .   M167
    44     WS-FILE-SWITCH2. . . . . . . .   M166 M516 M517 M518 M519
    61     WS-MONTH-NAME. . . . . . . . .   M227 M229 M232 M233 M311
    64     WS-MONTH-NUMBER
    69     WS-MONTH-TABLE . . . . . . . .   182
```

Figure 5.3 Cross-Reference of Data-Names.

invalid value. You would want to know where in the program the invalid data had been placed into the field (assuming the problem was not caused because the data item had never been initialized). Using COBOL II you usually only have to check those entries in the cross-reference that are preceded with an M, entries for group items which contain the field and are preceded with an M, or entries for redefined fields preceded with an M.

5.2.3 Cross-Reference of Procedures

The improvements to the Cross-Reference of Procedures are even more considerable than those to the data name cross-reference. Each reference is preceded by one of the codes shown at the top of the Fig. 5.4. The codes precisely define the reference to the field, e.g., whether a reference is due to a PERFORM or a GO TO.

```
PP 5668-958 IBM VS COBOL II Release 3.0 09/13/88
Context usage is indicated by the letter preceding a procedure-name reference.
These letters and their meanings are:
     A = ALTER (procedure-name)
     D = GO TO (procedure-name) DEPENDING ON
     E = End of range of (PERFORM) through (procedure-name)
     G = GO TO (procedure-name)
     P = PERFORM (procedure-name)
     T = (ALTER) TO PROCEED TO (procedure-name)
     U = USE FOR DEBUGGING (procedure-name)

Defined    Cross-reference of procedures    References

    140    A100-BAD-OPEN-FILE . . . . . .   P139
    148    A100-GOOD-OPEN-FILE
    301    COMPARE-DONE . . . . . . . . .   G285
    286    COMPARE-OVER-K . . . . . . . .   G270
    334    0200-CLEAR-AMOUNT-TABLE. . . .   P331
    336    0200-CLEAR-PROPERLY
    409    0300-END . . . . . . . . . . .   G382 G385 G388 G391 G394
    380    0300-1 . . . . . . . . . . . .   D376
    383    0300-2 . . . . . . . . . . . .   D376
    386    0300-3 . . . . . . . . . . . .   D376
    389    0300-4 . . . . . . . . . . . .   D376
    392    0300-5 . . . . . . . . . . . .   D376
    497    0400-ADD-AMOUNT. . . . . . . .   P494
    499    0400-ADD-QUICKLY
    511    0500-ADD-END . . . . . . . . .   E151 E163 E172
    508    0500-ADD-TOTALS. . . . . . . .   P151 P163 P172
    520    0500-SUBTRACT-END. . . . . . .   E176
    515    0500-SUBTRACT-TOTALS . . . . .   P176
    533    0500-SUM-END . . . . . . . . .   E190
    525    0500-SUM-TOTALS. . . . . . . .   P190
```

Figure 5.4 Cross-Reference of Procedures.

Defined	Cross-reference of programs	References
EXTERNAL	PROGEXT1	8
EXTERNAL	PROGEXT2	34
5	PROGRAM1	48
12	PROGRAM2	43 7
22	PROGRAM3	26 19
30	PROGRAM4	42 20
37	PROGRAM5	41 33
45	PROGRAM6	47 9

Figure 5.5 Sample Cross-Reference of Programs.

5.2.4 Cross-Reference of Programs

The Cross-Reference of Programs is new in Release 3. It shows the main program and each nested program that appears in the source code (see Fig. 5.5). It also shows all nonnested programs that are called (nested and nonnested programs are described in Sec. 8.2). The nonnested programs that are called are not defined in the program and are considered external programs. In the cross-reference, the non-nested programs are listed as EXTERNAL in the Defined column. The EXTERNAL definition should not be confused with the EXTERNAL attribute that can be used for files and data items in Release 3 (see Sec. 8.1). This EXTERNAL definition only means that the program does not appear in the source code file being compiled.

5.3 COMPILER OPTIONS

5.3.1 Options Shown in Listing

In VS COBOL the compiler options in effect appeared at the end of the listing, with many options appearing on each line. They were not in alphabetical order and you had to search through each option listed to find one in particular. You also had no way of knowing whether the options in effect were due to the defaults or because the defaults had been overridden.

COBOL II has greatly improved the listing of the compiler options. They now appear at the beginning of the listing and are in alphabetical order (QUOTE appears alphabetically where APOST would appear since either it or APOST is used) with one option on each line (see Fig. 5.6). If you request any default options to be overridden during a Release 2 compilation, the compiler produces the informational message "AN OPTIONS PARAMETER LIST WAS FOUND AS INPUT TO THE COMPILER AND WAS PROCESSED." as the first page in a listing. The Release 3 listing is an improvement. It gives the actual list of the parameters overridden above the list of compiler options used (see Fig. 5.6).

5.3.2 Locating Options in a Module

When a dump occurs, it may become necessary to determine the options with which a program was compiled. For example, a program may be producing incorrect numeric results and you wish to determine the NUMPROC and TRUNC options used to compile the program. This information is available in the program signature bytes (INFO. BYTES 1-6 at hexadecimal displacement 00002C in Fig. 5.7) that are located in the program initialization code of a COBOL II program. Similar code appears for every COBOL II program and is shown in the listing for programs compiled with the LIST option. Remember that the signature bytes contain the compile-time options, which are not necessarily the options with which the program will run. (Section 12.6 discusses the run-time options that may override the compile-time options.)

There are 25 signature bytes located near the beginning of every COBOL II load module. The first 5 signature bytes contain the options with which the program was compiled. Their values are shown in Fig. 5.8. The remaining bytes are not very useful since all the information they contain can be obtained from the source code. Bytes 6 and 7 contain information about the DATA DIVISION (which types of files are used, which clauses are used to describe data items); byte 8 shows which clauses are used in the ENVIRONMENT DIVISION; bytes 9 through 17 and bytes 21 through 25 show which verbs are used in the PROCEDURE DIVISION.

5.4 ERROR MESSAGES

One quite nice feature of COBOL II is that when the same error condition occurs many times in a program compilation, it is listed only once at the end of the compilation. It is produced the first time it occurs and contains the line numbers of all other instances where the same error condition resulted, as shown below:

```
15  IGYPS2121-S   "SUB1" was not defined as a data-name.  The statement
                  was discarded.

                  Same message on line:    14    19    20    24
```

This makes it much easier to correct your errors. For instance, if you forgot to define a subscript that was used 100 times, you might only

PP 5668-958 IBM VS COBOL II Release 3.0 09/13/88

Invocation parameters:
quote list trunc(std)

Options in effect:
        NOADV
          QUOTE
        NOAWO
          BUFSIZE(4096)
        NOCMPR2
        NOCOMPILE(E)
          DATA(31)
        NODBCS
        NODECK
        NODUMP
          DYNAM
        NOEXIT
        NOFASTSRT
        NOFDUMP
          FLAG(I,E)
        NOFLAGMIG
        NOFLAGSAA
        NOFLAGSTD
          LANGUAGE(EN)
        NOLIB
          LINECOUNT(54)
          LIST
          MAP
        NONAME
        NONUMBER
          NUMPROC(PFD)
          OBJECT
        NOOFFSET
        NOOPTIMIZE
          OUTDD(SYSOUT)
          RENT
          RESIDENT
        NOSEQUENCE
          SIZE(MAX)
          SOURCE
          SPACE(1)
        NOSSRANGE
          TERM
        NOTEST
          TRUNC(STD)
        NOVBREF
        NOWORD
        NOXREF
          ZWB

Figure 5.6   Listing of options used during the compilation of a COBOL II Release 3 program.

```
PP 5668-958 IBM VS COBOL II Release 3.0 09/13/88
000000                  PROG1  DS   0H
                               USING *,15
000000  47F0 F070        B    112(,15)          BYPASS CONSTANTS. BRANCH TO @STM
000004  23               DC   AL1(35)           SIGNATURE: LEN. PGM. I.D. CHARS.
000005  D7D9D6C7F1404040 DC   C'PROG1    '    @EPNAM:  PROGRAM NAME
00000D  40C3F240         DC   C' C2 '                   COMPILER = COBOL II
000011  F14BF34BF040     DC   C'1.3.0 '                 VERSION/RELEASE/MOD.
000017  F0F861F0F361F8F9 DC   C'08/03/89 '              DATE COMPILED
000020  F1F54BF4F14BF5F1 DC   C'15.41.51'               TIME COMPILED
000028  00000054         DC   A(*+44)          @APARM:  A(@PARMS)
00002C  6468ED440000     DC   X'6468ED440000'           INFO. BYTES 1-6
000032  0C0000000008     DC   X'0C0000000008'           INFO. BYTES 7-12
000038  002000000400     DC   X'002000000400'           INFO. BYTES 13-18
00003E  0000000100       DC   X'0000000100'             INFO. BYTES 19-23
000043  00               DC   X'00'                     RESERVED
000044  00000007         DC   X'00000007'               # DATA DIV. STMTS.
000048  0000000B         DC   X'0000000B'               # PROC. DIV. STMTS.
00004C  0000             DC   X'0000'                    INFO. BYTES 24-25
00004E  0000             DC   2X'00'                     RESERVED
```

Figure 5.7   Beginning of program initialization code for PROG1.

Byte #	Bit #	If Bit is On (Value=1)	If Bit is Off (Value=0)
1	0	ADV	NOADV
1	1	APOST	QUOTE
1	2	DATA(31)	DATA(24)
1	3	DECK	NODECK
1	4	DUMP	NODUMP
1	5	DYNAM	NODYNAM
1	6	FASTSRT	NOFASTSRT
1	7	FDUMP	NOFDUMP
2	0	LIB	NOLIB
2	1	LIST	NOLIST
2	2	MAP	NOMAP
2	3	NUM	NONUM
2	4	OBJ	NOOBJ
2	5	OFFSET	NOOFFSET
2	6	OPTIMIZE	NOOPTIMIZE
2	7	OUTDD supplies DDNAME	OUTDD uses default DDNAME
3	0	NUMPROC(PFD)	NUMPROC(NOPFD)
3	1	RENT	NORENT
3	2	RES	NORES
3	3	SEQUENCE	NOSEQUENCE
3	4	SIZE(MAX)	SIZE(value)
3	5	SOURCE	NOSOURCE
3	6	SSRANGE	NOSSRANGE
3	7	TERM	NOTERM
4	0	TEST	NOTEST
4	1	TRUNC(STD)	TRUNC(OPT)
4	2	User supplied reserved word list	Default reserved word list used
4	3	VBREF	NOVBREF
4	4	XREF	NOXREF
4	5	ZWB	NOZWB
4	6	NAME	NONAME
4	7	CMPR2	NOCMPR2
5	0	NUMPROC(MIG)	
5	1	NUMCLS	NONUMCLS
5	2	DBCS	NODBCS
5	3	AWO	NOAWO
5	4	TRUNC(BIN)	

Figure 5.8   Values of each bit in first 5 signature bytes. The values can be used to determine the options with which a program was compiled.

get one error message for this error and will be able to distinguish your other errors more easily. Furthermore, the smaller list of error messages will make you feel better.

Realize that when the FLAG option (discussed in Sec. 4.2) is used to imbed error messages within the source listing, if the same error message occurs many times, it will be repeated in each place that it occurs. It is only the error messages listed at the end of the compilation listing that are compressed by not repeating the same message many times.

5.5 CATALOGUED JCL PROCEDURES

There are five catalogued procedures supplied by IBM to perform one or more of the steps to compile, link-edit, and execute a COBOL II program. All of the procedure names begin with COB2U and are followed by a combination of the letters C (for a compilation), L (for a link-edit) and G (for go—to execute a program). The procedures and their functions are shown in Fig. 5.9.

The compilation step (in the four procedures that contain it) requires at least 640K (the default). It sometimes needs more storage depending upon the length and complexity of the program compiled. The SIZE compilation option used to specify the amount of storage for a compilation is discussed in Sec. 12.2.3.

The step names within the procedures are COB2 for the compile step, LKED for the link-edit step, and GO for the execution step. The PARM parameter on the EXEC statement for step COB2 is used to override default compilation options. Procedure COB2UCLG is shown in Fig. 5.10.

Procedure name	Procedure function
COB2UC	Compile a COBOL II program
COB2UCL	Compile and link-edit a COBOL II program
COB2UCLG	Compile, link-edit, and execute a COBOL II program
COB2UCG	Compile and execute a COBOL II program using the loader
COB2ULG	Link-edit and execute a COBOL II program

Figure 5.9   List of the IBM supplied catalogued procedures to compile, link-edit, and execute a COBOL II program.

```
//COB2UCLG PROC CMP='SYS1.COB2COMP',LIB='SYS1.COB2LIB'
//*             PROC FOR COBOL II - LINK AND GO
//COB2      EXEC PGM=IGYCRCTL,PARM='OBJECT',REGION=1024K
//STEPLIB   DD  DSNAME=&CMP,DISP=SHR
//SYSPRINT  DD  SYSOUT=A
//SYSLIN    DD  DSNAME=&&LOADSET,UNIT=SYSDA,DISP=(MOD,PASS),
//             SPACE=(TRK,(3,3)),DCB=(BLKSIZE=80,LRECL=80,RECFM=FB)
//SYSUT1    DD  UNIT=SYSDA,SPACE=(CYL,(1,1))
//SYSUT2    DD  UNIT=SYSDA,SPACE=(CYL,(1,1))
//SYSUT3    DD  UNIT=SYSDA,SPACE=(CYL,(1,1))
//SYSUT4    DD  UNIT=SYSDA,SPACE=(CYL,(1,1))
//SYSUT5    DD  UNIT=SYSDA,SPACE=(CYL,(1,1))
//SYSUT6    DD  UNIT=SYSDA,SPACE=(CYL,(1,1))
//SYSUT7    DD  UNIT=SYSDA,SPACE=(CYL,(1,1))
//LKED      EXEC PGM=IEWL,PARM='LIST,XREF,LET,MAP',COND=(5,LT,COB2),
//             REGION=512K
//SYSLIN    DD  DSNAME=&&LOADSET,DISP=(OLD,DELETE)
//         DD  DSNAME=SYSIN
//SYSLMOD   DD  DSNAME=&&GOSET(GO),DISP=(,PASS),UNIT=SYSDA,
//             SPACE=(CYL,(1,1,1))
//SYSLIB    DD  DSN=&LIB,DISP=SHR
//SYSUT1    DD  UNIT=SYSDA,SPACE=(CYL,(1,1))
//SYSPRINT  DD  SYSOUT=A
//GO        EXEC PGM=*.LKED.SYSLMOD,COND=((5,LT,LKED),(5,LT,COB2))
//STEPLIB   DD  DSNAME=&LIB,DISP=SHR
//SYSABOUT  DD  SYSOUT=A
//SYSDBOUT  DD  SYSOUT=A
//SYSUDUMP  DD  SYSOUT=A
```

Figure 5.10 Catalogued procedure COB2UCLG. The data set name for STEPLIB and SYSLIB are installation dependent.

6

COBOL II in
Special Environments

6.1 COBOL II AND CICS

COBOL II command level programs may be run under CICS Release 1.6 and newer releases. However, some of the features added in COBOL II Release 3 (discussed in Chaps. 7 and 8, e.g., nested programs, reference modification, lowercase characters in code, and global variables) require the CICS Release 2.1 translator run with the ANSI85 translator option. The translator option of COBOL2 is required for all COBOL II programs. Macro level is not supported under COBOL II.

COBOL II programs run under CICS may execute above the 16-megabyte line under XA or ESA (see Sec. 4.4). CICS programs link-edited as RMODE(ANY) will be loaded above the line and made permanently resident. Be aware that if RMODE(24) is specified for DFHECI (the COBOL stub link-edited with every COBOL II program), it will override the RMODE specified for a COBOL II program.

6.1.1 Restrictions Lifted

COBOL II has lifted a number of restrictions that existed under VS COBOL CICS. The INSPECT and UNSTRING statements may be used. The SERVICE RELOAD is not required in CICS COBOL II programs and is treated as a comment when coded. STOP RUN may be coded and is equivalent to coding an EXEC CICS RETURN to return to CICS; GOBACK may be coded and is equivalent to coding an EXEC CICS RETURN to return to CICS or a calling program; EXIT PROGRAM can also be coded to return to a calling program. GOBACK will work whether a program was invoked through an

EXEC CICS LINK, EXEC CICS XCTL, or a CALL statement while EXIT PROGRAM can only be used to return to a program that issued a CALL to it (EXIT PROGRAM is ignored in a program that received control through an EXEC CICS LINK or EXEC CICS XCTL).

The CALL statement can now be used to issue a static call (see Sec. 12.5.2) from a COBOL II program to another COBOL II program or to an assembler program. Issuing a static call is much more efficient than issuing an EXEC CICS LINK. In CICS, a COBOL II program cannot be called from a VS COBOL program. A called program can issue any CICS commands that would be allowed by the calling program. When the called program is processed by the CICS translator, which would be the case if the called program issues CICS requests, DFHEIBLK and DFHCOMMAREA must be passed as the first two parameters in the CALL. The CICS translator automatically inserts the two parameters into the USING clause of the PROCEDURE DIVISION statement in the called program.

Starting with CICS Release 1.7, dynamic calls to programs that do not request CICS services are allowed from CICS programs. Full dynamic call support, including dynamic calls to programs that contain CICS requests, are allowed for COBOL II programs run under CICS/MVS Version 2 Release 1.

You still cannot use the following COBOL verbs in CICS because they require operating system I/O functions: ACCEPT, CLOSE, DELETE, DISPLAY, MERGE, OPEN, READ, RERUN, REWRITE, SORT, START, and WRITE. Limited use of the SORT verb is allowed in COBOL II Release 3.1.

6.1.2   BLL CELLS No Longer Defined

The most dramatic change to coding CICS applications has come in BLL cell usage. The BLL cells are no longer coded, and CICS programs converted from VS COBOL to COBOL II must have their BLL structures removed from the LINKAGE SECTION. To enable the handling of the COBOL II BLL cells in an easier manner, enhancements were made to the COBOL II compiler. (Sec. 6.1.4 discusses the ADDRESS OF clause, which enables a program to establish addressability to fields in the LINKAGE SECTION.) There is less chance of error when using LINKAGE SECTION fields in CICS under COBOL II than there was in VS COBOL since the order and length of fields in the LINKAGE SECTION is not dependent upon the BLL cell definitions. Figure 6.1 shows a CICS program that was written to run with the VS COBOL compiler and an equivalent program written to run using COBOL II. Notice that the LENGTH option (discussed in Sec. 6.1.8) is no longer required in the READ and REWRITE statements.

```
000010 WORKING-STORAGE SECTION.
000020 01  TABLEX-LENGTH            PIC S9(9) COMP.
000030 01  RECORD-KEY               PIC X(10).
000040 LINKAGE SECTION.
000050 01  BLL-CELLS.
000060     05  FILLER               PIC S9(8) COMP.
000070     05  BLL-TABLEX1          PIC S9(8) COMP.
000080     05  BLL-TABLEX2          PIC S9(8) COMP.
000090 01  TABLEX.
000100     05  ENTRYX OCCURS 10 TIMES PIC X(500).
000110
000120 PROCEDURE DIVISION.
000130     EXEC CICS READ UPDATE
000140          DATASET('FILE1')
000150          RIDFLD(RECORD-KEY)
000160          SET(BLL-TABLEX1)
000170        . LENGTH(TABLEX-LENGTH)
000180          END-EXEC.
000190
000200     ADD 4096 BLL-TABLEX1 GIVING BLL-TABLEX2.
000210     ...
000220
000230     EXEC CICS REWRITE
000240          DATASET('FILE1')
000250          FROM(TABLEX)
000260          LENGTH(TABLEX-LENGTH)
000270          END-EXEC.
```

(a)

```
000010 WORKING-STORAGE SECTION.
000020 01  RECORD-KEY               PIC X(10).
000030*BLL CELLS ARE NO LONGER CODED AND INITIALIZED
000040 LINKAGE SECTION.
000050 01  TABLEX.
000060     05  ENTRYX OCCURS 10 TIMES PIC X(500).
000070
000080 PROCEDURE DIVISION.
000090     EXEC CICS READ UPDATE
000100          DATASET('FILE1')
000110          RIDFLD(RECORD-KEY)
000120          SET(ADDRESS OF TABLEX)
000130          END-EXEC.
000140     ...
000150
000160     EXEC CICS REWRITE
000170          DATASET('FILE1')
000180          FROM(TABLEX)
000190          END-EXEC.
```

(b)

Figure 6.1 Comparison of a VS COBOL CICS program
(a) and a COBOL II CICS program (b) that perform the
same function.

6.1.3   POINTER Fields

COBOL II data items may be used to hold addresses as pointers to storage areas. A data item used to hold an address is defined as USAGE IS POINTER and does not contain a PICTURE clause. POINTER fields are generated as a fullword (4 bytes) and contain an address. They have an implicit PICTURE of S9(9) COMP. POINTER fields may only be used in the SET statement, in relation conditions, and as parameters in a call (in the USING clause of a CALL statement, a PROCEDURE DIVISION, or an ENTRY statement). The COBOL II compiler prohibits the use of the UP BY or DOWN BY clauses of the SET statement to increment or decrement POINTER fields. POINTER fields may only be set to addresses or NULL(S).

When POINTER fields are used in an IF statement, they cannot use GREATER THAN, LESS THAN, or any relational operator other than EQUAL or NOT EQUAL. This restriction also applies to the ADDRESS OF special register, discussed next, which is implicitly defined as a POINTER field. POINTER fields may only be compared to other POINTER fields, the ADDRESS OF special register, or NULL(S).

COBOL II does not allow arithmetic functions to be performed upon fields defined as POINTER. However, if you wish to do arithmetic on the address contained in a POINTER field, you can code a field with a PICTURE S9(9) COMP, which REDEFINES the pointer, and then perform computations on the redefined field. Note that since POINTER items cannot be used in MOVE statements, they are ignored when a MOVE CORRESPONDING is done on a group item that contains POINTER fields.

6.1.4   ADDRESS OF Special Register

The ADDRESS OF clause allows addresses of data to be manipulated. It is a feature of the COBOL II compiler that did not exist in VS COBOL. It may be used in a SET or CALL statement. The ADDRESS OF clause is used with data names that are 01 or 77 levels in the LINKAGE SECTION and cannot be used upon fields in the WORKING-STORAGE SECTION. The clause is basically a way to refer to a BLL cell. (BLL cells are always used for LINKAGE SECTION fields in COBOL even though they are not explicitly defined in COBOL II CICS programs.) As an example, suppose that TABLEX-PTR is defined as USAGE IS POINTER, and TABLEX is an 01 level in the LINKAGE SECTION. SET TABLEX-PTR TO ADDRESS OF TABLEX will move the value of the BLL cell used for addressability to TABLEX to field TABLEX-PTR. When used in a CALL statement, the ADDRESS OF clause can be used to pass an address of data in the

LINKAGE SECTION, rather than the data itself, to another program. The address can then be used as a POINTER field in the called program.

Figure 6.2 shows PROGRAM1 issuing an EXEC CICS LINK command passing a COMMAREA to PROGRAM2. The COMMAREA contains POINTER fields that are used by PROGRAM2 to establish addressability to the data items referenced by these pointers. PROGRAM1 begins by requesting that the address of the TCTUA be placed into TCTUA-PTR. It then obtains a dynamic storage area and has the address of the area placed into TABLE1-PTR. Addressability to TABLE1 in PROGRAM1 is established with the SET statement on line 000140. After the EXEC CICS LINK is executed, the pointer fields in the COMMAREA are used by PROGRAM2 to get addressability to the data items in its LINKAGE SECTION (addressability to the COMMAREA is automatically established by CICS).

The EXEC CICS ADDRESS command (used to obtain the address of CICS areas such as the TCTUA) under COBOL II uses the ADDRESS OF clause rather than a BLL cell as a subparameter. For example, code that was EXEC CICS ADDRESS TWA(BLL-CELL) END-EXEC in VS COBOL is EXEC CICS ADDRESS TWA(ADDRESS OF TWA) END-EXEC in COBOL II.

6.1.5   CICS SET Parameter

The CICS changes mentioned so far in this chapter have led to the changes in the SET parameter used in CICS commands. For instance, take the case when addressability was established to TABLEX in the LINKAGE SECTION through a BLL cell named BLL-TABLEX1 (see the VS COBOL CICS program in Fig. 6.1). The syntax of using a SET parameter in CICS under VS COBOL is SET(BLL-TABLEX1). In COBOL II the syntax is SET(ADDRESS OF TABLEX) or SET(TABLEX-PTR), where TABLEX-PTR is a POINTER data item defined in the DATA DIVISION. Commands that contain the SET parameter are CONVERSE, GETMAIN, ISSUE RECEIVE, LOAD, POST, READ, READNEXT, READPREV, READQ, RECEIVE, RETRIEVE, SEND CONTROL, SEND PAGE, and SEND TEXT.

In addition to the updates to the SET options when converting a VS COBOL CICS program to COBOL II, CICS programs must also eliminate any other references to BLL cells. Programmers no longer have to worry about LINKAGE SECTION fields that are greater than 4096 bytes, which required more than one BLL cell to be initialized. Statements like ADD 4096 BLL-TABLEX1 GIVING BLL-TABLEX2 in Fig. 6.1, to address an area greater than 4096 bytes, should be deleted.

```
000010 PROGRAM-ID. PROGRAM1.
000020 DATA DIVISION.
000030 WORKING-STORAGE SECTION.
000040 01  PGM-COMMAREA.
000050     05  TCTUA-PTR          POINTER.
000060     05  TABLE1-PTR         POINTER.
000070 LINKAGE SECTION.
000080 01  TABLE1                 PIC X(5000).
000090
000100 PROCEDURE DIVISION.
000110     EXEC CICS ADDRESS TCTUA(TCTUA-PTR) END-EXEC.
000120     EXEC CICS GETMAIN SET(TABLE1-PTR)
000130                         LENGTH(5000) END-EXEC.
000140     SET ADDRESS OF TABLE1 TO TABLE1-PTR.
000150     EXEC CICS LINK PROGRAM('PROGRAM2')
000160                      COMMAREA(PGM-COMMAREA) END-EXEC.
```

(a)

```
000010 PROGRAM-ID. PROGRAM2.
000020 DATA DIVISION.
000030 LINKAGE SECTION.
000040 01  PGM-COMMAREA.
000050     05  TCTUA-PTR          POINTER.
000060     05  TABLE1-PTR         POINTER.
000070 01  TCTUA-AREA             PIC X(50).
000080 01  TABLE1                 PIC X(5000).
000090
000100 PROCEDURE DIVISION.
000110     SET ADDRESS OF TCTUA-AREA TO TCTUA-PTR.
000120     SET ADDRESS OF TABLE1 TO TABLE1-PTR.
```

(b)

Figure 6.2 How the ADDRESS OF special register and POINTER fields can be used to pass addressability of areas from (a) PROGRAM1 to (b) PROGRAM2.

Once addressability is established, additional BLL cells after the first are automatically set by the COBOL II compiler. The new method should prevent many storage violations that occurred when a program failed to properly define or properly initialize multiple BLL cells for a LINKAGE SECTION field. Storage overlays may still occur when a program is not recompiled after the length of a copy member it uses is decreased.

For efficiency reasons, the COBOL II SET statement should be used instead of the CICS ADDRESS statement whenever possible. As an example, SET ADDRESS OF TABLEX TO TABLEX-PTR should be coded instead of EXEC CICS ADDRESS SET(ADDRESS OF TABLEX) USING(TABLEX-PTR) END-EXEC. Code generated by the

COBOL II compiler in-line can be executed in a fraction of the time required to call a CICS function to perform the same function.

6.1.6 NULL POINTERs

The keywords NULL or NULLS are interchangeable and may be used with fields defined as USAGE IS POINTER or with the ADDRESS OF special register. They set a field to an invalid address and can be used at the end of a list of addresses to show that you are at the end of the chain (discussed in Sec. 6.1.7). NULL(S) can be used with the VALUE clause, the SET statement, and in conditional expressions such as in an IF statement. Their value is considered a nonnumeric zero and should not be considered as low-values (hexadecimal '00000000'). Make sure not to perform arithmetic on a POINTER field (which is normally not allowed but can be done using the method described in Sec. 6.1.3) when it contains a NULL value.

6.1.7 Linked Lists

By using the ADDRESS OF, POINTER, and NULL features of the COBOL II compiler, it is now possible for a COBOL program to establish a linked or double-linked, chained list. This is normally a programming technique that is reserved for system programs written in assembler language. However, IBM includes an overview of this technique in their manuals and even uses it in the sample programs supplied on the COBOL II product tape.

A list is a set of items, which can be a group of records. In a linked list, the items have pointers that connect them to one another. The pointers can go in a forward direction (from the first record to the second, second record to the third, etc.), backward (from the last record to next to the last, etc.), or in both directions. If the pointers only go in one direction (either forward or backward), it is a single-linked list. A double-linked list has pointers going in a forward and a backward direction. Figure 6.3 illustrates how the pointers in a double-linked list look. FIRST-REC-PTR begins the forward pointer chain and LAST-REC-PTR begins the backward pointer chain.

A COBOL program normally reads and processes one record at a time from a file. When lists are used, many records may all be kept in storage at the same time. The pointers enable the records to be transversed in order after they are all read. Figure 6.4 illustrates a COBOL II CICS program written to handle a double-linked list.

I do not see the technique of using linked lists as a reasonable method for coding a COBOL II program. It requires precision of manipulating addresses. Although the code used to process a list is not

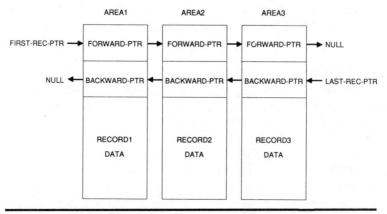

Figure 6.3   Illustration of the pointers in a double-linked list.

long, COBOL programmers who are not familiar with it may have difficulty following it. Errors in creating or processing a linked list can easily lead a program into using a tremendous amount of storage or going into a loop. This is because the technique for using linked lists often involves the use of obtaining a GETMAINed area for each link in the chain, establishing forward and backward pointers in each GETMAINed area to point to the preceding and next GETMAINed area, and using NULL pointers to show the ends of the list.

6.1.8   LENGTH OF Special Register

The LENGTH OF clause is a COBOL II feature that allows a program to access the length of any data field (e.g., MOVE LENGTH OF RECORD1 TO REC1-LENGTH). Like address fields, lengths have implicit definitions of S9(9) COMP. While the LENGTH OF clause is defined under the CALL statement in the COBOL II Release 2 manual, it may be used in any statement that allows a numeric data item, except that it cannot be used as a receiving field or as a subscript. When the length of a table entry is requested, a subscript need not be supplied and the length used will be of a single occurrence. Note also each character in a DBCS data item requires 2 bytes of storage and counts as 2 in the length.

LENGTH OF can be used on a data item even if addressability has not been established to it. For example, if you define a record definition in the LINKAGE SECTION and have not yet begun using the record, you can still obtain its length. This would be helpful in a case where you needed the length to do a GETMAIN for an area to hold a record you are going to create. (In a batch program you can use the

```
000010 DATA DIVISION.
000020 WORKING-STORAGE SECTION.
000030 01  FIRST-REC-PTR            USAGE IS POINTER VALUE NULL.
000040 01  LAST-REC-PTR             USAGE IS POINTER VALUE NULL.
000050 01  WS-RECORD                PIC X(500).
000060 01  FIRST-REC-SWITCH         PIC X VALUE 'Y'.
000070     88  FIRST-RECORD         VALUE 'Y'.
000080 01  RECORD-KEY               PIC X(5) VALUE '88888'.
000090 ...
000100 LINKAGE SECTION.
000110 01  LINK-RECORD.
000120     05  LINK-REC-FORWARD-PTR   USAGE IS POINTER.
000130     05  LINK-REC-BACKWARD-PTR  USAGE IS POINTER.
000140     05  RECORD-DATA-FIELD1     PIC X(492).
000150     05  ...
000160 ...
000170 PROCEDURE DIVISION.
000180     EXEC CICS HANDLE ENDFILE(FORWARD-PROCESSING)
000190                 END-EXEC.
000200     EXEC CICS STARTBR DATASET('FILE1') RIDFLD(RECORD-KEY)
000210                 END-EXEC.
000220 GET-NEXT-RECORD.
000230     EXEC CICS READNEXT DATASET('FILE1') INTO(WS-RECORD)
000240                 END-EXEC.
000250     EXEC CICS GETMAIN SET(ADDRESS OF LINK-RECORD)
000260                 LENGTH(500) END-EXEC.
000270     MOVE WS-RECORD TO LINK-RECORD.
000280*UPDATE CURRENT RECORD POINTERS
000290     SET LINK-REC-FORWARD-PTR TO NULL.
000300     SET LINK-REC-BACKWARD-PTR TO LAST-REC-PTR.
000310
000320     SET LAST-REC-PTR TO ADDRESS OF LINK-RECORD.
000330*UPDATE PRIOR RECORD TO POINT TO CURRENT RECORD
000340     IF FIRST-RECORD
000350         MOVE 'N' TO FIRST-REC-SWITCH
000360     ELSE
000370         SET ADDRESS OF LINK-RECORD TO LINK-REC-BACKWARD-PTR
000380         SET LINK-REC-FORWARD-PTR TO LAST-REC-PTR.
000390     GO TO GET-NEXT-RECORD.
000400
000410*FORWARD PROCESSING THROUGH CHAINED LIST
000420 FORWARD-PROCESSING.
000430     SET ADDRESS OF LINK-RECORD TO FIRST-REC-PTR.
000440     PERFORM UNTIL ADDRESS OF LINK-RECORD = NULL
000450         ...
000460         SET ADDRESS OF LINK-RECORD TO
000470                 LINK-REC-FORWARD-PTR
000480     END-PERFORM.
000490
000500*BACKWARD PROCESSING THROUGH CHAINED LIST
000510 BACKWARD-PROCESSING.
000520     SET ADDRESS OF LINK-RECORD TO LAST-REC-PTR.
000530     PERFORM UNTIL ADDRESS OF LINK-RECORD = NULL
000540         ...
000550         SET ADDRESS OF LINK-RECORD TO
000560                 LINK-REC-BACKWARD-PTR
000570     END-PERFORM.
```

Figure 6.4 CICS program that processes a double-linked list of records.

LENGTH OF clause on a record definition in an FD at any time, even if the file is not opened.)

The LENGTH OF clause has enhanced COBOL/CICS processing. When the FROM and INTO options are used in an EXEC CICS command, the LENGTH, FLENGTH, FROMLENGTH, MAXLENGTH, MAXFLENGTH, DESTIDLENG, and VOLUMELENG no longer have to be coded. However, these options can still be coded if you wish to use a length other than the length a data item was defined with in the DATA DIVISION.

The ADDRESS OF, the USAGE IS POINTER, and the LENGTH OF clauses may also be used by batch COBOL II programs.

6.1.9   Other CICS Changes

The COBOL II compiler option DBCS cannot be used with CICS Release 1.7 nor can DBCS data names, literals, or any nonnumeric literals containing DBCS characters. (DBCS support is being added to new releases of CICS. CICS/ESA Release 3.1 was announced with extended DBCS support.) When a CICS EXEC command is coded, the space character must be used between words wherever a space, semicolon, or comma would normally be allowed in a batch COBOL II program. Any nested programs in Release 3 (see Sec. 8.2) that use the EIB or DFHCOMMAREA of CICS must be passed the EIB and DFHCOMMAREA from the outer programs that call the nested program.

6.1.10   Debugging Under CICS

The batch debugger available through the TEST compiler option is available under CICS and is described in Sec. 4.7.2. Additionally, there are a number of non-IBM debuggers available for use under CICS [including INTERTEST, On-line Software International; Advanced Debugging System (ADS), Gary Bergman Associates, Inc.; CA-EZTEST/CICS, Computer Associates; and CICS dBUG-AID, Compuware].

A formatted dump (the FDUMP option of the compiler is described in Sec. 12.4.2) is also available under CICS. The output is written to temporary storage and can be browsed using the CEBR transaction. There are two major considerations when using the FDUMP option. It requires additional virtual storage to process, which may affect program performance. It should not be used in an online production environment. A more important potential problem is that the temporary storage used by FDUMP is not automatically freed. It is the responsibility of the programmer to manually free it. If this is not done, temporary storage may be held and other transactions may become suspended until the temporary storage is freed.

Be aware that if an ABEND occurs after a CICS program executes an EXEC CICS HANDLE ABEND statement, control will go to the procedure name specified in the statement. In this case COBOL II ABEND processing, including FDUMP processing, will be bypassed.

6.2   COBOL II PROGRAMS RUNNING UNDER IMS

COBOL II programs that are written to run under IMS basically use the same standard COBOL II syntax used by non-IMS programs. The specifics for IMS programs include a few coding restrictions, specific compiler options to be used, link-edit requirements, and rules for running VS COBOL programs under IMS using the COBOL II libraries.

6.2.1   Coding Restrictions

COBOL II programs (as well as VS COBOL programs) that are Message Processing Programs (MPPs) have a number of restrictions. They cannot issue any I/O commands that are not done by IMS. The CLOSE, DELETE, OPEN, READ, REWRITE, START, and WRITE statements cannot be used. The ACCEPT, DISPLAY, INSPECT, RECEIVE, SEND, STOP RUN, and UNSTRING statements are not allowed in VS COBOL programs that execute under IMS; all but RECEIVE and SEND may now be used under COBOL II.

6.2.2   Compiler Options

COBOL II programs that make calls to IMS must be compiled with the DATA(24) compiler option (see Sec. 4.4 for more details about the DATA option). Even though COBOL II IMS programs may run above the 16-megabyte line, IMS requires that all data passed to it be below the 16-megabyte line. If, for performance reasons, you wish to run your IMS program above the 16-megabyte line, the RENT and RES compiler options are additionally required. (COBOL II programs may only run above the line when these two options are used.)

The other reason for using certain options in a COBOL II compilation of an IMS program is to enable the program to be preloaded by IMS. This is an IMS performance option that can enable a transaction to execute faster. A copy of the program remains in storage and does not have to be loaded for each use after the first. The RENT and RES options must be used for programs that are always or sometimes preloaded.

A systems staff will have the maximum flexibility in tuning an IMS region when all COBOL II programs in the region were compiled with the DATA(24), RENT, and RES options. This will allow programs to run either above or below the 16-megabyte line. It is therefore recommended that the three options always be used.

6.2.3 Link-Edit Requirements

When running under IMS, any COBOL load modules that exclusively contain COBOL II programs compiled with the RENT compiler option should be link-edited with the RENT linkage-editor option (which specifies that a single copy of a load module can be executed concurrently by multiple tasks). When a COBOL II program compiled with the RENT option is link-edited with other programs (not necessarily COBOL II programs), you may specify whichever linkage-editor options are necessary to run the other programs. COBOL II is flexible enough to run with whichever linkage-editor options you choose. If the other programs are VS COBOL programs that will be preloaded, they should be link-edited with the REUS option; if the VS COBOL programs will not be preloaded, they should not be link-edited as REUS.

6.2.4 Running VS COBOL Programs Under IMS Using the COBOL II Libraries

Performance will normally be degraded when running VS COBOL programs under IMS using the COBOL II run-time libraries. Each time an IMS application program is executed using the COBOL II libraries, the COBOL II environment gets rebuilt. This occurs even if no COBOL II programs exist in the application.

The LIBKEEP run-time option (which is set at installation time and cannot be set through the EXEC PARM parameter in the JCL) can be used to keep library routines in storage until a task terminates. Additionally, for efficiency reasons, it is recommended that the highly used COBOL run-time library routines be preloaded. These include IGZCPAC (general library routines that are used most often), IGZCPCO (MVS- and MVS/XA-specific library routines), IGZEINI (controls initialization of the RES environment), IGZEPCL (performs partition level termination functions), IGZEPSU (performs partition level initialization functions), and IGZCTCO (contains the thread level communications block).

6.3 COBOL II PROGRAMS RUNNING UNDER CMS

6.3.1 CMS Differences

Almost all features of COBOL II that are supported under MVS are also supported under CMS. The SORT and MERGE statements are not supported by IBM except in virtual machines running CMS under VM/SP in 370 mode, or VM/XA in 370 mode. However, there are sort/merge utilities from other vendors that do support internal sorts under CMS.

The ON OVERFLOW and ON EXCEPTION clauses of the CALL statement (see Sec. 7.5) are not supported in CMS. OPEN EXTEND (used for adding records at the end of a file) is not allowed. There are minor differences in I/O processing, but they are rarely noticeable. For instance, the REEL clause of the CLOSE statement is not supported and neither are spanned records. (All of the restrictions listed in this paragraph have been removed in COBOL II Release 3.1.)

The IGZBRDGE macro (described in Sec. 12.5.2) that changes static calls to dynamic calls cannot be used.

6.3.2 CMS Compiler Options

The OSDECK option was used with VS COBOL to instruct the compiler under CMS to create an object deck that will not be run under CMS. This option is no longer supported. It is not needed since the same text deck is used whether it is run under CMS or MVS. The only difference in compiler options for a compilation done under CMS rather than under MVS is the choice of the DISK, PRINT, or NOPRINT options. You can only choose one of the three; they function in the same way they did under VS COBOL. These options direct the listing either to your virtual disk (DISK), virtual printer (PRINT), or to neither (NOPRINT); DISK is the default. If the listing is written to disk, the program name becomes the filename and the filetype is set to LISTING.

6.3.3 Program Compilation Under CMS

Program compilation is performed through the use of the COBOL2 command. The command is entered as follows:

```
COBOL2 pgmname (options
```

where "pgmname" is the name of the program (its filetype must be COBOL) and "options" are the specific compiler options to be used. In

Release 2, entering the compilation options is as in VS COBOL. After the opening left parenthesis, each option is separated from the next option by a space. Additionally, when an option has a subparameter, the subparameter must be enclosed in spaces rather than in parentheses (e.g., DATA 24). In VS COBOL and Release 2, each option cannot exceed eight characters and any entered option whose full name is more than eight characters must be abbreviated. The limit of eight characters was a CMS restriction. CMS used to truncate each input parameter to eight characters.

The new versions of CMS allow an extended parameter list which does not truncate parameters. COBOL II Release 3 takes advantage of this and no longer requires that any option names be abbreviated when entered. However, the syntax necessary for requesting compiler options in Release 3 can lead to confusion. For instance, if you enter the NUMPROC(PFD) option with spaces instead of parentheses surrounding PFD, it will not be handled properly and will produce an error. The facts to remember are:

- Each option may be separated from the other options by either a space or a comma.

- Spaces or commas must be consistent within the command. (You cannot place a comma between some options and a space between others.)

- Option subparameters must be enclosed in spaces or parentheses.

- Enclosing subparameters within spaces or parentheses must be consistent within the command.

- The subparameters of new Release 3 options [e.g., TRUNC(BIN), NUMPROC(PFD)] must be enclosed in parentheses. This means that if you use one of the new options containing subparameters and also use other options that have subparameters, all subparameters must be enclosed in parentheses. I therefore recommend that you always enclose subparameters in parentheses. Be careful to observe this rule when updating EXECs to use the new options.

This command will receive an error and prevent compilation:

```
COBOL2 PROGRAM1 (DATA 24 NUMPROC MIG
```

Compilation will proceed after the following commands are entered but an option will be ignored by the compiler. (DATA is ignored in the first command and FLAG is ignored in the second command.)

```
COBOL2 PROGRAM1 (DATA 24 NUMPROC(MIG)
COBOL2 PROGRAM1 (DATA(24) FLAG I
```

A message will be generated that parentheses were added to the following command but all options will be accepted:

```
COBOL2 PROGRAM1 (DATA 24 FLAG I
```

This contains the proper syntax for requesting a Release 3 compilation:

```
COBOL2 PROGRAM1 (DATA(24) NUMPROC(MIG)
```

6.3.4 Executing Under CMS

The COBOL II libraries are required to run under CMS. Assume that your COBOL II text library is called VSC2LTXT, your COBOL II load library is called VSC2LOAD, and your VS COBOL load library is called OSVSLOAD. To make the text library available to LOAD or INCLUDE commands processed under CMS, issue the following statement:

```
GLOBAL TXTLIB VSC2LTXT
```

To make the load libraries available to the OSRUN command or to ATTACH, LOAD, LINK, or XCTL macros executed, issue either:

```
GLOBAL LOADLIB VSC2LOAD
```

if all programs to be run were compiled with COBOL II or

```
GLOBAL LOADLIB VSC2LOAD OSVSLOAD
```

if some programs to be run were compiled with VS COBOL.

COBOL II Release 3

Part 2 of this book deals with the features of Release 3 that are different from those of Release 2. The changes to Release 3 are so comprehensive that it could have, and probably should have, been called COBOL III Release 1. Chapter 7 deals with the updates that make Release 3 programs function differently from VS COBOL and/or COBOL II Release 2 programs. Whether or not you are presently using Release 2, you should read this chapter very carefully. Some code produces no errors or warnings but does not function in the same manner in Release 3 as it did in VS COBOL and in Release 2.

Although there is a compiler option (CMPR2) that can be used under Release 3 to make a program function in the same manner it did in Release 2, this feature prevents the use of a number of Release 3 features. A program may be hard to maintain if this feature is used as a crutch. You may suddenly want to update the program using some Release 3 feature that is not allowed or forget to compile with the CMPR2 option and get unexpected results.

Chapter 8 discusses the new features that have been added to Release 3. They are quite interesting and include the concept of nested programs, i.e., coding many PROCEDURE DIVISIONs within the same source program.

Release 3 Updates

Release 3 of the COBOL II compiler incorporates many of the enhancements listed in the American National Standard Programming Language COBOL (often called the ANSI standard) of 1985.

7.1 CMPR2 OPTION

Not only have a number of new features been added to Release 3 of COBOL II, but there are a number of statements which execute differently between Release 2 and Release 3 of COBOL II. A compiler option of CMPR2 has been added to Release 3 that, when used, allows a Release 2 program, without modification, to execute under Release 3 and yield the same results. When this option is used, many new features of Release 3 are not available to the program. To have the compiler list those statements in a Release 2 program or a VS COBOL program that may behave differently under Release 3, use the FLAGMIG option in addition to the CMPR2 option. (FLAGMIG cannot be used without the CMPR2 option.) When the FLAGMIG and CMPR2 options are used together to find the changes that must be made to a program, the NOCOMPILE option (described in Sec. 12.2.1) should be used as well. This will prevent an object deck from being created, thereby making the compilation more efficient. (You can also compile programs under VS COBOL Release 2.4 using the MIGR option to determine which statements will cause problems to the COBOL II compiler.)

Although it will require additional resources, certainly time and money, you may want to convert your Release 2 programs to Release 3. I am sure that many programming managers do not want to consider this, especially those that have spent a considerable amount of effort converting VS COBOL programs to COBOL II Release 2. However, the fact remains that the compiler will continue to be updated and old programs will have to be maintained. Some program updates will either call on the features in Release 3 or those in future releases. Some of these features are not available when the CMPR2 option is used. Additionally, a program may be inadvertently recompiled without the CMPR2 option in the future and the message indicating that a feature that may behave slightly differently in Release 3 might be overlooked by a programmer. To further confuse matters, it will be quite cumbersome to keep track of all programs in production that must be compiled with CMPR2 and those that do not require it. For all the reasons above, I strongly recommend any company planning to convert from VS COBOL to COBOL II to definitely convert to Release 3, not Release 2. Otherwise, you may have to convert twice.

7.2 ALPHABETIC CONDITION

When a field is checked for ALPHABETIC under Release 3, lowercase letters (as well as uppercase letters) will make the test true. In VS COBOL and COBOL II Release 2 only uppercase letters satisfied the test. Release 3 also allows the class test for ALPHABETIC-LOWER and ALPHABETIC-UPPER. A field is considered ALPHABETIC-LOWER only if all of the characters in the field are lowercase alphabetic characters between *a* and *z*, or are spaces, while it is considered ALPHABETIC-UPPER only if all of the characters in the field are uppercase alphabetic characters between A and Z, or are spaces. The ALPHABETIC-UPPER clause in Release 3 produces the same results that the ALPHABETIC clause in VS COBOL and COBOL II Release 2 produced.

A field may be tested for ALPHABETIC in Release 3 by coding IF FIELD1 ALPHABETIC or IF FIELD1 IS ALPHABETIC. In all clauses that the keyword IS appears in Release 3, it does not have to be specified. Until Release 3, a field with a PICTURE that only contained the symbols A and B was considered ALPHABETIC. It is considered ALPHANUMERIC-EDITED in Release 3.

7.3 OCCURS DEPENDING ON

A full understanding of the OCCURS DEPENDING ON clause is quite difficult in Release 3. Before proceeding, it is necessary to define what the object of the OCCURS DEPENDING ON clause is. The object of the clause is the data item that defines the number of times that a field occurs. FIELD1 is the object in the following code:

```
000010     05  FIELD1                    PIC S9(4) COMP.
000020     05  FIELD2 OCCURS 10 TO 50 TIMES
000030              DEPENDING ON FIELD1  PIC X(5).
```

The processing of the clause depends upon:

- Whether the object of the OCCURS DEPENDING ON exists in the same group item as the field that contains the clause.
- Whether the OCCURS DEPENDING ON field has another field that follows it but is not subordinate to it, and both fields are contained within the same group. A field not subordinate to it would mean that the field has a level number that is equal to or lower than the field containing the clause.
- Whether the group item containing both the object of the clause and the field with the clause is used as the sending field or the receiving field in a MOVE statement.

When a group item contains a data item which has the OCCURS DEPENDING ON clause, all cases but one will use the actual length of the data item. The only time when the maximum rather than the actual length is used is when all of the following are true: the group item is a receiving field, it contains the object field, and the group item contains no data items following it that are not subordinate to it.

All cases illustrated in Fig. 7.1 use the actual length of the OCCURS DEPENDING ON field. The length of the data moved to or from the variable length field depends on the value of the object field.

Figure 7.2 shows code that uses the maximum rather than the actual length of an OCCURS DEPENDING ON field when the program is run under Release 3 (when run under VS COBOL or Release 2, the program used the actual length). TABLE2 used in the figure is the same as TABLE2 used in Fig. 7.1. When the maximum length is used rather than the actual length, the COBOL II compiler generates much more efficient code even though more data is probably moved. The object code generated for moving the maximum length is a single Move Character (MVC) rather than a number of instructions including a perform of COBOL-generated code (see Sec. 2.2).

The difference between the MOVE involving ENTIRE-TABLE2 in Fig. 7.2 and the MOVE involving ENTIRE-TABLE2 on line 000290 in Fig. 7.1 is that in Fig. 7.2 ENTIRE-TABLE2 is a receiving rather than a sending field. The difference between the MOVE to TABLE3-PART1 on line 000300 in Fig. 7.1 and the MOVE to ENTIRE-TABLE2 in Fig. 7.2 is that TABLE3-PART1 is in a group which contains a subordinate data item while ENTIRE-TABLE2 does not have a subordinate data item. When the maximum length is used in a move of a variable length data field, neither a decimal data exception nor a storage overlay can occur. This is true even if the object field of the OCCURS

```
000010 DATA DIVISION.
000020 WORKING-STORAGE SECTION.
000030 01  TABLE1.
000040     05  ENTRY1 OCCURS 10 TO 50 TIMES
000050         DEPENDING ON NUM-ENT-TAB1  PIC X.
000060 01  NUM-ENT-TAB1            PIC S9(4) COMP.
000070 01  HOLD-TABLE1            PIC X(50).
000080
000090 01  TABLE2.
000100     05  ENTIRE-TABLE2.
000110         10 NUM-ENT-TAB2         PIC S9(4) COMP.
000120         10 ENTRY2 OCCURS 10 TO 50 TIMES
000130            DEPENDING ON NUM-ENT-TAB2  PIC X.
000140 01  HOLD-TABLE2            PIC X(52).
000150
000160 01  TABLE3.
000170     05  TABLE3-PART1.
000180         10 NUM-ENT-TAB3         PIC S9(4) COMP.
000190         10 ENTRY3 OCCURS 10 TO 50 TIMES
000200            DEPENDING ON NUM-ENT-TAB3   PIC X.
000210     05  TABLE3-PART2          PIC X(20).
000220 01  HOLD-TABLE3            PIC X(52).
000230
000240 PROCEDURE DIVISION.
000250     ...
000260     MOVE 20 TO NUM-ENT-TAB1 NUM-ENT-TAB2 NUM-ENT-TAB3.
000270     MOVE TABLE1 TO HOLD-TABLE1.
000280     MOVE HOLD-TABLE1 TO TABLE1.
000290     MOVE ENTIRE-TABLE2 TO HOLD-TABLE2.
000300     MOVE ENTIRE-TABLE2 TO TABLE3-PART1.
000310     MOVE TABLE3-PART1 TO HOLD-TABLE3.
000320     MOVE HOLD-TABLE3 TO TABLE3-PART1.
```

Figure 7.1 Example of when a MOVE statement uses the actual length of a field defined with the OCCURS DEPENDING ON clause rather than the maximum length.

DEPENDING ON has invalid decimal data or an invalid decimal value before the move is executed. Since the maximum length is used, the object field is not used.

As shown in Fig. 7.2, the maximum length of a group item is sometimes used for a variable length field. Since confusion may occur between the case of moving to TABLE3-PART1 in Fig. 7.1 when the maximum length is not used and the case of moving to ENTIRE-TABLE2 in Fig. 7.2 when the maximum length is used, a warning message has been added to the compiler. When the maximum length is not used (in a case such as TABLE3-PART1), the compiler will issue a message indicating that the actual length was used (the 1985 ANSI COBOL standard states that the maximum length is used). Note also

```
000010 DATA DIVISION.
000020 WORKING-STORAGE SECTION.
000030 01  TABLE2.
000040     05  ENTIRE-TABLE2.
000050         10 NUM-ENT-TAB2                PIC S9(4) COMP.
000060         10 ENTRY2 OCCURS 10 TO 50 TIMES
000070            DEPENDING ON NUM-ENT-TAB2   PIC X.
000080 01  HOLD-TABLE2                        PIC X(52).
000090
000100 PROCEDURE DIVISION.
000110     ...
000120     MOVE HOLD-TABLE2 TO ENTIRE-TABLE2.
```

Figure 7.2 Example of when a MOVE statement uses the
maximum length of a field defined with the OCCURS
DEPENDING ON clause rather than the actual length.

that when the actual length is used, the field defining the number of
occurrences must be set prior to the move to the group item.

It seems rather strange that IBM gives a warning message only in
one of the cases when the actual length is used. Since there are many
cases when the actual length is used and only one case when the maximum length is used, it seems to me that a warning message should be
issued when the maximum length is used. Remember that the warning message issued when the actual length of the data field is used
only occurs in one of several cases.

Be aware that it is not only the MOVE statement that can use the
maximum rather than the actual length of a variable length field. The
ACCEPT, READ...INTO, RELEASE...FROM, RETURN...INTO,
REWRITE...FROM, STRING...INTO, UNSTRING...INTO, and
WRITE...FROM also may use the maximum length.

7.4 RECORD CLAUSE

7.4.1 Matching Record Definitions

The record definitions (01 levels) in the FD determine the file format
(fixed or variable) in VS COBOL and COBOL II Release 2. This is not
necessarily true in Release 3. If the RECORD CONTAINS clause specifies a single integer (e.g., RECORD CONTAINS 80 CHARACTERS,
not RECORD CONTAINS 50 TO 100 CHARACTERS), the file is considered fixed length to COBOL II regardless of the record definitions.

Additionally, the Release 3 compiler no longer forces the record definitions to exactly match the RECORD CONTAINS clause. For instance, a file can be defined with a RECORD CONTAINS 80 CHAR-
ACTERS and have two 01 levels defining the record, one for 60 bytes

and one for 70 bytes. In this case, the RECORD CONTAINS clause overrides the lengths of the record definitions. The file will be considered as containing fixed-length, 80-byte records, but when the records in the FD are used in the program, they are truncated to 60 or 70 bytes. You might want to use code like this when you want a program to only be sensitive to the beginning of a fixed-length record and not have access to the end, which will be truncated in storage.

7.4.2   Variable Length Record Size

If you ever wanted to obtain the length of a variable length record read in VS COBOL, or even in COBOL II Release 2, you had to use some tricky and specialized code. COBOL never allowed you, as part of its standard syntax, to access the record length of a variable length record. This length is contained in a 4-byte Record Descriptor Word (RDW). When a variable length record exists on disk, on tape, or in a buffer, it is preceded by the RDW. The first 2 bytes of the RDW contain the record length in binary; the last 2 bytes are reserved for system use.

After a variable length record was read, a program was always able to obtain the RDW through the use of the trick shown in Fig. 7.3. While it is illegal to use a literal of 0 as a subscript, a data item containing 0 used as a subscript actually comes in handy. Since a subscript of 1 points to the first entry in a table, a 0 subscript points to the position in storage that is one entry length above the table. A table with 4-byte entries can be used to define a variable length record. The record length of a variable length record begins 4 bytes before the data so a 0 subscript used on a table with 4-byte entries will point to the record length.

The obscure method shown in Fig. 7.3 need not be coded any more. If you find any programs that use it, you should now update them since COBOL II Release 3 does let you obtain, by using the RECORD clause, the length of a variable length record. The RECORD clause can be coded in an FD as follows:

```
RECORD IS VARYING IN SIZE FROM x TO y CHARACTERS
DEPENDING ON data-item.
```

where x and y are integers and "data-item" is a numeric field in the DATA DIVISION. The PICTURE clause for "data-item" cannot contain a sign. (If it does, a severe error message occurs during compilation.) The reason for this restriction defies the imagination.

Most of the parts of the RECORD clause are optional. When x is specified, it is the minimum number of characters in a record in the file, while y specifies the maximum record size in the file. The mini-

```
000010 DATA DIVISION.
000020 FILE SECTION.
000030 FD  INPUT-FILE
000040     BLOCK CONTAINS 0 RECORDS
000050     LABEL RECORDS ARE STANDARD
000060     RECORDING MODE IS V.
000070 01  INPUT-RECORD.
000080     05  EACH ENTRY OCCURS 1 TO 500 TIMES
000090             DEPENDING ON FIELD1  PIC X.
000100 01  FILLER.
000110     05  FIND-LENGTH-ENTRY OCCURS 2 TIMES.
000120         10  VAR-LENGTH      PIC S9(4) COMP.
000130         10  FILLER          PIC XX.
000140 WORKING-STORAGE SECTION.
000150 01  SUB1               PIC S9(4) COMP VALUE ZERO.
000160 01  REC-LENGTH         PIC S9(4) COMP.
000170 01  FIELD1             PIC S9(3) COMP-3.
000180 ...
000190 PROCEDURE DIVISION.
000200     ...
000210     MOVE VAR-LENGTH (SUB1) TO REC-LENGTH.
```

Figure 7.3 Code that can be used in IBM mainframe COBOL to obtain the length of a variable length record.

mum and maximum record sizes are not necessarily the number of character positions with which the record is defined. They can be greater if the SYNCHRONIZED clause appears on a data item, causing slack bytes to be added. When either the FROM or TO portions are not specified in the RECORD clause, the minimum or maximum record lengths are determined from the record definitions of the file.

The most interesting part of the clause for experienced VS COBOL or COBOL II programmers is the "DEPENDING ON data-item" portion, which is optional. When it is specified, "data-item" will contain the record length after a READ or RETURN statement is executed. The length is not the length value in the RDW. The RDW length includes itself while the length returned in "data-item" is only the length of the data portion of the record. For instance, if the data portion of a variable length record is 100 bytes, COBOL will return 100 in "data-item," but the length value in the RDW is 104.

If "data-item" is coded in the RECORD IS VARYING clause, it must be filled in with the record length of a record to be written with the RELEASE, REWRITE, or WRITE statement. Note that if a RETURN or READ statement fails to obtain a record (e.g., an end-of-file condition), the value in "data-item" is not changed. When a RELEASE, REWRITE, or WRITE statement is executed on a variable length file that does not have the RECORD IS VARYING clause, or has the clause without the "DEPENDING ON data-item" portion, the length of the record written will be determined from the length of the record used in the RELEASE, REWRITE, or WRITE statement.

For READ and RETURN statements containing the INTO clause, the value that is put into "data-item" by the COBOL I/O routines (or the value that would have been there if either the RECORD IS VARYING clause or the "DEPENDING ON data-item" portion is not coded) is used as the length of the sending field. This leads to interesting results. Figure 7.4 shows a program that has record definitions of 60 and 75 bytes but contains a RECORD IS VARYING clause that defines the records as 60 to 80 bytes. The program can therefore process a file containing records up to 80 bytes long (but will not be able to process a file containing longer records). If a record is read that contains between 76 and 80 bytes, the read is successful but IN-STATUS-CODE is set to 04. This indicates that the record available in the FD is truncated since the largest record description is not large enough. However, although the record in the FD is truncated, the entire record without truncation is read into WS-IN-REC. This is because the move is done using the value of IN-SIZE. The compiler generates an informational message in the listing stating that the largest record (IN-REC2) was used for the READ...INTO. However, this is not really true since truncation does not occur for WORKING-STORAGE field WS-IN-REC.

7.5   CALL...ON OVERFLOW

VS COBOL and Release 2 allowed the coding of an ON OVERFLOW clause in a CALL statement. The ON OVERFLOW clause enabled a program to do its own error recovery. If not enough storage was available to process a CALL that did not contain the clause, the program would ABEND; if not enough storage was available to process a CALL containing the clause, the program would execute the imperative statement specified in the clause and continue processing.

In Release 3 there is an ON EXCEPTION clause which is exactly equivalent to the Release 3 ON OVERFLOW clause. However, while both clauses are available in Release 3, neither clause functions exactly the same way as the ON OVERFLOW clause in Release 2. The ON OVERFLOW clause in Release 2 only applied to the condition when not enough storage was available to load a program. In Release 3, the imperative statement in an ON OVERFLOW or ON EXCEPTION clause is executed for a wider range of errors encountered during the loading of a program, such as when an I/O error occurs. If a Release 2 program was using the ON OVERFLOW clause to trigger an error message and ABEND, the code will not have to be updated to run properly under Release 3. However, if a program was using the

```
000010 ENVIRONMENT DIVISION.
000020 INPUT-OUTPUT SECTION.
000030 FILE-CONTROL.
000040     SELECT INPUT-FILE ASSIGN TO S-INFILE
000050         FILE STATUS IS IN-STATUS-CODE.
000060
000070 DATA DIVISION.
000080 FILE SECTION.
000090 FD  INPUT-FILE
000100     BLOCK CONTAINS 0 RECORDS
000110     RECORD IS VARYING IN SIZE FROM 60 TO 80 CHARACTERS
000120         DEPENDING ON IN-SIZE
000130     LABEL RECORDS ARE STANDARD.
000140 01  IN-REC1              PIC X(60).
000150 01  IN-REC2              PIC X(75).
000160
000170 WORKING-STORAGE SECTION.
000180 01  IN-SIZE              PIC 9(3) COMP-3.
000190 01  IN-STATUS-CODE       PIC XX.
000200 01  WS-IN-REC            PIC X(80).
000210 PROCEDURE DIVISION.
000220     OPEN INPUT INPUT-FILE.
000230     READ INPUT-FILE INTO WS-IN-REC
000240         AT END ...
```

Figure 7.4 Example of RECORD IS VARYING clause with a larger value than the record descriptions.

error condition to go into a recovery routine to release storage so that the program causing the overflow could be loaded, the method may not work. If the error condition in Release 3 is incurred because of an I/O error, different recovery procedures apply; ABENDing will usually be the method of choice.

Note that the NOT ON EXCEPTION clause has been added to Release 3. It is used to give alternative processing to the ON EXCEPTION clause and does not have any effect unless the ON EXCEPTION clause is coded in the same CALL statement. (There is still no NOT ON OVERFLOW clause.) When running using CMS under VM, neither the ON OVERFLOW nor the ON EXCEPTION clauses were supported until COBOL II Release 3.1.

7.6 EXIT STATEMENT

The EXIT statement had to be the only statement in a paragraph in VS COBOL and COBOL II through Release 2. Under Release 3, the EXIT statement no longer has to be alone in a paragraph. The IBM *VS COBOL II Application Programming Language Reference* manual states the following: "The sentence must be the only sentence in the paragraph (this restriction is not enforced)." It seems rather bizarre that the compiler would be changed to stop enforcing a restriction that prevented coding errors. I would much rather have compilation errors than production run-time errors. For instance, in Fig. 7.5 the DISPLAY statement on line 000080 will execute when the PERFORM on line 000020 is executed. The code would have produced an error during compilation using Release 2. Converted programs will not have any problems with the lifting of the restriction. However, the error of inadvertently coding other statements within the same paragraph as an EXIT statement may now make a program run incorrectly since the compiler will not inform you of the error.

```
000010 PROCEDURE DIVISION.
000020     PERFORM PARA1 THRU PARA1-END.
000030     ...
000040 PARA1.
000050     DISPLAY 'EXECUTING PARA1'.
000060 PARA1-END.
000070     EXIT.
000080     DISPLAY 'AFTER EXIT IN PARA1-END'.
```

Figure 7.5 The Release 3 compiler executes statements after an EXIT in a paragraph and does not inform you of the condition.

7.7 EXIT PROGRAM

The EXIT PROGRAM statement exists in both Release 2 and Release 3 but is not widely used. When coded in a main program, it serves no function, and when executed, processing continues as if it had not been coded. In a called program, the EXIT PROGRAM statement returns control to the calling program. Until Release 3, it had to be the only statement in a paragraph. It now can be coded in a paragraph that contains other statements.

In VS COBOL and up through and including COBOL II Release 2, a GOBACK or EXIT PROGRAM had to be coded to return to a calling program. If either a main program or a called program executed past the last line of code without issuing one of these statements, VS COBOL produced a User 519 ABEND while COBOL II Release 2 produces an error message and ABENDs with a User 1037.

COBOL II will still ABEND in Release 3 if you execute past the last line of code in a main program. However, if you proceed past the last line of code in a called program, an implicit EXIT PROGRAM statement is executed and control returns to the calling program. Therefore neither an EXIT PROGRAM, GOBACK, or STOP RUN statement is required in a Release 3 called program. The compiler no longer issues a warning message when none of these statements appear in a program.

I do not recommend that you code programs that use the implicit EXIT PROGRAM. It may confuse the person who will maintain the program. Furthermore, if you have a logic error in the program and proceed past the last line accidentally, you will return to the calling program. I think this was a poor "enhancement" to the compiler. For debugging purposes, you may want to put a call to a user ABEND routine as the last line in a program, just in case control passes to it accidentally. This would in effect reinstate the ABEND that had always existed to catch this type of error.

7.8 PERFORM STATEMENTS

7.8.1 PERFORM Ranges

When a VS COBOL or COBOL II program executes a PERFORM statement, the object code saves a return address so that when the end of the performed procedure is reached, control will return to the statement following the PERFORM. In VS COBOL and Release 2, until the end of the performed procedure is reached, this address will remain set. At the end of the performed procedure, the address is reset to its initial setting (pointing to the next paragraph). If the procedure executes without being performed (e.g., the procedure is entered by a GO TO), processing will continue with the next sequential paragraph. The resetting of the address in a called program is different in Release 3. In a called program running under Release 3, not only is the return address of a performed procedure reset when its end is reached, but it is also reset upon each entry into the called program. Each time a program is called, exit from procedures will execute as if the program was called for the first time. This is how COBOL should have always worked. In VS COBOL and Release 2, the return address of a performed procedure was left in its last used state when a GOBACK or EXIT PROGRAM was issued. While the change to Release 3 normally will not cause any changes in execution, poor programming techniques such as exiting performed procedures with a GO TO or GOBACK before they finish execution could lead to called programs that will behave differently.

7.8.2 PERFORM VARYING Differences

Release 3 instituted a very subtle change to the way a PERFORM VARYING statement is executed. It will very rarely affect a program but when it does, it will be extremely difficult to debug. The main difference in processing can be seen in Fig. 7.6. In Release 2, when the

```
000010 DATA DIVISION.
000020 WORKING-STORAGE SECTION.
000030 01   TAB1.
000040      05  LEVEL1   OCCURS 5 TIMES.
000050          10   LEVEL2 OCCURS 5 TIMES PIC X.
000060 01   SUB1                 PIC S9 COMP-3.
000070 01   SUB2                 PIC S9 COMP-3.
000080 01   PERFORM-COUNT        PIC 9(3) COMP-3 VALUE ZERO.
000090
000100 PROCEDURE DIVISION.
000110      PERFORM PARA1 THRU PARA1-END
000120          VARYING SUB1 FROM +1 BY +1
000130          UNTIL SUB1 > 5
000140          AFTER SUB2 FROM SUB1 BY +1
000150          UNTIL SUB2 > 5.
000160      DISPLAY 'PERFORM-COUNT: ' PERFORM-COUNT.
000170      STOP RUN.
000180 PARA1.
000190      MOVE 'X' TO LEVEL2 (SUB1, SUB2).
000200      ADD +1 TO PERFORM-COUNT.
000210      DISPLAY '(' SUB1    ', ' SUB2 ')'.
000220 PARA1-END. EXIT.
```

(a)

Output Using VS COBOL or COBOL II
Release 2

(1, 1)
(1, 2)
(1, 3)
(1, 4)
(1, 5)
(2, 1)
(2, 2)
(2, 3)
(2, 4)
(2, 5)
(3, 2)
(3, 3)
(3, 4)
(3, 5)
(4, 3)
(4, 4)
(4, 5)
(5, 4)
(5, 5)
PERFORM-COUNT: 019

Output Using COBOL II Release 3

(1, 1)
(1, 2)
(1, 3)
(1, 4)
(1, 5)
(2, 2)
(2, 3)
(2, 4)
(2, 5)
(3, 3)
(3, 4)
(3, 5)
(4, 4)
(4, 5)
(5, 5)
PERFORM-COUNT: 015

(b)

Figure 7.6   Example of a PERFORM statement (a) that produces different results (b) in Release 3 than it would in VS COBOL or COBOL II Release 2.

condition in the AFTER clause (SUB2 > 5) was true, SUB2 was set to the value of SUB1 and then SUB1 was incremented by 1. In Release 3, the processes are done in the reverse order. When SUB2 > 5 is true, SUB1 is incremented by 1 and then SUB2 is set to the value of SUB1. The practical differences in execution will occur when the data items in the PERFORM VARYING depend upon one another. If SUB2 began from a numeric literal or any field other than SUB1, the PERFORM statement would execute the same under Release 2 and Release 3. When the PERFORM statement in Fig. 7.6 is executed under Release 3, it is executed 15 times while in VS COBOL or COBOL II Release 2 it is executed 19 times. Figure 7.7 shows code that when run under Release 3 produces equivalent results to the code in Fig. 7.6 running under VS COBOL or Release 2.

7.9 NEW FILE STATUS CODES ADDED

In addition to the extended VSAM file status information that has been added to COBOL II, Release 3 has added a considerable number of new codes for the standard 2-byte file status. Whereas the Release 2 manual listed 18 possible file status codes, the Release 3 manual lists 33. COBOL II Release 2 programs compiled under Release 3 with the CMPR2 option will still only return the 18 possible codes used in Re-

```
000010 DATA DIVISION.
000020 WORKING-STORAGE SECTION.
000030 01  TAB1.
000040     05  LEVEL1   OCCURS 5 TIMES.
000050        10  LEVEL2 OCCURS 5 TIMES PIC X.
000060 01  SUB1                 PIC 9 COMP-3.
000070 01  SUB2                 PIC 9 COMP-3.
000080 01  PERFORM-COUNT        PIC 9(3) COMP-3 VALUE ZERO.
000090
000100 PROCEDURE DIVISION.
000110     MOVE 1 TO SUB1 SUB2.
000120     PERFORM UNTIL SUB1 > 5
000130        PERFORM UNTIL SUB2 > 5
000140           MOVE 'X' TO LEVEL2 (SUB1, SUB2)
000150           ADD +1 TO PERFORM-COUNT
000160           DISPLAY '(' SUB1   ', ' SUB2 ')'
000170           ADD 1 TO SUB2
000180        END-PERFORM
000190        MOVE SUB1 TO SUB2
000200        ADD 1 TO SUB1
000210     END-PERFORM.
000220     DISPLAY 'PERFORM-COUNT: ' PERFORM-COUNT.
000230     STOP RUN.
```

Figure 7.7 Code that runs under Release 3 to produce equivalent results to the code in Fig. 7.6 running under VS COBOL or Release 2.

lease 2. Note that some error conditions that previously caused ABENDs under VS COBOL and COBOL II Release 2 will, under Release 3, return a status code indicating an error but will continue processing. The complete list of status codes is shown in Fig. 7.8. The codes are broken up into six categories depending on the first digit of the file status.

The OPTIONAL clause can be coded on a SELECT statement to indicate that a file does not have to be available to the program when it runs (a DD statement may not exist in the JCL). An optional input file receives an end-of-file condition when the first record is read, processing in the same manner as if a DD DUMMY statement has been coded in the JCL for a nonoptional file. Some of the file status codes in Fig. 7.8 are for OPTIONAL files. For instance, if you issue an OPEN EXTEND for a nonOPTIONAL file that does not exist, a file status of 35 is returned; if it is defined as OPTIONAL, a file status of 05 is received. Release 3 now allows all types of VSAM files to be OPTIONAL.

The new status codes are very helpful. Many errors in VS COBOL and COBOL II that used to be combined under the error code of "92 - logic error" are now quite explicit. For instance, a 41 is an attempt to OPEN a file that had already been opened and a 42 is an attempt to CLOSE a file that had not been opened. The list of the Release 3 status codes and their corresponding status code values in VS COBOL (and Release 2) is given in Fig. 7.9.

I have seen programmers spend many hours each time they received a nonspecific logic error. IBM should have added these more explicit codes years ago.

7.10   TABLE HANDLING CHANGES

7.10.1   Subscripting and Indexing Changes

In Release 3 tables may be defined with up to seven levels, allowing seven levels of subscripting or indexing (VS COBOL and Release 2 only allowed three levels). Subscripts and indexes may both be coded in the same statement to access a data item. Also, subscripts may be coded in the form of "subscript + x" or "subscript - x," where x is an integer. This form of coding is called "relative subscripting" and had previously only been allowed for indexes.

7.10.2   VALUE Clause in Tables

The VALUE clause may be specified on a field that contains an OCCURS clause or a field subordinate to a data item containing an OCCURS clause. When the VALUE clause is used on a data item that

FILE STATUS value	Description
	Successful completions
00	The code successfully executed.
02	Successful completion but a duplicate key condition was detected in a VSAM file. If a READ was issued, it indicates that the next key on the file is the same as the one just read (the current key). For a WRITE or a REWRITE, it indicates that another record on the file contains the same key in the alternate index. These conditions exist when duplicate keys are allowed through the WITH DUPLICATES clause on the SELECT statement.
04*	A READ statement successfully executed, but the length of the record did not conform to the file attributes of the file. This means that the record was read but may have been truncated because the record definitions were not large enough to hold the entire record.
05*	An OPEN statement was successfully executed for an OPTIONAL file which does not exist. The file will be created if the statement is an OPEN I-O or OPEN EXTEND.
07*	Either an OPEN statement was issued with the NO REWIND clause or a CLOSE statement was issued with a NO REWIND, FOR REMOVAL, FOR REEL, or UNIT clause. The file was not on a reel device. (This error applies to QSAM files only.)
	At end conditions
10	An end-of-file condition has occurred. Control will pass to the paragraph specified in the AT END clause, if one is specified. This status is reached after all records in a data set have been processed or when the first READ is issued to an OPTIONAL file that does not exist.
14*	A sequential READ statement was issued for a VSAM relative record data set. The value of the relative record number exceeded the largest relative record number allowed for the file.
	Invalid key conditions
21	A prime key sequence error has occurred when processing a KSDS or RRDS VSAM file. Either the key was changed between the execution of a READ and a REWRITE statement or the requirement of successively higher key values was violated. Ascending key sequence is required when a KSDS file is opened in EXTEND mode or when a KSDS file is opened for output and has ORGANIZATION IS SEQUENTIAL coded in the SELECT statement.
22	A duplicate key error has occurred in a KSDS or RRDS VSAM file for one of the following reasons: • A READ or REWRITE of a record with a duplicate prime key in a KSDS VSAM file. • A WRITE or REWRITE of a record with a duplicate alternate key when the DUPLICATE phrase was not used in the SELECT statement to allow duplicate alternate keys in the file. • A WRITE of a duplicate key in a relative (RRDS) VSAM file.
23	Record not found in a KSDS or RRDS VSAM file. A READ statement was attempted with a nonexistent key, or a START or random READ statement was issued on an OPTIONAL file that was not present.

Figure 7.8 Chart of the FILE STATUS codes available under Release 3. Codes that did not exist until Release 3 are marked with an asterisk.

FILE STATUS value	Description
	Invalid key conditions
24	Either an out-of-space condition has occurred on a VSAM keyed file (KSDS) or a WRITE to a VSAM relative file (RRDS) used a relative record number where the value in the relative record number exceeded the largest relative record number allowed for the file.
	Permanent data error conditions
30	A permanent I/O error occurred such as a data check or a parity check.
34	An out-of-space condition has occurred on a sequential file (QSAM) when a WRITE was executed.
35*	An OPEN statement with either the INPUT, I-O, or EXTEND clauses was attempted on a file that does not exist. A DD statement is probably missing from the JCL. This error will not occur if a file is defined as OPTIONAL.
37*	The options on an OPEN statement were incompatible with the file being processed. It can occur when a file is not on a mass storage device. Possible reasons are: • The OUTPUT or EXTEND options were specified but WRITE statements were not allowed for the file. • The INPUT option was specified but READ statements were not allowed for the file. • The I-O option was specified but either READ or WRITE statements were not allowed for the file.
38*	An OPEN statement was issued for a file that had been closed with the LOCK option. This applies to QSAM files only.
39*	An OPEN failed because of a conflict between the file description in the program and the actual file attributes. It could be because of a conflict in the file organization, prime key position, alternate key position, the code set, the maximum record size, the record format, or the block size.
	Logic error conditions
41*	An OPEN statement was issued for a file that was already OPEN.
42*	A CLOSE statement was issued for a file that was not OPEN.
43*	A READ statement did not successfully execute either before: • A REWRITE issued upon a mass storage file processed in sequential access mode. • A REWRITE or DELETE statement upon an indexed or relative file in sequential access mode.
44*	Either an attempt was made to REWRITE a record that was not the same size as the record that was read, or a WRITE or REWRITE was issued for a record that was either smaller or larger than the limits of the record size as defined in the RECORD IS VARYING clause in the FD. This error only applies to QSAM files.
46*	A sequential READ statement has been issued upon an open file in which either an end-of-file condition has occurred, or the prior READ failed and sequential positioning is not in effect.
47*	A READ statement was issued upon a file that was not opened in INPUT or I-O mode.

Figure 7.8   (*Continued*)

FILE STATUS value	Description
	Logic error conditions
48*	A WRITE statement was issued upon a file that was not opened in OUTPUT, I-O, or EXTEND mode.
49*	A REWRITE or DELETE statement was issued for a file that was not opened in I-O mode.
	Other implementation dependent errors
90	A program logic error has occurred.
91	A password failure has occurred when processing a VSAM file.
92	A program logic error has occurred.
93	A VSAM resource was not available.
94	File positioning did not exist (there was no current record pointer) when a sequential processing request was issued. (This error only occurs when the CMPR2 compiler option is in effect.)
95	Incomplete or invalid file information was available for a VSAM file.
96	No DD statement was specified in the JCL for a VSAM file.
97	An OPEN statement successfully executed for a VSAM file but a VERIFY had to be issued for the file.

Figure 7.8 *(Continued)*

occurs many times, each occurrence is set to the value coded. In Fig. 7.10, all 175 entries in TABLE-MIXED are set to +999.

Figure 7.11 shows where the VALUE clause can and cannot be used in relation to the OCCURS DEPENDING ON clause. The VALUE clause for SUBORDINATE-DATA is valid, but a VALUE clause for NON-SUBORDINATE would cause an error. Subordinate to a field means that another field follows with a higher level number (e.g., SUBORDINATE-DATA is subordinate to ENTRY1 in Fig. 7.11). The VALUE clause can be coded on an item containing OCCURS DEPENDING ON or on one of the elementary fields subordinate to it, if it is a group item; it cannot be specified for a data item that follows, but is not subordinate to, a data item that contains the OCCURS DEPENDING ON clause (e.g., NON-SUBORDINATE in Fig. 7.11).

7.11 SORT AND MERGE STATEMENTS

The SORT and MERGE statements in Release 3 allow multiple GIVING clauses and the SORT allows WITH DUPLICATES IN ORDER. Figure 7.12 shows a SORT statement using these new options. When the WITH DUPLICATES IN ORDER clause is not coded, the sort can process with increased efficiency, not worrying about the sorted order when records containing keys with the same value are sorted; when it is coded, the sort must preserve the order of records in

Release 3 Status Code	VS COBOL and Release 2 Status Code
00	00
02	02
04	00 for VSAM (no status code existed for QSAM).
05	00 for VSAM (no status code existed for QSAM).
07	No status code existed. This error only applies to QSAM.
10	10
14	No status code existed. This error only applies to VSAM.
21	21
22	22
23	23
24	24
30	30
34	34
35	93 or 96
37	93 for QSAM files. 96 for VSAM files.
38	92 This error only applies to QSAM.
39	95
41	92
42	92
43	92
44	92
46	92
47	92
48	92
49	92
90	90
91	91
92	92 This error only applies to QSAM files.
93	93
94	94
95	95
96	96
97	97 This error only applies to VSAM files.

Figure 7.9   Comparison of new status codes in Release 3 and their counterparts in VS COBOL and Release 2. Explanations of the status codes can be found in Fig. 7.8.

```
000010 DATA DIVISION.
000020 WORKING-STORAGE SECTION.
000030 01  TABLE-MIXED.
000040     05  MIXED1 OCCURS 7 TIMES.
000050         10  MIXED2 OCCURS 5 TIMES.
000060             15  MIXED3 OCCURS 5 TIMES PIC S9(3) VALUE +999.
```

Figure 7.10   How the VALUE clause can be used within a table under Release 3.

```
000010 DATA DIVISION.
000020 WORKING-STORAGE SECTION.
000030 01   VAR-NUM                  PIC S9(3) COMP-3.
000040 01   VARIABLE-GROUP.
000050      05   ENTRY1   OCCURS 1 TO 5 TIMES DEPENDING ON VAR-NUM.
000060           10   SUBORDINATE-DATA  PIC X(5) VALUE '12345'.
000070      05   NON-SUBORDINATE      PIC X(5).
```

Figure 7.11 How the VALUE clause can be used with an OCCURS
DEPENDING ON group under Release 3.

```
000010 PROCEDURE DIVISION.
000020      SORT SORT-FILE
000030           ON ASCENDING KEY SORT-KEY
000040           WITH DUPLICATES IN ORDER
000050           USING IN-FILE
000060           GIVING OUT-FILE1
000070           GIVING OUT-FILE2.
```

Figure 7.12 Code containing a SORT with
multiple GIVING clauses and a WITH
DUPLICATES IN ORDER clause.

the input file (or passed by the input procedure) that contain equal
keys. Some sort utilities such as SyncSort and DFSORT allowed you
to request this option in the past. Since the WITH DUPLICATES IN
ORDER clause will decrease the efficiency of a sort, it should only be
coded when absolutely necessary.

7.12 FILLER DATA NAME

The FILLER clause is no longer required. Although it may save time
in typing in a program, it will probably take most programmers a little time to get used to. The code in Fig. 7.13 shows code that will compile properly in Release 3.

```
000010 DATA DIVISION.
000020 WORKING-STORAGE SECTION.
000030 01   REPORT-DATE              PIC X(8) VALUE '02/01/90'.
000040 01   REDEFINES REPORT-DATE.
000050      05   WS-MONTH            PIC XX.
000060      05                       PIC X.
000070      05   WS-DAY              PIC XX.
000080      05                       PIC X.
000090      05   WS-YEAR             PIC XX.
```

Figure 7.13 FILLER data items no longer have to have the word
FILLER explicitly coded.

7.13   DE-EDITING OF NUMERIC EDITED FIELDS

Numeric edited items may be de-edited, allowing a numeric edited field to be moved to a numeric field. In Fig. 7.14, line 000060 would have caused a compilation error in VS COBOL or COBOL II Release 2. This statement is allowed in Release 3. It is usually considerably more efficient to move a numeric field to another numeric field rather than moving a numeric edited field to a numeric field. A first thought might be that de-editing is somewhat useless, since if you were able to edit a data item, you already have the information and do not need access to the edited field. However, de-editing does have significant applications. For instance, if an optical scanner was used to read a report and you wish to place the report values into numeric fields, de-editing can be used. Also, if you had a machine-readable copy of a spreadsheet or of any report in which the numeric values were not available other than in edited form, de-editing can allow you to process the values in numeric form.

You could always have de-edited a field manually, but the code was convoluted. You had to put leading zeros back in, and strip out the sign and decimal point. De-editing makes the code clearer and simpler.

7.14   BINARY AND PACKED-DECIMAL FIELDS

Binary fields defined as COMP or COMP-4 may now be defined as BINARY, and packed decimal fields defined as COMP-3 may now be defined as PACKED-DECIMAL. There is no difference in processing between equivalent formats on an IBM mainframe (e.g., COMP-3 versus PACKED-DECIMAL). However, differences in data representation may occur between COMP and BINARY fields if COBOL II code is run on other SAA machines (see Sec. 8.6.3).

```
000010 DATA DIVISION.
000020 WORKING-STORAGE SECTION.
000030 01  AGE                   PIC S9(3) COMP-3
000040 01  EDIT-AGE              PIC ZZ9-.
000050 PROCEDURE DIVISION.
000060     MOVE EDIT-AGE TO AGE.
```

Figure 7.14   Example of de-editing allowed in Release 3. The code would have produced a compilation error in VS COBOL or Release 2.

7.15 UPPER- AND LOWERCASE CODE

Figure 7.15 shows how COBOL code may be in both upper- and lowercase (lowercase was only previously allowed in literals). The three MOVE statements are equivalent since the compiler makes no differentiation between upper- and lowercase letters (except in literals). Upper- and lowercase code is allowed in other languages such as C and Pascal. C is case sensitive (a word in uppercase is not considered the same as the same word in lowercase, e.g., "FIELD" and "field" would be considered as different items) while Pascal and COBOL II Release 3 are not case sensitive. I strongly recommend that you keep your programs as case sensitive as possible. There is no reason to assume that COBOL will not become case sensitive in the future. Programmers are used to reading uppercase COBOL code and it makes sense to continue in this manner. If you do decide to code in lowercase or in a mixture of upper and lower, be consistent and document the coding methodology that you use. For instance, you may want to code the names of all constant fields in uppercase and the names of all other fields in lowercase.

7.16 NONNUMERIC LITERALS

Nonnumeric literals may be specified in hexadecimal in Release 3. To do so, code an X followed by the hexadecimal constant within quotes (or apostrophes if you use the APOST compiler option). Each two hexadecimal characters represent 1 byte (see Fig. 7.16).

Nonnumeric literals may be up to 160 characters in length (VS COBOL allowed up to 120 characters). In Release 3 they may contain intervening blank lines. The intervening blank lines are ignored and are not considered part of the literal. (They caused a compilation error in VS COBOL and in Release 2.) I see no reason why you would ever want a blank line in the middle of defining a literal, but it is allowed.

```
000010 Data Division.
000020 WORKING-STORAGE SECTION.
000030 01   AGE                     PIC S9(3) PACKED-DECIMAL.
000040 01   field-one               pic s9(4) binary.
000050
000060 PROCEDURE DIVISION.
000070      MOVE FIELD-ONE TO AGE.
000080      MOVE FIELD-one TO age.
000090      move fieLD-oNE TO aGe.
```

Figure 7.15 Example showing mixture of upper- and lowercase letters in code.

```
000010 DATA DIVISION.
000020 WORKING-STORAGE SECTION.
000030 01  HEX-TABLE1-INIT           VALUE X'004C003C009C'.
000040     05  TABLE1-ENTRY OCCURS 3 TIMES  PIC S9(3) COMP-3.
000050 01  BIG-DATA-VALUE            PIC X(160)
000060     VALUE 'This is a very long nonnumeric literal that gets con
000070-    'tinued throughout this line and onto the next line.  It ca
000080
000090-    'n contain up to 160 characters'.
```

Figure 7.16 Hexadecimal values and literals up to 160 bytes may be coded.

7.17 RELATION CONDITIONS

Relation conditions under Release 3 include < =, LESS OR EQUAL, LESS THAN OR EQUAL TO, > =, GREATER OR EQUAL, and GREATER THAN OR EQUAL TO. The first three forms are all equivalent and may be used interchangeably; the same is true of the last three forms.

7.18 INTERMEDIATE RESULTS

The ON SIZE ERROR always applies to final results of MULTIPLY and DIVIDE statements in VS COBOL, COBOL II Release 2, and COBOL II Release 3. Intermediate results on MULTIPLY and DIVIDE statements may cause an ON SIZE ERROR in VS COBOL and Release 2, whereas they do not in Release 3.

7.19 ADD...TO...GIVING

It is interesting that the syntax of a COBOL statement was updated because so many programmers kept making the same coding mistake. While in VS COBOL and COBOL II through Release 2, ADD A B GIVING C was correct syntax, ADD A TO B GIVING C was not. While an ADD...TO...GIVING statement only caused a warning message in VS COBOL, it caused a severe error in Release 2 of COBOL II. This increased conversion problems. The TO verb will not cause a warning or error message if used in Release 3 in an ADD statement with the GIVING option (the TO verb is still required in ADD statements that do not contain the GIVING option).

7.20 OBSOLETE ELEMENTS OF COBOL

The IBM Release 3 manuals list many statements and clauses that are obsolete and will be removed from the next revision of the ANSI

COBOL standard. While these statements may be coded in a Release 3 program, it is unclear whether IBM expects to remove them from the compiler at a later date. I expect they will and strongly recommend that the "obsolete elements" of the compiler no longer be used. It would have been better for IBM to have deleted them, since conversions from VS COBOL to COBOL II Release 2 are extensive already, and conversions from COBOL II Release 2 to COBOL II Release 3 will probably be done as well.

7.20.1 LABEL RECORDS Clause

In VS COBOL, an error message would result if the LABEL RECORDS clause was not specified in a File Description (FD). It is also required in an FD under Release 2. In Release 3 the LABEL RECORDS clause (LABELS RECORDS ARE STANDARD, LABEL RECORDS ARE OMITTED) is no longer a required statement. Furthermore, like the other COBOL clauses discussed in this section, it will be removed from the next revision of the ANSI COBOL standard. The TOTALING AREA and TOTALED AREA clauses on the LABEL RECORDS clause were used for user label processing in VS COBOL. They are not supported under COBOL II.

The DATA RECORDS and VALUE OF clauses used in an FD are also considered obsolete. Both clauses are syntax checked but have no effect on program execution.

7.20.2 ALTER Statement and Altered GO TO

The ALTER statement is now officially considered obsolete. This will make programmers who write structured code quite happy since they all considered the ALTER statement obsolete years ago. The ALTER statement was always considered confusing and for many years almost every company has restricted its use or strongly recommended that it not be used.

7.20.3 Optional Paragraphs in the IDENTIFICATION DIVISION

The REMARKS paragraph has been removed in COBOL II. However, the AUTHOR, INSTALLATION, DATE-WRITTEN, DATE-COMPILED, and SECURITY paragraphs are still allowed. They are considered obsolete. Comments should be coded instead of any of these paragraphs.

7.20.4   Other Obsolete Elements

The ENTER statement is checked for syntax during compilation but
has no effect on the execution of a program. The RERUN (that specified checkpoint records are used) and the MULTIPLE FILE TAPE
clauses (that specified more than one file shared the same physical
reel) in I-O-CONTROL are considered obsolete. The DEBUG-ITEM
special register, debugging sections, and the DEBUGGING declarative will also be removed from the next revision of the ANSI COBOL
standard.

7.21   FILE ORGANIZATION

The keyword ORGANIZATION need not be coded in the SELECT
statement in a Release 3 program. Whereas you used to have to code a
clause like:

```
000010 SELECT IN-FILE ASSIGN TO INFILE
000020     ORGANIZATION IS INDEXED.
```

you can now simply code:

```
000010 SELECT IN-FILE ASSIGN TO INFILE INDEXED.
```

7.22   STRING AND UNSTRING

The receiving field specified in the INTO clause of a STRING statement may be a group item in Release 3. UNSTRING changes are more
complex. Subscripts, lengths, and location information were analyzed
as the statement executed in Release 2. This meant that the information could be affected by results that were stored in the receiving
fields during execution of the statement. In Release 3 the subscripts,
length, and location information, as well as any reference modifications (see Sec. 8.4), are all done before the statement executes. This
may lead to different results.

7.23   NOT AT END, NOT INVALID KEY

The READ and RETURN statements have been updated to allow NOT
AT END. This gives the programmer the option to code AT END, NOT
AT END, or both within each statement. Figure 7.17 illustrates its
use.

Similar to the way NOT AT END is allowed as well as AT END, the
NOT INVALID KEY clause may be used in statements that allow
INVALID KEY. These are the DELETE, READ, REWRITE, START,
and WRITE statements. The NOT INVALID KEY clause may be used

```
000010 DATA DIVISION.
000020 FILE SECTION.
000030 FD  INPUT-FILE
000040     BLOCK CONTAINS 0 RECORDS
000050     LABEL RECORDS ARE STANDARD.
000060 01  INPUT-RECORD           PIC X(80).
000070 WORKING-STORAGE SECTION.
000080 01  WS-RECORDS-READ        PIC S9(5) COMP-3 VALUE ZERO.
000090 01  WS-END-OF-FILE         PIC X VALUE 'N'.
000100
000110 PROCEDURE DIVISION.
000120     READ INPUT-FILE
000130         AT END
000140             MOVE 'Y' TO WS-END-OF-FILE
000150         NOT AT END
000160             ADD +1 TO WS-RECORDS-READ
000170             ...
```

Figure 7.17   Use of the NOT AT END clause in a READ statement.

in a statement whether or not the statement contains the INVALID
KEY clause.

7.24   NOT ON SIZE ERROR

The NOT ON SIZE ERROR clause may be specified in COBOL II programs within the statements that previously allowed the ON SIZE
ERROR clause. These are the ADD, COMPUTE, DIVIDE, MULTIPLY,
and SUBTRACT statements. Statements within the ON SIZE ERROR
clause are executed if the result of an arithmetic operation is too large to
be placed in the receiving field; statements within a NOT ON SIZE ER-
ROR will be executed when the result fits into the receiving field.

7.25   PROGRAM COLLATING SEQUENCE

PROGRAM COLLATING SEQUENCE can be coded in the OBJECT-
COMPUTER paragraph to override the standard EBCDIC collating
sequence. When coded, it affects the INSPECT, STRING, and
UNSTRING statements. (It also affects nonnumeric keys in a MERGE
or SORT when the COLLATING SEQUENCE is not specified in the
SORT or MERGE statement.) The PROGRAM COLLATING
SEQUENCE affects nonnumeric comparisons. In VS COBOL and Release 2 it affects both explicitly coded conditions and implicitly performed conditions (those comparisons which the compiler deems necessary to perform) in INSPECT, STRING, and UNSTRING
statements. In Release 3 the PROGRAM COLLATING SEQUENCE
only affects explicitly coded conditions in these statements.

Chapter 8

New Release 3 Features

8.1 EXTERNAL ATTRIBUTES

8.1.1 EXTERNAL Attribute in the WORKING-STORAGE SECTION

Among the most interesting features added to Release 3 is the EXTERNAL attribute. If many Release 3 programs wish to use the same field, such as a count of the number of records read, they may all share the same field without passing it between programs with a CALL statement. As an example, if REC-COUNT is to be shared in many programs, all programs would define the field as "01 REC-COUNT PIC S9(3) EXTERNAL." The EXTERNAL clause can only be used for data items that are defined on the 01 level in the WORKING-STORAGE SECTION. When a data item is defined as EXTERNAL, any subordinate data items are also considered as EXTERNAL. This includes explicitly defined indexes (e.g., 10 INDEX1 USAGE IS INDEX) but excludes implicitly defined indexes (e.g., INDEXED BY INDEX1). Also, note that an EXTERNAL data item cannot have a VALUE clause coded with it. Figure 8.1 shows a

```
000010 DATA DIVISION.
000020 WORKING-STORAGE SECTION.
000030 01  REC-COUNT                PIC S9(3) EXTERNAL.
000040 01  GROUP-EXT-ITEM EXTERNAL.
000050     05  FIELD1               PIC S9(5) COMP-3.
000060     05  TABLE1.
000070         10  ENTRY1 OCCURS 10 TIMES
000080                 INDEXED BY ENTRY1-INDEX  PIC X(20).
```

Figure 8.1 Example of a program using EXTERNAL data fields.

program in which all data items in WORKING-STORAGE, except for ENTRY1-INDEX, are EXTERNAL.

Since EXTERNAL fields are shared by definition, the EXTERNAL clause is therefore not allowed in the LINKAGE SECTION. However, this does not mean that a field defined as EXTERNAL cannot be passed to another program or that a called program cannot code the field without the EXTERNAL attribute in its LINKAGE SECTION. While it would make no sense to code this way in a called COBOL II program, it would make sense if a COBOL II program was calling a VS COBOL program, a Release 2 program, or a program written in another language (PL/I, FORTRAN, Assembly, etc.).

8.1.2   EXTERNAL Attribute With Files

The EXTERNAL attribute gives added flexibility to programs since it may be used for files as well as data items. No longer do you have to specifically write an I/O module just to read and write files shared by many programs. Files processed with any access method (e.g., QSAM, VSAM) may be defined as EXTERNAL, and the READ and WRITE statements in each program will all access the same file (see Fig. 8.2). For instance, a common report file that has records added to it from many different programs can now have the WRITE statements placed into each program using the file. An EXTERNAL file, like a standard file, should only be opened and closed once. An indicator defined as EXTERNAL in WORKING-STORAGE could be shared by all programs using the file to show that the file was opened or closed.

8.2   NESTED PROGRAMS

Among the most enigmatic enhancements to the COBOL II compiler is the concept of nested (or contained) programs, the ability to code multiple PROCEDURE DIVISIONs within a single source program. Most programmers have enough of a problem coding one PROCEDURE DIVISION in a program. The new implementation allows multiple IDENTIFICATION DIVISION and END PROGRAM statements indicating where each nested program begins and ends. Nested programs are given control in the same manner as nonnested programs, through a CALL statement. While a CALL to a nested program will function with the efficiency of a PERFORM rather than a CALL, which is quite good, I see this nested program feature adding to the complexity of COBOL code, not diminishing it.

Each nested program must have an IDENTIFICATION DIVISION, but the other divisions are optional; ENVIRONMENT DIVISION, DATA DIVISION, and PROCEDURE DIVISION do not have to be

```
000010 PROGRAM-ID. MAINPROG.
000020 ENVIRONMENT DIVISION.
000030 INPUT-OUTPUT SECTION.
000040 FILE-CONTROL.
000050      SELECT OUT-FILE ASSIGN TO S-OUTFILE.
000060 DATA DIVISION.
000070 FILE SECTION.
000080 FD   OUT-FILE EXTERNAL.
000090 01   OUT-RECORD          PIC X(80).
000100 WORKING-STORAGE SECTION.
000110 01   REC-COUNT           PIC S9(3) EXTERNAL.
000120 01   MAINPROG-DATA       PIC X(200).
000130
000140 PROCEDURE DIVISION.
000150      OPEN OUTPUT OUT-FILE.
000160      CALL 'WRITEPG1'.
000170      CALL 'WRITEPG2'.
000180      ...
```

(a)

```
000010 PROGRAM-ID. WRITEPG1.
000020 ENVIRONMENT DIVISION.
000030 INPUT-OUTPUT SECTION.
000040 FILE-CONTROL.
000050      SELECT OUT-FILE ASSIGN TO S-OUTFILE.
000060 DATA DIVISION.
000070 FILE SECTION.
000080 FD   OUT-FILE EXTERNAL.
000090 01   OUT-RECORD          PIC X(80).
000100 WORKING-STORAGE SECTION.
000110 01   WRITEPG1-DATA       PIC X(500).
000120 01   REC-COUNT           PIC S9(3) EXTERNAL.
000130
000140 PROCEDURE DIVISION.
000150      ...
000160      WRITE OUTPUT-RECORD.
000170      ADD +1 TO REC-COUNT.
```

(b)

```
000010 PROGRAM-ID. WRITEPG2.
000020 ENVIRONMENT DIVISION.
000030 INPUT-OUTPUT SECTION.
000040 FILE-CONTROL.
000050      SELECT OUT-FILE ASSIGN TO S-OUTFILE.
000060 DATA DIVISION.
000070 FILE SECTION.
000080 FD   OUT-FILE EXTERNAL.
000090 01   OUT-RECORD          PIC X(80).
000100 WORKING-STORAGE SECTION.
000110 01   REC-COUNT           PIC S9(3) EXTERNAL.
000120
000130 PROCEDURE DIVISION.
000140      ...
000150      WRITE OUTPUT-RECORD.
000160      ADD +1 TO REC-COUNT.
```

(c)

Figure 8.2 Example of three programs using an
EXTERNAL file. The records written in
WRITEPG1 (*b*) and WRITEPG2 (*c*) are added to
the file opened in MAINPROG (*a*).

coded. This does not mean that a division header does not have to be coded when the division exists in a program. For instance, you cannot leave out the DATA DIVISION in a program that has a WORKING-STORAGE SECTION. What it means is that when a program has no data defined, the DATA DIVISION may be left out (this possibility will make more sense after you understand GLOBAL data items, discussed in Sec. 8.2.2).

Reading a program which does not contain division headers may take some getting used to. I strongly recommend that you continue to code the division header statements in your programs even when the division has no information in it. This will explicitly show the empty division and will make the program clearer to follow.

The program name on the PROGRAM-ID statement may be up to 30 characters. The characters used and the length of a program name follow the same rules that are required for a paragraph name. This is to make the name used in a CALL statement similar to the name used in a PERFORM statement. The first characters of the main (outermost) program must still be alphabetic and only the first eight characters of the main program are used by the system (e.g., the program name on an EXEC statement in the JCL). The outermost program and all of its nested programs are placed into a single object deck and load module, and only the outermost program can be called from another separately compiled program.

The CONFIGURATION SECTION can only be coded in the outermost program. The end of each nested program must be marked with an END PROGRAM statement which contains the name of the PROGRAM-ID.

To understand which nested programs can call which other nested programs, the terms "directly contained program" and "indirectly contained program" must be understood. A directly contained program within a program is any other program at the next lower nesting level. An indirectly contained program is a program that is more than one nesting level below another program. Figure 8.3 shows an example of directly and indirectly contained nested programs. PROGRAM2 and PROGRAM5 are directly contained within PROGRAM1. PROGRAM3 and PROGRAM4 are directly contained in PROGRAM2 and indirectly contained in PROGRAM1.

8.2.1 COMMON Attribute

The COMMON clause can be coded on the PROGRAM-ID of a program to increase the scope of programs that can call it. COMMON may only be coded on a contained program. When it is not coded on a PROGRAM-ID clause of a contained program, the contained program

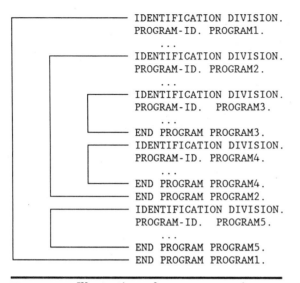

```
                            IDENTIFICATION DIVISION.
                            PROGRAM-ID. PROGRAM1.
                                ...
                            IDENTIFICATION DIVISION.
                            PROGRAM-ID. PROGRAM2.
                                ...
                            IDENTIFICATION DIVISION.
                            PROGRAM-ID.  PROGRAM3.
                                ...
                            END PROGRAM PROGRAM3.
                            IDENTIFICATION DIVISION.
                            PROGRAM-ID. PROGRAM4.
                                ...
                            END PROGRAM PROGRAM4.
                            END PROGRAM PROGRAM2.
                            IDENTIFICATION DIVISION.
                            PROGRAM-ID.  PROGRAM5.
                                ...
                            END PROGRAM PROGRAM5.
                            END PROGRAM PROGRAM1.
```

Figure 8.3 Illustration of program nesting levels.

may only be called by a program in which it is directly contained; when the COMMON clause is coded on a PROGRAM-ID, the program may be called from any other program that is either directly or indirectly contained within the same program in which the COMMON program is contained.

As an example, look at Fig. 8.4. If the COMMON clause was not coded on PROGRAM4 and PROGRAM6, PROGRAM3 would not be able to call them. This is because PROGRAM4 and PROGRAM6 are not directly contained within PROGRAM3. When they contain the COMMON clause, they may both be called by PROGRAM3 since they are directly contained in PROGRAM1, which indirectly contains PROGRAM3.

8.2.2 GLOBAL Attribute

The complexity of nested programs is increased through the use of GLOBAL variables. GLOBAL variables are data items which may be used by any nested program. They should not be confused with EXTERNAL data items that may be used by any Release 3 program, whether nested or not. All data items not declared as GLOBAL are considered local; they are only known to the program using the data item. When the GLOBAL clause is coded on a data item, it is available for use in all programs either directly or indirectly contained within the program, as well as being available within the program in which it is declared. The GLOBAL clause can be used in the FILE SECTION

```
000010 IDENTIFICATION DIVISION.
000020 PROGRAM-ID. PROGRAM1.
000030 ENVIRONMENT DIVISION.
000040 DATA DIVISION.
000050 01  FIELD1            PIC S9(4) COMP.
000060 01  COUNTER1G         PIC S9(4) COMP GLOBAL.
000070 PROCEDURE DIVISION.
000080     CALL 'PROGRAM2'.
000090     STOP RUN.
000100
000110 IDENTIFICATION DIVISION.
000120 PROGRAM-ID. PROGRAM2.
000130 DATA DIVISION.
000140 WORKING-STORAGE SECTION.
000150 01  COUNTER1G         PIC S9(4) COMP GLOBAL.
000160 01  COUNTER2G         PIC S9(4) COMP GLOBAL.
000170 PROCEDURE DIVISION.
000180
000190     DISPLAY 'PROGRAM2 IS RUNNING'.
000200     EXIT PROGRAM.
000210 IDENTIFICATION DIVISION.
000220 PROGRAM-ID. PROGRAM3.
000230 PROCEDURE DIVISION.
000240     DISPLAY 'PROGRAM3 IS RUNNING'.
000250     EXIT PROGRAM.
000260 END PROGRAM PROGRAM3.
000270
000280 IDENTIFICATION DIVISION.
000290 PROGRAM-ID. PROGRAM4 IS COMMON.
000300 PROCEDURE DIVISION.
000310     DISPLAY 'PROGRAM4 IS RUNNING'.
000320     EXIT PROGRAM.
000330
000340 IDENTIFICATION DIVISION.
000350 PROGRAM-ID. PROGRAM5.
000360 PROCEDURE DIVISION.
000370     DISPLAY 'PROGRAM5 IS RUNNING'.
000380     EXIT PROGRAM.
000390 END PROGRAM PROGRAM5.
000400
000410 END PROGRAM PROGRAM4.
000420 END PROGRAM PROGRAM2.
000430
000440 IDENTIFICATION DIVISION.
000450 PROGRAM-ID. PROGRAM6 IS COMMON.
000460 PROCEDURE DIVISION.
000470     DISPLAY 'PROGRAM6 IS RUNNING'.
000480     EXIT PROGRAM.
000490 END PROGRAM PROGRAM6.
000500
000510 END PROGRAM PROGRAM1.
```

Figure 8.4 Use of COMMON and GLOBAL attributes in a nested program structure containing six programs.

```
Nested Program CALLs Allowed
Program     Can CALL Program      Reason
PROGRAM1    PROGRAM2              Directly contained
            PROGRAM6              Directly contained
PROGRAM2    PROGRAM3              Directly contained
            PROGRAM4              Directly contained
            PROGRAM6              It is COMMON
PROGRAM3    PROGRAM4              It is COMMON
            PROGRAM6              It is COMMON
PROGRAM4    PROGRAM5              Directly contained
            PROGRAM6              It is COMMON
PROGRAM5    PROGRAM6              It is COMMON
PROGRAM6    None
```

Note: PROGRAM5 cannot call PROGRAM4 because it would be a recursive call that is not allowed. PROGRAM6 cannot call PROGRAM4 because PROGRAM6 is not directly or indirectly contained in PROGRAM2.

```
Data Item Usage Allowed
Program     Data Item                   Reason
PROGRAM1    FIELD1                       Defined in program
            COUNTER1G of PROGRAM1        Defined in program
PROGRAM2    COUNTER1G of PROGRAM2        Defined in program
            COUNTER2G                    Defined in program
PROGRAM3    COUNTER1G of PROGRAM2        Defined in outer program
            COUNTER2G                    Defined in outer program
PROGRAM4    COUNTER1G of PROGRAM2        Defined in outer program
            COUNTER2G                    Defined in outer program
PROGRAM5    COUNTER1G of PROGRAM2        Defined in outer program
            COUNTER2G                    Defined in outer program
PROGRAM6    COUNTER1G of PROGRAM1        Defined in outer program
```

Note: Programs that are contained in both PROGRAM1 and PROGRAM2 will have access to COUNTER1G defined in PROGRAM2 rather than PROGRAM1. This is because a program uses the GLOBAL definition of a data item in an inner program in which it is defined rather than a GLOBAL definition in an outer program.

Figure 8.4 *(Continued)*

or the WORKING-STORAGE SECTION but may only be coded on 01 level data items. Any data item subordinate to a GLOBAL data item is considered GLOBAL. This includes explicitly defined indexes, implicitly defined indexes, and condition names (88 levels). The GLOBAL attribute cannot be used on two different data items within the same DATA DIVISION if they both contain the same name.

When the compiler attempts to resolve the reference to a data item, it first searches the program containing the reference for the data item and, if not found, searches for a GLOBAL data item (with the same name) within each of the outer programs in which the program is nested. As soon as a match is found, the field found is used as the referenced field. The search will stop even if another data field with the same name is defined as GLOBAL in another program and would have been found had the search continued outwardly through other nested programs.

File Descriptions (FDs), as well as data items, may be declared as GLOBAL. Any program directly or indirectly contained within the program which has the GLOBAL File Description can use the file. The record description within a GLOBAL FD is automatically considered GLOBAL and the GLOBAL clause does not have to be coded on it. However, the GLOBAL clause can be coded on the record description when it is not on the FD. In this case the record is available for use in the contained programs while issuing I/O upon the file is not. The GLOBAL attribute, like the EXTERNAL attribute, may not be used in the LINKAGE SECTION.

Figure 8.4 is an example showing a number of nested programs that use the COMMON and GLOBAL clauses. It shows which programs may call others and which programs have access to GLOBAL data items.

COBOL programs may never make recursive calls (they may not call themselves). This becomes somewhat more complicated with nested programs. In the example in Fig. 8.4, after PROGRAM4 calls PROGRAM5, PROGRAM5 cannot call PROGRAM4. It would essentially be considered a recursive call.

8.2.3 Uses of Nested Programs

A dynamic CALL statement (see Sec. 12.5.2) under COBOL II takes much longer than the same CALL statement issued under VS COBOL (often more than twice as long). Nested programs can be called with the efficiency of a PERFORM. In cases where a short program is called many times and efficiency is a major concern, it would be worthwhile to combine the two programs, making the called program a nested program. It can sometimes cut the run-time in half. Realize that this technique could be used upon VS COBOL programs that have been migrated to COBOL II Release 3 as well as new Release 3 programs that are written.

If you decide to nest programs, each PROCEDURE DIVISION can still be written by a different programmer as might be done when separate programs were written. You can combine the programs into one by putting COPY statements into the main program.

It has always been a problem to test a program that calls a second program, when you are waiting for another programmer to finish coding the second program. While you were always able to code a stub program (a program that sets a few parameters and does a GOBACK), it required the writing, compiling, and link-editing of a separate program. If a few programs were all called and you were awaiting their completion, it became a burden to prepare many small stub programs for testing. With nested programs allowed under Release 3, you can now code stub programs as nested programs, eliminating the need for multiple compiles and link-edits.

8.3   INITIAL ATTRIBUTE

Programs may now contain the INITIAL attribute in the PROGRAM-ID as follows:

```
000010 PROGRAM-ID. PROGRAM1 IS INITIAL PROGRAM.
```

The INITIAL attribute informs the compiler that each time the program is called, the program is to be in its initial state. This means that each time the program is entered, all WORKING-STORAGE fields will have the initial values that are coded for them. WORKING-STORAGE fields that do not contain a VALUE clause (including EXTERNAL data items that cannot have a VALUE clause) are not affected by the INITIAL attribute.

On all static calls issued under VS COBOL or COBOL II Release 2 (and when the INITIAL attribute is not used under Release 3) the called program is only in its initial state on the first call (refer to Sec. 12.5.2 for a discussion of static and dynamic calls). Additional calls to a statically called program will find WORKING-STORAGE data in the last-used state. For example, suppose a called program contained WORKING-STORAGE data item "01 FIELD1   PIC S9(7)V99 COMP-3 VALUE ZERO." If the called program did not contain the INITIAL attribute and had added five dollars to FIELD1 on the first call, on the second entry to the program FIELD1 will still contain the five dollars; if the INITIAL attribute had been coded for the called program, on the second entry to the program FIELD1 will be zero.

Before the INITIAL attribute was added to the compiler, there had previously been no standard way to place a statically called COBOL program into its initial state. Note that the INITIAL attribute applies to all directly and indirectly contained programs within a program.

When a dynamic call is made to a program, as with a static call, all subsequent calls will normally find the WORKING-STORAGE data in the called program in the state that it had previously been in. In COBOL II, as well as in VS COBOL, the CANCEL verb (e.g., CANCEL 'PROGRAM1') allows a program to be logically deleted from memory. CANCEL may only be used with a program that was dynamically called (a CANCEL statement issued for a statically called program has no effect). If a CANCEL is issued upon a program, the program will be in its initial state when it is called again.

Coding the INITIAL attribute on a program that is called dynami-

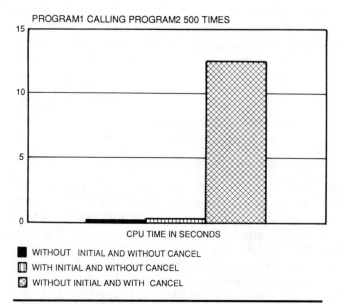

PROGRAM1 CALLING PROGRAM2 500 TIMES

CPU TIME IN SECONDS

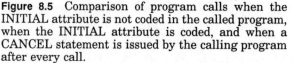

■ WITHOUT INITIAL AND WITHOUT CANCEL
▥ WITH INITIAL AND WITHOUT CANCEL
▨ WITHOUT INITIAL AND WITH CANCEL

Figure 8.5 Comparison of program calls when the INITIAL attribute is not coded in the called program, when the INITIAL attribute is coded, and when a CANCEL statement is issued by the calling program after every call.

cally will have the same logical effect as issuing a CANCEL for the program before issuing the next CALL to it. However, the CANCEL command gives a program more flexibility since it allows you to put the program into its initial state selectively, rather than upon every invocation. In cases where you want the program in its initial state on every CALL, it is clearer to use the INITIAL attribute. The INITIAL attribute also works infinitely faster than CANCEL. On a very small program that calls another small program, the execution times can be seen in Fig. 8.5.

Be very careful when using the INITIAL attribute on any program that contains files. All files that are not defined with the EXTERNAL attribute are closed when the program returns control to the calling program.

8.4   REFERENCE MODIFICATION

The colon (:) was not a valid character in COBOL code until Release 3. It is now allowed as a separator character used to delimit values in what the COBOL II manuals call "reference modification." This feature allows part of a data item (a substring) to be used without defining the breakdown of the data item in the DATA DIVISION.

8.4.1   Integer Constants as Reference Modifiers

Reference modification may only be used with fields in DISPLAY format. Reference modification has the format DATA-FIELD $(x{:}y)$, where x is the beginning character position (relative to 1) to be used in DATA-FIELD and y is the number of bytes. For example, MOVE FIELD1 (3:7) TO FIELD2 will move the third through ninth bytes of FIELD1 to FIELD2. The number of bytes moved from the sending field do not have to be coded in a reference modification [e.g., MOVE FIELD1 (3:) TO FIELD2]. If not coded, all bytes through the end of the field are moved.

When reference modification is used, it can allow you to code fewer fields in the DATA DIVISION since reference modifications can define the subfields to be acted upon. However, I recommend caution when using it solely for this reason. A program may become confusing when someone attempts to interpret the modifiers and must then determine the meaning of the subfields without having any descriptive names. While reference modifications detract from the clarity of a program using fields that occur in fixed positions within a data item, it adds clarity to code which processes fields whose length or beginning position is variable.

8.4.2   Data Items as Reference Modifiers

Reference modification to a data item can be done using other data items and arithmetic expressions as well as with literals. Until reference modification was added to the compiler, some simple functions required complex code. Take the case when FULL-NAME contains a person's full name beginning with the first name and LAST-NAME-BEGIN contains the character position where the first character of the last name begins. If you wanted to move the person's last name to field LAST-NAME, you either had to move each character separately (the first segment of code in Fig. 8.6) or use the slick method of a double OCCURS DEPENDING ON (the second segment of code in the figure). The last segment of code in Fig. 8.6 shows how simply the solution can now be coded using data items as reference modifiers to FULL-NAME.

```
000010 DATA DIVISION.
000020 WORKING-STORAGE SECTION.
000030 01   FULL-NAME.
000040      05   FULL-CHAR        PIC X OCCURS 40 TIMES.
000050 01   LAST-NAME.
000060      05   LAST-CHAR        PIC X OCCURS 20 TIMES.
000070 01   LAST-NAME-BEGIN       PIC S9(3) COMP-3.
000080 01   SUB-FULL             PIC S9(4) COMP.
000090 01   SUB-LAST             PIC S9(4) COMP.
000100 PROCEDURE DIVISION.
000110      ...
000120      MOVE +1 TO SUB-LAST.
000130      PERFORM MOVE-LAST THRU MOVE-END
000140          VARYING SUB-FULL FROM LAST-NAME-BEGIN BY +1
000150          UNTIL SUB-FULL IS GREATER THAN 40 OR
000160                SUB-LAST IS GREATER THAN 20.
000170      ...
000180 MOVE-LAST.
000190      MOVE FULL-CHAR (SUB-FULL) TO LAST-CHAR (SUB-LAST).
000200      ADD +1 TO SUB-LAST.
000210 MOVE-END. EXIT.
```

(a)

```
000010 DATA DIVISION.
000020 WORKING-STORAGE SECTION.
000030 01   FULL-NAME.
000040      05   EACH-FIRST OCCURS 1 TO 40 TIMES
000050           DEPENDING ON SUB-FULL1      PIC X.
000060      05   FULL-LAST.
000070          10   EACH-LAST  OCCURS 1 TO 40 TIMES
000080               DEPENDING ON SUB-FULL2      PIC X.
000090 01   LAST-NAME             PIC X(20).
000100 01   LAST-NAME-BEGIN       PIC S9(3) COMP-3.
000110 01   SUB-FULL1            PIC S9(4) COMP.
000120 01   SUB-FULL2            PIC S9(4) COMP.
000130 PROCEDURE DIVISION.
000140      ...
000150      SUBTRACT +1 FROM LAST-NAME-BEGIN GIVING SUB-FULL1.
000160      SUBTRACT SUB-FULL1 FROM 40 GIVING SUB-FULL2.
000170      MOVE FULL-LAST TO LAST-NAME.
```

(b)

```
000010 DATA DIVISION.
000020 WORKING-STORAGE SECTION.
000030 01   FULL-NAME             PIC X(40).
000040 01   LAST-NAME             PIC X(20).
000050 01   LAST-NAME-BEGIN       PIC S9(3) COMP-3.
000060 PROCEDURE DIVISION.
000070      ...
000080      MOVE FULL-NAME (LAST-NAME-BEGIN: )
000090                  TO LAST-NAME.
```

(c)

Figure 8.6 Three methods of isolating a person's last name
from a field containing the first name followed by the last
name. The last method (c) is the simplest and clearest and is
only allowed in COBOL II Release 3.

8.4.3 Reference Modifiers with Variable Length Fields

The length used when doing a variable length move can be dependent upon how the variable length field is defined in the program. The maximum length rather than the actual length might be used when you really want the actual length to be used. Data movement involving OCCURS DEPENDING ON fields is discussed in detail in Sec. 7.3. In the example in Fig. 8.7, line 000140 will use the maximum length of TABLE1 when the MOVE is executed, wiping out any information that you may have wanted to preserve at the end of the field. You may have only wanted to change the city in the address but leave the state code and zip code as is. Line 000150 shows how reference modification can be used to move CITY-NAME to the first 10 bytes of TABLE1 and not affect the last 10 bytes of TABLE1 (on line 000150 where the field length is not given in a reference modification, the actual length until the end of the data item is used). Even though one line in the code uses the actual length and another uses the maximum length, no error messages, not even informational messages, are produced by the COBOL II compiler. The implementation of the lengths used for variable length fields is confusing. You must be very careful in coding if you are to obtain the desired results when dealing with variable length fields.

8.4.4 Subscripting and Reference Modification Combined

Reference modification and subscripting (or indexing) can both be used on the same field, in the same statement of a COBOL II program.

```
000010 WORKING-STORAGE SECTION.
000020 01   VAR-TAB1.
000030      05   ADDR-LENGTH1        PIC S9(3) COMP-3 VALUE +10.
000040      05   TABLE1.
000050          10   EACH-ENTRY OCCURS 1 TO 20 TIMES
000060               DEPENDING ON ADDR-LENGTH1    PIC X.
000070 01   VAR-TAB2.
000080      05   ADDR-LENGTH2        PIC S9(3) COMP-3 VALUE +10.
000090      05   TABLE2.
000100          10   CITY-NAME       PIC X(10) VALUE 'BROOKLYN, '.
000110          10   STATE-ZIP-CODE  PIC X(10) VALUE 'NY    11201'.
000120 PROCEDURE DIVISION.
000130      ...
000140      MOVE VAR-TAB2 TO VAR-TAB1.
000150      MOVE VAR-TAB2 TO VAR-TAB1 (1: ).
```

Figure 8.7 How reference modification can force the COBOL II compiler to use the actual length, rather than the maximum length, of a variable length table.

```
000010 DATA DIVISION.
000020 WORKING-STORAGE SECTION.
000030 01   TABLE1.
000040       05   ENTRY1 OCCURS 20 TIMES   PIC X(15).
000050 01   SUB1                           PIC S9(4) COMP.
000060 01   FIELD1                         PIC X(7).
000070 PROCEDURE DIVISION.
000080       ...
000090       MOVE ENTRY1 (SUB1) (5:7) TO FIELD1.
```

Figure 8.8 Example of how subscripts are used together
with reference modification.

The subscript always appears first in the code. The example in Fig. 8.8
shows how the code will look.

8.4.5   Compilation Error Messages Affected
by Reference Modification

When an undefined field is found during compilation and the field is
followed by a second field that is defined and enclosed in parentheses,
the VS COBOL and COBOL II Release 2 compilers assume that the
second field is a subscript. The Release 3 compiler sometimes assumes
that the second field is a reference modification. You therefore get an
error message indicating that an expected reference modification was
not found. The error does not occur if the field in parentheses is followed by a colon, in which case the compiler realizes that it is definitely a reference modification. It really makes no difference whether
the error is assumed as a reference modification error rather than a
subscripting error except that you should be aware of this fact. Otherwise the error message might lead you in the wrong direction.

8.5   REPLACE STATEMENT

The REPLACE statement has been added to the COBOL II language
in Release 3. This is not the same as the REPLACING option of the
COPY statement. The REPLACE statement does not produce any executable code. Similar to the REPLACING option, REPLACE specifies
a word or words in a COBOL II program and other word or words that
will be substituted for them when the program is compiled. The main
difference between the REPLACING option of the COPY statement
and the REPLACE statement is that the REPLACING option acts
only upon the COPY member for which it is specified, while the
REPLACE statement acts upon part of or an entire program.

   The REPLACE statement stays in effect until another REPLACE

statement appears in the code. If you wish to cancel the effect of a REPLACE statement and want no other replacements to be made in the program, a REPLACE OFF statement can be coded. Compiling with the LIB option is a requirement when the REPLACE statement is used.

A first thought might be that the statement seems to be rather excessive since all modern program editors allow a global change, which is just as fast and makes the program easier to follow than using a REPLACE statement. However, the fact that the REPLACE statements work after COPY members are copied into a program makes it a neat shorthand form of specifying REPLACING on many COPY members used in a program. Additionally, for conversion purposes, it may come in handy. For instance, suppose many programs and COPY members were using a field called DAY-OF-WEEK. DAY-OF-WEEK is a COBOL II reserved word in Release 3. If the COPY members in use were supplied by a vendor and should not be changed, adding a REPLACE statement to every program to change DAY-OF-WEEK to another name would be the simplest way to ease the conversion to Release 3.

A more complex example would be when a programmer wanted to change the name of all occurrences of the DAY-OF-WEEK field but also wanted to add code to use the ACCEPT statement with the DAY-OF-WEEK option. REPLACE statements could be added to accomplish this. The code to do so is illustrated in Fig. 8.9. The REPLACE statement on line 000010 remains in effect until explicitly terminated on line 000110. Any references to DAY-OF-WEEK in MEMBER1 or MEMBER2, as well as the reference on line 000070, will be changed to THE-WEEK-DAY. No REPLACE statement is in effect when the ACCEPT statement on line 000120 is processed, so it is not changed.

8.6 NEW COMPILER OPTIONS

8.6.1 AWO Option

The AWO compiler option is a nice addition to Release 3. It is used for efficient processing of blocked variable length output records in QSAM files and serves the equivalent function of the APPLY WRITE-ONLY clause coded within the I-O-CONTROL paragraph. It requests COBOL to place the maximum number of records into each block rather than allowing COBOL to write blocks that are only partially full (refer to Sec. 11.8.1 for a more complete description). Programs writing variable length records can run more efficiently if you recompile them with the AWO option; you no longer have to change

```
000010 REPLACE ==DAY-OF-WEEK== BY ==THE-WEEK-DAY==.
000020 DATA DIVISION.
000030 WORKING-STORAGE SECTION.
000040 COPY MEMBER1.
000050 COPY MEMBER2.
000060 01  FIELD1                  PIC X(6).
000070 01  DAY-OF-WEEK             PIC X.
000080
000090 PROCEDURE DIVISION.
000100     . . .
000110     REPLACE OFF.
000120     ACCEPT FIELD1 FROM DAY-OF-WEEK.
000130     REPLACE ==DAY-OF-WEEK== BY ==THE-WEEK-DAY==.
000140     MOVE 'Y' TO DAY-OF-WEEK.
000150     . . .
```

(a)

```
000001    000010 REPLACE ==DAY-OF-WEEK== BY ==THE-WEEK-DAY==.
000002    000020 DATA DIVISION.
000003    000030 WORKING-STORAGE SECTION.
             . . .
000007    000070 01  THE-WEEK-DAY            PIC X.
000008    000080
000009    000090 PROCEDURE DIVISION.
000010    000100     . . .
000011    000110     REPLACE OFF.
000012    000120     ACCEPT FIELD1 FROM DAY-OF-WEEK.
000013    000130     REPLACE ==DAY-OF-WEEK== BY ==THE-WEEK-DAY==.
000014    000140     MOVE 'Y' TO THE-WEEK-DAY.
000015    000150     . . .
```

(b)

Figure 8.9 Example of code using the REPLACE statement (a) and the compiler listing produced (b).

the program itself. When the option is used, COBOL II produces an informational message informing you of each file that will be affected by the option.

Restrictions in VS COBOL for files processed with APPLY WRITE-ONLY have been eliminated in COBOL II. This also applies when the AWO option is used. The output record was restricted from containing any fields that were the object of an OCCURS DEPENDING ON clause, and you were not allowed to move to any subfields in the output record (you were only able to move to the 01 level). Be careful when using the APPLY WRITE-ONLY clause or the AWO option with EXTERNAL files. If either affects a file, all programs that contain the file should be compiled with the AWO compiler option (or should contain the APPLY WRITE-ONLY clause).

8.6.2   TRUNC Option

The TRUNC and NOTRUNC options that were supported in VS COBOL and COBOL II Release 2 have been removed and are replaced with the TRUNC(STD), TRUNC(OPT), and TRUNC(BIN) options in Release 3. The TRUNC(STD) option works the same way the VS COBOL TRUNC option used to work. The TRUNC(BIN) produces similar results to the VS COBOL NOTRUNC option, allowing a binary field to be truncated based upon the maximum value in the binary field (halfword, fullword, doubleword), not the maximum value based upon the PICTURE clause. The TRUNC(OPT) option was added for performance reasons to generate the most efficient code, either truncating to the length of the PICTURE clause or the binary field. It processes in a similar manner to the NOTRUNC option in COBOL II Release 2. This option should only be used when a program's logic never allows the value of binary fields to exceed the number of digits defined in their PICTURE clauses. For more information on the various TRUNC options, refer to Sec. 12.5.1.

8.6.3   FLAGSAA Option

As Systems Application Architecture (SAA) becomes more popular, it may be helpful for companies planning to use it to check their programs to ensure that they are using the subset of the COBOL II language supported by SAA. The COBOL II compiler supplies the FLAGSAA option to fill this need. Any incompatibilities between the COBOL II program and SAA are listed as warning messages in the listing. The FLAGSAA option can only be used when NOCMPR2 is in effect (the CMPR2 option allows Release 2 programs to run under Release 3 without modification). Other options that are necessary for SAA compatibility are ADV, DYNAM, NONUM, NOSEQ, NUMPROC(NOPFD), QUOTE, RES, TRUNC(STD), and ZWB.

A number of features allowed for SAA COBOL did not exist in the COBOL II compiler until Release 3. Some programmers are therefore under the impression that all features of Release 3 are SAA compatible. This is not true. SAA does support many features that were added to COBOL II in Release 3 (e.g., seven levels of subscripting, relative subscripting, lowercase code, and the NOT AT END clause). However, many features added to Release 3 are flagged as nonconforming to the SAA language element so that the program using them may not be portable. For instance, reference modification, hexadecimal literals, de-editing, and the NUMPROC(PFD) compiler options are all flagged as nonconforming. This seems blatantly silly since IBM makes the rules for both SAA and Release 3. Perhaps they feel that adding the Release 3 features to the SAA COBOL compiler on other machines (such as the AS/400) will be too much work.

There are a few important points to understand when coding COBOL programs to be run under SAA. The processing of intermediate results and the ON SIZE ERROR clause are system specific. It is therefore recommended that the ADD, SUBTRACT, MULTIPLY, and DIVIDE statements be used rather than the COMPUTE statement. This will minimize the differences that may occur when an SAA compatible program runs in different operating environments. Defining a data item as COMP makes it system dependent because it instructs the compiler to use the most efficient data representation for the item. While fields defined as either COMP or BINARY in Release 3 will produce exactly the same code, this is not necessarily true for other SAA COBOL compilers (e.g., COMP signifies internal decimal on the AS/400). Another difference between SAA implementations is that some use EBCDIC characters (e.g., COBOL II under MVS) while ASCII characters are used for COBOL/2 running under OS/2. You must therefore be careful when using the REDEFINES clause to define a data item with a different usage than the data item being redefined or when comparing numeric and nonnumeric data items. Results may be system dependent and the program may not be portable.

8.6.4 LANGUAGE Option

The LANGUAGE option is used to specify that compiler output be in either mixed-case English (LANGUAGE = EN), uppercase English (LANGUAGE = UE), or Japanese (LANGUAGE = JA or LANGUAGE = JP). The output affected includes the diagnostic messages and headings. The Japanese language may only be used at installations that have installed the Japanese National Language Feature. The default of ENGLISH seems a reasonable choice while the uppercase option of UE can be used by those used to reading listings in uppercase.

8.6.5 DBCS Option

The DBCS compiler option is often not required for a program using DBCS characters. It only instructs the compiler that hexadecimal codes of '0E' (SHIFT-OUT) and '0F' (SHIFT-IN) are to be processed as shift control characters when they appear in nonnumeric literals. When the option is not in effect, these hexadecimal values are accepted as actual values and cause no special processing. This option must be used when EBCDIC and DBCS characters are mixed within a nonnumeric literal (refer to Sec. 3.7 for more information on DBCS characters).

```
PP 5668-958 IBM VS COBOL II Release 3.0 09/13/88
PL SL
----+-*A-1-B--+----2----+-----3----+----4----+----5----+----6
        000010 IDENTIFICATION DIVISION.
        000020 PROGRAM-ID. PROGRAM1.
        000030 PROCEDURE DIVISION.
        000040     CALL 'PROGRAM2'.
        000050     STOP RUN.
        000060
1       000070 IDENTIFICATION DIVISION.
1       000080 PROGRAM-ID. PROGRAM2 INITIAL.
1       000090 DATA DIVISION.
1       000100 WORKING-STORAGE SECTION.
1       000110   01  COUNT-PROGS-2-3-4    PIC S9(3) GLOBAL.
1       000120 PROCEDURE DIVISION.
1       000130     DISPLAY 'PROGRAM2 IS RUNNING'.
1       000140     EXIT PROGRAM.
2       000150 IDENTIFICATION DIVISION.
2       000160 PROGRAM-ID. PROGRAM3.
2       000170 PROCEDURE DIVISION.
2       000180     DISPLAY 'PROGRAM3 IS RUNNING'.
2       000190     EXIT PROGRAM.
2       000200 END PROGRAM PROGRAM3.
2       000210
2       000220 IDENTIFICATION DIVISION.
2       000230 PROGRAM-ID. PROGRAM4 IS COMMON.
2       000240 PROCEDURE DIVISION.
2       000250     DISPLAY 'PROGRAM4 IS RUNNING'.
2       000260     EXIT PROGRAM.
2       000270
3       000280 IDENTIFICATION DIVISION.
3       000290 PROGRAM-ID. PROGRAM5.
3       000300 PROCEDURE DIVISION.
3       000310     DISPLAY 'PROGRAM5 IS RUNNING'.
3       000320     EXIT PROGRAM.
3       000330 END PROGRAM PROGRAM5.
3       000340
2       000350 END PROGRAM PROGRAM4.
2       000360
1       000370 END PROGRAM PROGRAM2.
1       000380
1       000390 IDENTIFICATION DIVISION.
1       000400 PROGRAM-ID. PROGRAM6 IS COMMON.
1       000410 PROCEDURE DIVISION.
1       000420     DISPLAY 'PROGRAM 6 IS RUNNING'.
1       000430     EXIT PROGRAM.
1       000440 END PROGRAM PROGRAM6.
1       000450
        000460 END PROGRAM PROGRAM1.
```

Figure 8.10 Multiple nested programs and a Release 3 listing
showing the nesting levels of the programs.

8.7 PROGRAM NESTING LEVELS IN THE COMPILER LISTING

Release 3 allows nested programs, which were discussed in Sec. 8.2. The program listing now includes the program nesting level (PL) to go along with this new feature. The main program has no nesting level and the PL is left blank. Nested programs at the level below the main program are considered as nesting level 1, a program nested within this program is given a nesting level of 2, etc. (see Fig. 8.10).

Part 3

Programming Techniques

Coding technique, other than structure, is often overlooked in modern COBOL programs. This is quite unfortunate, since poor technique can cause more inefficiencies and program errors than poor structure. Chapter 9 deals with movement of data, arithmetic operations, and how to purposely ABEND a COBOL II program. Although data movement is among the most fundamental requirements of coding a program, a precise understanding of data movement in COBOL is rarely achieved.

Chapter 10 gives an overview of COBOL II efficiency. While efficiency should rarely be regarded as the main consideration when writing a program, it is all too often overlooked. Millions of dollars worth of computers are purchased in situations where the expense could have been avoided had good programming technique been used during program coding. Specific techniques for writing efficient code are discussed in Chap. 11. While finesse is required for some of them, many will become second nature to a programmer who has spent the time to study them.

COBOL II programs, even to a greater extent than VS COBOL, are affected by the options used during compilation. The compiler options are discussed in Chap. 12. Some, such as TRUNC, must be understood. For example, using the wrong subparameter with TRUNC may cause a program to obtain incorrect results or ABEND.

It is in vogue to accept as normal an environment in which programmers do not understand the implications of their own code, relying upon the wide array of debugging and optimization products. However, often overlooked is the fact that programmers who lack the detailed knowledge of COBOL will also be lacking in productivity. Anyone who suggests that programmers attempt to use a programming language without understanding the important intricacies of the language is asking the programmers to stumble around in the dark. The time spent by a programmer to understand a language, rather than blindly code it, will end up as cost efficient, since coding errors will be resolved considerably faster. Rather than companies running to upgrade to faster machines to run their programs, let them run to educate their programmers, their most valuable resource. This rearrangement of priorities will translate into dollars saved and more knowledgeable programmers ready to meet the new technical challenges ahead.

9

Coding Techniques

9.1 MOVEMENT OF DATA IN COBOL II

Movement of data is among the most basic part of any computer program. When data movement is done improperly, a program exception such as an 0C7 may ensue; if you are less fortunate, you will get erroneous results, possibly causing you to spend many hours to resolve the problem.

While many of the basic principles of data movement have remained the same from VS COBOL, some have changed considerably. Most data items can be used in a MOVE statement, as well as some special registers. Index data items and pointers cannot be used in a MOVE statement. Even when these fields exist in a group that is used in a MOVE CORRESPONDING statement, they are not moved.

9.1.1 Elementary Versus Group Moves

A programmer must first realize that there are two types of moves: elementary item moves and group item moves. An elementary item is not further broken down and is therefore not a group item; it may, however, be an item within a group. The COBOL II compiler considers movement from an elementary item to another elementary item an elementary move. All other moves are group moves; at least one of the fields in the move is a group data item. The critical point to remember in a group move is that no data conversion takes place when the data is moved. That means that a packed decimal field (COMP-3) will not be unpacked when moved to a nonpacked (DISPLAY) data item and vice versa.

9.1.2 Moves Involving Numeric Data

Moves involving numeric data seem to cause programmers many problems. In the code in Fig. 9.1, statement 000080 will cause a deci-

```
000010 DATA DIVISION.
000020 WORKING-STORAGE SECTION.
000030 01  FIELD1.
000040      05  FIELD2          PIC S9(3).
000050 01  FIELD3               PIC S9(3) COMP-3 VALUE +123.
000060 PROCEDURE DIVISION.
000070      MOVE FIELD3 TO FIELD1.
000080      ADD +1 TO FIELD2.
```

Figure 9.1 Example of a MOVE statement that does not cause the proper conversion of data. This causes a subsequent decimal data exception (0C7).

mal data exception (0C7). A field defined with a PIC of COMP-3 is moved to a group level on line 000070 and no conversion takes place. After the MOVE instruction is executed, FIELD1 (and therefore FIELD2) will contain a hexadecimal value of '123C40'. This is not a valid display numeric value and will cause a decimal data exception if it is used in an arithmetic operation.

Another piece of code that places invalid data into a COMP-3 field is shown in Fig. 9.2. It initializes a group level rather than the elementary fields themselves. The zeros moved to the group level will be character zeros rather than packed decimal zeros. After line 000060 in Fig. 9.2 is executed, each of the three occurrences of FIELD1 will contain hexadecimal values of 'F0F0'. The fields do not have valid signs (the signs are 0) and each field contains invalid digits (F). A decimal data exception will occur if any of the occurrences of FIELD1 are used in arithmetic operations as on line 000070. Note that TABLE1 could have been initialized properly if either line 000040 contained a VALUE ZERO clause or if line 000060 was an INITIALIZE TABLE1 statement.

9.1.2.1 Decimal point alignment

In elementary moves data conversion takes place depending upon the definition of the receiving data item. When data is moved between any combination of numeric and numeric-edited fields, alignment by

```
000010 DATA DIVISION.
000020 WORKING-STORAGE SECTION.
000030 01  TABLE1.
000040      05  FIELD1 OCCURS 3 TIMES   PIC S9(3) COMP-3.
000050 PROCEDURE DIVISION.
000060      MOVE ZEROS TO TABLE1.
000070      ADD +1 TO FIELD1 (1).
```

Figure 9.2 Improper table initialization. A decimal data exception (0C7) will occur on line 000070.

```
000010 DATA DIVISION.
000020 WORKING-STORAGE SECTION.
000030 01   FIELD1              PIC S9(5) COMP-3 VALUE +12345.
000040 01   FIELD2              PIC Z(3).99.
000050 PROCEDURE DIVISION.
000060     MOVE FIELD1 TO FIELD2.
```

Figure 9.3 Example showing decimal point alignment during a move of numeric fields. High-order truncation of digits occurs.

decimal point always occurs. When a field does not contain a decimal point, the decimal point is assumed to be after the last digit in the field. In Fig. 9.3, after line 000060 is executed, FIELD2 will contain 345.00, not 123.45. If the receiving field does not contain enough digits before the decimal point to hold the significant digits of the sending field, the high-order digits will be truncated (as in Fig. 9.3); if the receiving field does not contain enough digits after the decimal point to hold the significant digits of the receiving field, low-order digits will be lost.

9.1.2.2 Unsigned fields

An elementary move of numeric data into an unsigned field usually will strip the sign from the field, making the receiving field positive (it was always stripped under VS COBOL but depends upon compiler options under COBOL II). When the code on line 000080 in Fig. 9.4 executes, FIELD2 will have a value of positive 05, not negative 05. The code on line 000090 is trickier. Many programmers think that the result will either be an 0C7 decimal data exception or that the code will put a '5-' into FIELD2. Neither of these choices is correct when the NUMPROC(NOPFD) or NUMPROC(MIG) compiler options are used on the program. Execution of line 000090 will set FIELD2 to 50 when these options are used. When the NUMPROC(PFD) option is used to compile the program, FIELD2 will be set to '5-'. The movement

```
000010 DATA DIVISION.
000020 WORKING-STORAGE SECTION.
000030 77   FIELD1              PIC X(2) VALUE '5-'.
000040 77   FIELD2              PIC 9(2).
000050 77   FIELD3              PIC S9(2) VALUE -05.
000060
000070 PROCEDURE DIVISION.
000080     MOVE FIELD3 TO FIELD2.
000090     MOVE FIELD1 TO FIELD2.
```

Figure 9.4 Example of data movement to an unsigned field. Execution results will differ depending upon the compiler options used.

of data on line 000090 follows two rules of movement of elementary numeric fields:

1. When the sending data item is alphanumeric, the field is treated as if it was an unsigned integer.

2. When the receiving data item is unsigned, the absolute (positive) value of the data item is moved.

When the code executes, the sending field which has a hexadecimal value of 'F560' gets a positive sign and becomes hexadecimal 'F5F0'. This is a decimal 50. The receiving field is therefore set to 50. When the NUMPROC(PFD) option is used during compilation, the compiler assumes that the sending field contains a positive sign and does not modify it.

While this example may seem rather abstract, it can occur with some frequency in the online environment. For instance, if an operator accidentally enters a 5- into a numeric field, rather than a 59, a CICS program should realize the invalid data and report the error. However, some CICS programs move the data (often described as alphanumeric) to an unsigned numeric field before doing a numeric check. This is incorrect. As can be clearly seen, a numeric check of FIELD2 will usually not fail (depending upon compiler options) if placed into the code in Fig. 9.4.

9.1.2.3 Moves involving floating insertion editing

Numeric data may be moved to data items defined with floating-insertion editing symbols. The floating-insertion symbols of $, +, and − can be used in a PICTURE clause. The plus sign inserts a + if the edited number is positive and a − if the edited number is negative; the minus sign will insert a − if the edited number is negative and a space if it is positive. When the code in Fig. 9.5 executes under COBOL II, FIELD2 will be set to $12,345.00, FIELD3 will be set to +12,345.00, and FIELD4 will be set to $ 12,345.00. Had FIELD1 been equal to zero, the results would have been $.00, spaces, and $ .00.

Floating-insertion editing caused confusion for VS COBOL programmers. When programmers did not carefully read the IBM reference manual, they assumed fields like FIELD2 and FIELD3 were properly defined. However, the VS COBOL compiler had an idiosyncrasy and required at least two floating-insertion symbols to precede the first comma in a PICTURE clause. If only one preceded it, as in FIELD2 and FIELD3 in Fig. 9.5, the first symbol would be considered a fixed symbol and would always be inserted. The other symbols in the PICTURE would be considered floating-insertion symbols. If the PICTURE clause for FIELD2 in Fig. 9.5 was used in a VS COBOL pro-

```
000010 DATA DIVISION.
000020 WORKING-STORAGE SECTION.
000040 77    FIELD1              PIC S9(5) COMP-3 VALUE +12345.
000030 77    FIELD2              PIC $,$$$,$$$.99.
000030 77    FIELD3              PIC +,+++,+++.++.
000030 77    FIELD4              PIC $ZZZ,ZZZ.99.
000050
000060 PROCEDURE DIVISION.
000070      MOVE FIELD1 TO FIELD2 FIELD3 FIELD4.
```

Figure 9.5 Floating-insertion editing using certain PICTURE clauses produces different results under VS COBOL and COBOL II.

gram, the result of executing line 000090 would yield two dollar signs for the value in FIELD2.

This confusing situation does not exist in COBOL II since a single floating-insertion symbol is allowed before a comma. You only have to worry about truncation. Make sure to code enough floating-insertion symbols so that one represents each digit in the sending field and one additional symbol so that the insertion symbol appears in the result.

9.1.3 De-Editing

The code on line 000070 in Fig. 9.6 would have caused a compilation error in VS COBOL or COBOL II Release 2. Numeric-edited fields were not allowed to be moved to numeric fields. This type of data movement is allowed in Release 3. It is called de-editing and code is generated which first moves the edited field into a temporary numeric field and then moves the temporary field to the receiving field. If a sign is available in the edited field, the sign will be preserved in the receiving field.

9.1.4 DBCS Data Items

When a DBCS data item (see Sec. 3.7) is used as a sending field, it can only be moved to another DBCS data item or a group item; when a DBCS data item is used as a receiving field, only another DBCS data

```
000010 DATA DIVISION.
000020 WORKING-STORAGE SECTION.
000030 77    FIELD1              PIC S9(5)V99 COMP-3.
000040 77    FIELD2              PIC Z(3).99-.
000050 PROCEDURE DIVISION.
000060      MOVE 23.45 TO FIELD2.
000070      MOVE FIELD2 TO FIELD1.
```

Figure 9.6 De-editing is now allowed in Release 3.

item, a group item, or SPACES can be moved to it. If a receiving DBCS data item is larger than the sending data item, the receiving data item will be padded with DBCS spaces on the right.

9.2 WORKING WITH MULTIPLE FIELDS

9.2.1 Moving to Multiple Fields

Any subscript or length calculation of a sending field is evaluated only once, before the sending field is moved to any receiving data item. Any subscript or length calculation necessary for a receiving field is done immediately before the data is moved to the receiving field. These rules are significant when there are multiple receiving fields in a MOVE statement and movement of data to one field could affect the movement of data to another field. The example in Fig. 9.7 shows one such possibility which might not yield the results that one would expect. When the code on line 000100 is executed, the value of SUB1 used when moving to ENTRY2 (SUB1) is the value that SUB1 contained before the statement executed, not the value that was just placed into SUB1 by the statement.

9.2.2 Adding to Multiple Fields

The result of an ADD statement can be placed into multiple fields as shown in Fig. 9.8. The processing is similar and consistent with the way the MOVE statement executes.

```
000010 DATA DIVISION.
000020 WORKING-STORAGE SECTION.
000030 01   SUB1                      PIC S9(3) COMP-3.
000040 01   TABLE1.
000050      05  ENTRY1 OCCURS 5 TIMES  PIC S9(3) COMP-3.
000060 01   TABLE2.
000070      05  ENTRY2 OCCURS 5 TIMES  PIC S9(3) COMP-3.
000080 PROCEDURE DIVISION.
000090      ...
000100      MOVE ENTRY1 (SUB1) TO SUB1 ENTRY2 (SUB1).
000110
000120*THE CODE ON LINE 000100 IS NOT THE SAME AS THE NEXT 2 LINES
000130      MOVE ENTRY1 (SUB1) TO SUB1.
000140      MOVE ENTRY1 (SUB1) TO ENTRY2 (SUB1).
000150
000160*THE CODE ON LINE 000100 IS ACTUALLY EXECUTED AS FOLLOWS
000170      MOVE ENTRY1 (SUB1) TO TEMP-SUB.
000180      MOVE TEMP-SUB TO SUB1.
000190      MOVE TEMP-SUB TO ENTRY2 (SUB1).
```

Figure 9.7 How COBOL II executes movement of data to multiple fields in a MOVE statement. Note: TEMP-SUB is a temporary storage field in the TGT (the TGT is described in Chap. 14).

```
000010 DATA DIVISION.
000020 WORKING-STORAGE SECTION.
000030 01  SUB1                      PIC S9(3) COMP-3.
000040 01  TABLE1.
000050     05  ENTRY1 OCCURS 5 TIMES  PIC S9(3) COMP-3.
000060 01  FIELD1                    PIC S9(3) COMP-3.
000070 01  FIELD2                    PIC S9(3) COMP-3.
000080
000090 PROCEDURE DIVISION.
000100     ...
000110     ADD FIELD1 FIELD2 TO SUB1 ENTRY1 (SUB1).
000120
000130*THE CODE ON LINE 000110 IS NOT THE SAME AS THE NEXT 2 LINES
000140     ADD FIELD1 FIELD2 TO SUB1.
000150     ADD FIELD1 FIELD2 TO ENTRY1 (SUB1).
000160
000170*THE CODE ON LINE 000110 IS ACTUALLY EXECUTED AS FOLLOWS
000180     ADD FIELD1 FIELD2 GIVING TEMP-SUB.
000190     ADD TEMP-SUB TO SUB1.
000200     ADD TEMP-SUB TO ENTRY1 (SUB1).
```

Figure 9.8 How COBOL II handles addition when multiple receiving fields are used in an ADD statement. Note: TEMP-SUB is a temporary storage field in the TGT (the TGT is described in Chap. 14).

9.3 TRUNCATION DURING FIXED-POINT ARITHMETIC OPERATIONS

When truncation occurs during arithmetic computations, no error occurs. The ON SIZE ERROR clause can be coded to give control to a routine should truncation occur. Truncation of binary data fields (COMP or BINARY) depends upon the TRUNC option used during compilation (see Sec. 12.5.1). High-order truncation of packed decimal (COMP-3 or PACKED-DECIMAL) and DISPLAY fields occurs based upon the number of digits defined for the field. Figure 9.9 shows an ADD instruction that yields a result of 2, not 1002. The MULTIPLY then sets FIELD2 equal to 994, not 1994. No error occurs when either the ADD or the MULTIPLY is executed.

```
000010 DATA DIVISION.
000020 WORKING-STORAGE SECTION.
000030 01  FIELD1                    PIC S9(3) COMP-3 VALUE +997.
000040 01  FIELD2                    PIC S9(3) COMP-3 VALUE +5.
000050
000060 PROCEDURE DIVISION.
000070     ADD FIELD1 TO FIELD2.
000080     MULTIPLY FIELD1 BY FIELD2.
```

Figure 9.9 Truncation of high-order digits occurs during the ADD and the MULTIPLY, but COBOL II does not generate an error during program execution.

9.4   FLOATING-POINT PRECISION

Floating-point numbers are defined with a USAGE of COMP-1 or COMP-2. COMP-1 numbers are 4 bytes long and are used for single precision; COMP-2 numbers are 8 bytes long and are used for double precision. Any arithmetic operation in a COBOL II program done in floating point will require the compiler to convert any fixed-point numbers used in the computation to floating point.

You can write code that moves numbers from fixed-point fields to floating-point fields and vice versa. However, rounding problems can occur during the conversion from one numeric format to another. If you want the results to be accurate, you must follow certain rules. Accuracy will be guaranteed if you move a fixed-point number containing a value of six significant digits or less to a COMP-1 field and then move the number back to the fixed-point field. If the number has more than six significant digits, the first six digits will always end up exact but the others may not be. For fixed-point values moved to COMP-2 fields and then back to the sending field, fields of 15 significant digits or less will always remain exactly the same; fields greater than 15 significant digits will maintain accuracy for at least the first 15 digits.

For floating-point values moved to fixed-point fields, the number of digits required to guarantee accuracy is not what you might expect. To maintain accuracy of a COMP-1 value moved to a fixed-point field which will be returned to the COMP-1 field, the fixed-point field must have at least nine digits. If the fixed-point field has more than nine digits, all digits after the first nine are set to zero. A COMP-2 field must be moved to a field of 18 digits to maintain accuracy if it is to be moved back to the COMP-2 field.

Be careful when doing any comparisons of floating-point fields unless they both have the same precision, i.e., COMP-1 with COMP-1 or COMP-2 with COMP-2. If the precision is not the same, values that you expect to be the same may be slightly different because of the precision differences.

9.5   USER REQUESTED ABENDS

You can request COBOL II to cause a User ABEND in the same manner that a VS COBOL program requested it, by calling routine ILBOABN0. This method should not be used in CICS where the EXEC CICS ABEND command is available. The call passes a positive dump code value of less than 4096 as a COMP field of four digits. The dump code value used should not be between 1000 and 1999. These User ABENDs are reserved for COBOL II's own use and are used when COBOL II determines an error condition and decides to ABEND a pro-

```
000010 DATA DIVISION.
000020 WORKING-STORAGE SECTION.
000030 01   DUMP-CODE              PIC S9(4) COMP VALUE +2345.
000040 PROCEDURE DIVISION.
000050     ...
000060     CALL 'ILBOABNO' USING DUMP-CODE.
```

Figure 9.10   Standard way to cause a User ABEND under COBOL II.

```
000010 DATA DIVISION.
000020 WORKING-STORAGE SECTION.
000030 01   FIELD1                 PIC 9(3) COMP-3.
000040 01   FIELD2                 PIC 9(3) COMP-3.
000050 PROCEDURE DIVISION.
000060     ...
000070     ADD FIELD1 TO FIELD2.
```

Figure 9.11   Nonstandard way to ABEND a VS COBOL program. The program may not ABEND under COBOL II.

gram. If a field greater than 4096 is passed to ILBOABN0, the field is divided by 4096 and the remainder becomes the ABEND code. The example in Fig. 9.10 shows how to ABEND a COBOL program with an ABEND code of 2345.

Beware of using the nonstandard method of ABENDing a program that is shown in Fig. 9.11. Some programs ABEND by performing arithmetic on uninitialized packed decimal fields. The code in Fig. 9.11 yields a decimal data exception (0C7) under VS COBOL but may not ABEND under COBOL II. It will ABEND under COBOL II if the NUMPROC(MIG) or NUMPROC(PFD) options are used during compilation but will not ABEND if the NUMPROC(NOPFD) option is used. When the NUMPROC(NOPFD) option is used to compile a program, the code produced inserts a proper sign into any unsigned field, even if it contains nonnumeric data. This may turn an uninitialized field into a valid numeric number.

10

Efficient Coding Overview

10.1 WHY CODING EFFICIENCY STILL MAKES SENSE

"Computers are now so fast that it doesn't matter how inefficient your program is." "Concentrate on the application, not the program." "Spend your time on a structured program, not a technically efficient program." These frequently used adages are becoming more and more uncritically accepted by data processing management. The saying used to be, "It is important to write efficient code." Why has this idea fallen out of favor in recent years?

It is indisputable that efficient code is at least sometimes necessary. As companies grow, so does the amount of data they process. When the rate of increase of data processed exceeds the rate of increase in the speed of computers, additional processing time can become critical. If a production run cannot complete within the batch window (between the time a company ends daily processing in the evening and begins the next day's activities), a company cannot function. Furthermore, even if a job can process in this time frame, any programming problems become major ones. The schedule may be too tight to allow for a rerun.

I have a friend who has written part of the operating system for the F16 fighter jet. Imagine a missile coming at your jet. When the program designed to automatically perform defensive maneuvers executes or when it requests services of the operating system, you do not want the sudden realization that your program is running very slowly because of inefficient code. You better hope that you can get your parachute and bail out more efficiently than your defensive program is processing.

Efficient programs certainly save money. At the end of 1984 I spent over a month updating COBOL programs that ran on an IBM 3081.

By using techniques detailed in this part of the book, I was able to save between 15 and 95 percent of the CPU time for each program. This saved a major company over $30,000 each time the programs were executed, which was a few times per year. One program which originally ran in over 3 hours CPU time was changed to run in less than 1 hour while another was changed from running over 15 minutes to less than 1 minute.

It is quite apparent that efficiency is not always of primary importance. If a programmer writes code that will run only once, a very small program that runs quickly, or a program that processes a small amount of data, extra time spent in making the program run faster is not cost effective. Yet, with a proper understanding of the concepts of COBOL efficiency, the basics of which can be learned in about 2 days, one can learn to write efficient code as quickly as inefficient code. Although it may be hard for some to break bad habits, it is much easier than one thinks to be able to code efficiently.

10.2   EFFICIENT CODE IS EASIER TO FOLLOW

Efficiency is unfortunately considered something that, when added to a program, makes the program more convoluted and harder to maintain. While in some highly technical pieces of code that strain the limits of COBOL this is the case, this code is rarely added for efficiency alone. It is a fallacy that efficient code must be difficult code. One often overlooked valuable result of efficient code is that the programming logic is often easier to follow. Consider the example in Fig. 10.1, which locates a month name based upon the numeric value of the month. Which of the code segments do you find easier to read and understand? The code in the second program runs much faster than the code in the first program.

10.3   EFFICIENT CODE CAN BE WRITTEN JUST AS QUICKLY

Figure 10.2 illustrates two different pieces of code that serve the same function. Although the code segments look quite similar and would take approximately the same amount of time to write, one of the segments runs about 3 times as fast as the other. By the time you have finished Chaps. 10 and 11, it should be quite apparent as to which is the faster running code.

```
000010 DATA DIVISION.
000020 WORKING-STORAGE SECTION.
000030 77  MONTH-NUMBER           PIC 99.
000040 77  MONTH-NAME             PIC X(9).
000050 01  MONTH-TABLE.
000060     05  FILLER             PIC X(11) VALUE '01JANUARY  '.
000070     05  FILLER             PIC X(11) VALUE '02FEBRUARY '.
000080     05  FILLER             PIC X(11) VALUE '03MARCH    '.
000090     05  FILLER             PIC X(11) VALUE '04APRIL    '.
000100     05  FILLER             PIC X(11) VALUE '05MAY      '.
000110     05  FILLER             PIC X(11) VALUE '06JUNE     '.
000120     05  FILLER             PIC X(11) VALUE '07JULY     '.
000130     05  FILLER             PIC X(11) VALUE '08AUGUST   '.
000140     05  FILLER             PIC X(11) VALUE '09SEPTEMBER'.
000150     05  FILLER             PIC X(11) VALUE '10OCTOBER  '.
000160     05  FILLER             PIC X(11) VALUE '11NOVEMBER '.
000170     05  FILLER             PIC X(11) VALUE '12DECEMBER '.
000180 01  FILLER REDEFINES MONTH-TABLE.
000190     05  MONTH-ENTRY OCCURS 12 TIMES
000200         ASCENDING KEY IS MONTH-TAB-NUMBER
000210         INDEXED BY MONTH-INDEX.
000220     10  MONTH-TAB-NUMBER PIC 99.
000230     10  MONTH-TAB-NAME   PIC X(9).
000240 PROCEDURE DIVISION.
000250     ...
000260     SEARCH ALL MONTH-ENTRY
000270         WHEN MONTH-TAB-NUMBER (MONTH-INDEX) = MONTH-NUMBER
000280             MOVE MONTH-TAB-NAME (MONTH-INDEX) TO MONTH-NAME.
```

(a)

```
000010 DATA DIVISION.
000020 WORKING-STORAGE SECTION.
000030 77  MONTH-NUMBER           PIC 99.
000040 77  MONTH-NAME             PIC X(9).
000050 01  MONTH-TABLE.
000060     05  FILLER             PIC X(9) VALUE 'JANUARY  '.
000070     05  FILLER             PIC X(9) VALUE 'FEBRUARY '.
000080     05  FILLER             PIC X(9) VALUE 'MARCH    '.
000090     05  FILLER             PIC X(9) VALUE 'APRIL    '.
000100     05  FILLER             PIC X(9) VALUE 'MAY      '.
000110     05  FILLER             PIC X(9) VALUE 'JUNE     '.
000120     05  FILLER             PIC X(9) VALUE 'JULY     '.
000130     05  FILLER             PIC X(9) VALUE 'AUGUST   '.
000140     05  FILLER             PIC X(9) VALUE 'SEPTEMBER'.
000150     05  FILLER             PIC X(9) VALUE 'OCTOBER  '.
000160     05  FILLER             PIC X(9) VALUE 'NOVEMBER '.
000170     05  FILLER             PIC X(9) VALUE 'DECEMBER '.
000180 01  FILLER REDEFINES MONTH-TABLE.
000190     05  MONTH-ENTRY OCCURS 12 TIMES PIC X(9).
000200 PROCEDURE DIVISION.
000210     ...
000220     MOVE MONTH-ENTRY (MONTH-NUMBER) TO MONTH-NAME.
```

(b)

Figure 10.1 Inefficient (*a*) and efficient (*b*) coding examples to obtain a month name based upon its numeric value.

```
000010 DATA DIVISION.
000020 WORKING-STORAGE SECTION.
000030 01  MONTH-NUMBER            PIC 99.
000040 01  FINISHED-INDICATOR      PIC XXX.
000050 PROCEDURE DIVISION.
000060     ...
000070     IF MONTH-NUMBER IS GREATER THAN 12
000080         MOVE 'YES' TO FINISHED-INDICATOR.
```

(a)

```
000010 DATA DIVISION.
000020 WORKING-STORAGE SECTION.
000030 01  MONTH-NUMBER            PIC XX.
000040 01  FINISHED-INDICATOR      PIC X.
000050 PROCEDURE DIVISION.
000060     ...
000070     IF MONTH-NUMBER IS GREATER THAN '12'
000080         MOVE 'Y' TO FINISHED-INDICATOR.
```

(b)

Figure 10.2 Inefficient (a) and efficient (b) IF statements. The efficient method can execute more than 3 times as fast.

10.4 PROGRAM MONITORS AND CODE OPTIMIZERS

It often pays to scrutinize existing code and improve its speed. A COBOL program of 1500 lines that has already been written can be reviewed and updated to run faster in less than a day, and I have rarely, if ever, seen a program that cannot be made to run at least 15 percent faster. One quick approach is to install a program monitor and determine the exact points in your system where excess CPU time is being used. These are the points at which you can concentrate your efficiency efforts.

Perhaps you are convinced that efficiency in COBOL programs is important but that it can be accomplished by one of the fine COBOL optimizer programs on the market. An optimizer can only make the best out of the code it is given; it cannot rewrite the logic. While it may increase the speed of a poorly written program, this is no substitution for well-written code that is optimized. Figure 10.3 is an example of code in which the placement of a MULTIPLY statement, a very slow function, can be optimized easily by a person but the placement would not be improved upon by an optimizing compiler. The MULTIPLY is performed 25 times in the first segment of code but only once in the second.

Some fairly simple optimizations are often overlooked. Figure 10.4

```
000010 DATA DIVISION.
000020 WORKING-STORAGE SECTION.
000030 01   TOTAL-FIELD            PIC S9(9) COMP-3.
000040 01   SUB1                   PIC S9(4) COMP.
000050 01   TEMP-RESULT            PIC S9(9) COMP-3.
000060 01   TABLE1.
000070      05  ENTRY1 OCCURS 25 TIMES PIC S9(7) COMP-3.
000080
000090 PROCEDURE DIVISION.
000100      ...
000110      MOVE ZERO TO TOTAL-FIELD.
000120      PERFORM
000130          VARYING SUB1 FROM +1 BY +1
000140          UNTIL SUB1 > 25
000150      MULTIPLY ENTRY1 (SUB1) BY 7 GIVING TEMP-RESULT
000160      ADD TEMP-RESULT TO TOTAL-FIELD
000170      END-PERFORM.
```

(a)

```
000010 DATA DIVISION.
000020 WORKING-STORAGE SECTION.
000030 01   TOTAL-FIELD            PIC S9(9) COMP-3.
000040 01   SUB1                   PIC S9(4) COMP.
000050 01   TABLE1.
000060      05  ENTRY1 OCCURS 25 TIMES PIC S9(7) COMP-3.
000070
000080 PROCEDURE DIVISION.
000090      ...
000100      MOVE ZERO TO TOTAL-FIELD.
000110      PERFORM
000120          VARYING SUB1 FROM +1 BY +1
000130          UNTIL SUB1 > 25
000140      ADD ENTRY1 (SUB1) TO TOTAL-FIELD
000150      END-PERFORM.
000160      MULTIPLY TOTAL-FIELD BY 7 GIVING TOTAL-FIELD.
```

(b)

Figure 10.3 Example of how inefficient code can be made efficient by a human but would not be made as efficient by using the optimization option of the compiler. (*a*) Inefficient code; (*b*) efficient code.

shows how inefficient code can be made more efficient by combining operations. Only five rather than nine ADD statements are necessary in the code. A programmer can easily change code that an optimizer program would not improve.

10.5 INSTRUCTION SPEEDS

Chapter 11 describes a number of techniques that enable a COBOL II program to run faster. The list is fairly extensive but does not specify

```
000010 WORKING-STORAGE SECTION.
000020 01   SUB-TOTAL              PIC S9(9)V99 COMP-3 VALUE ZERO.
000030 01   GRAND-TOTAL            PIC S9(9)V99 COMP-3 VALUE ZERO.
000040 01   WRITE-COUNT            PIC S9(7) COMP-3 VALUE ZERO.
000050
000060 PROCEDURE DIVISION.
000070      . . .
000080      ADD REC1-AMOUNT TO SUB-TOTAL.
000090      ADD REC1-AMOUNT TO GRAND-TOTAL.
000100      ADD 1 TO WRITE-COUNT.
000110      WRITE RECORD1.
000120      ADD REC2-AMOUNT TO SUB-TOTAL.
000130      ADD REC2-AMOUNT TO GRAND-TOTAL.
000140      ADD 1 TO WRITE-COUNT.
000150      WRITE RECORD2.
000160      ADD REC3-AMOUNT TO SUB-TOTAL.
000170      ADD REC3-AMOUNT TO GRAND-TOTAL.
000180      ADD 1 TO WRITE-COUNT.
000190      WRITE RECORD3.
```

(a)

```
000010 WORKING-STORAGE SECTION.
000020 01   SUB-TOTAL              PIC S9(9)V99 COMP-3 VALUE ZERO.
000030 01   GRAND-TOTAL            PIC S9(9)V99 COMP-3 VALUE ZERO.
000040 01   WRITE-COUNT            PIC S9(7) COMP-3 VALUE ZERO.
000050
000060 PROCEDURE DIVISION.
000070      . . .
000080      ADD REC1-AMOUNT TO SUB-TOTAL.
000090      WRITE RECORD1.
000100      ADD REC2-AMOUNT TO SUB-TOTAL.
000110      WRITE RECORD2.
000120      ADD REC3-AMOUNT TO SUB-TOTAL.
000130      WRITE RECORD3.
000140      ADD 3 TO WRITE-COUNT.
000150      ADD SUB-TOTAL TO GRAND-TOTAL.
```

(b)

Figure 10.4 Combining repetitious operations can increase efficiency.
(a) Inefficient code; (b) efficient code.

every possible efficiency. It serves as a strong foundation and a point
from which one can proceed to learn other efficiencies. The coding sug-
gestions serve to encourage programmers to examine new techniques
of their own. By using COBOL II Procedure Maps (produced with
LIST compiler option), which contain the assembler language listing
of a program, programmers can extend their ability through the study
of the assembler code produced for different methods of COBOL coding. One can also experiment by running two different programs that
produce the same results and comparing the CPU usage of each.

For many years, IBM has not published the speed of each instruction on its mainframe processors. One reason is that the timings vary depending upon the multiprogramming environment. However, the relative timings of the instructions can generally be measured. As an aid in computing timing differences when comparing code in a Procedure Map, Fig. 10.5 contains relative timings of various 370 instructions. The timings are not meant to be absolute, since they will vary depending upon processor speed. They also cannot be exact, even as relative timings, since instruction speed may slightly vary from model to model and can sometimes significantly vary between IBM and compatible mainframe manufacturers. They are meant as a guide to determine whether one instruction sequence is considerably faster than another.

10.6   GENERAL COBOL II EFFICIENCY DIFFERENCES FROM VS COBOL

As far as efficiency is concerned under COBOL II, there have been changes that affect it in both directions. The code produced for subscripting and indexing has been improved and is now shorter. Loading of BL cells is also done in a more efficient manner than in VS COBOL, and in many instances loading of a BL cell is no longer needed. On the other hand, some code produced in COBOL II is considerably less efficient than in VS COBOL. In the statement IF FIELD1 (SUB1) = 1 OR 2 OR 3 OR 4 OR 5, the displacement computation for FIELD1 was done only once in VS COBOL while in COBOL II it may be recomputed five times. Even when the COBOL II optimizer is used, it still may recompute the same displacement five separate times.

10.6.1   The IBM Optimizer

The IBM optimizer creates some interesting efficiencies in the object code. For instance, if you PERFORM a paragraph in a program, the optimizer may copy the code to make it an in-line PERFORM. In-line PERFORMs do not require object code to branch to another area in the program and then return, and therefore execute faster than out-of-line PERFORMs. The optimizer will change out-of-line PERFORMs to in-line PERFORMs until a program size limit is reached. If the program size increases by more than 50 percent, PERFORMs are no longer changed to in-line. Executable code for the performed paragraph is always produced in the paragraph's original position.

PERFORMs can be prevented from being moved in-line by placing the performed paragraph in a section with a different priority number than the priority number of the section that contains the PERFORM

Instruction	Operation code	Mnemonic	Format	Relative time	
Add Register	1A	AR	RR	5	
Add	5A	A	RX	9	
Add Packed	FA	AP	SS	77	(+)
Add Halfword	4A	AH	RX	9	
And Immediate	94	NI	SI	9	
Branch And Link Register	05	BALR	RR	10	(++)
Branch And Link	45	BAL	RX	15	
Branch on Condition Register	07	BCR	RR	4	(++)
Branch on Condition	47	BC	RX	5	(++)
Branch on Count Register	06	BCTR	RR	4	(++)
Compare	59	C	RX	9	
Compare Packed	F9	CP	SS	35	(+)
Compare Halfword	49	CH	RX	9	
Compare Logical Immediate	95	CLI	SI	5	
Compare Logical Character	D5	CLC	SS	15	(+)
Convert to Binary	4F	CVB	RX	15	
Convert to Decimal	4E	CVD	RX	20	
Divide Register	1D	DR	RR	135	
Divide	5D	D	RX	135	
Divide Packed	FD	DP	SS	185	(+)
Edit	DE	ED	SS	72	(+)
Load Register	18	LR	RR	5	
Load	58	L	RX	5	
Load Address	41	LA	RX	5	
Load Halfword	48	LH	RX	9	
Move Immediate	92	MVI	SI	5	
Move Character	D2	MVC	SS	30	(+)
Multiply Register	1C	MR	RR	67	
Multiply	5C	M	RX	63	
Multiply Packed	FC	MP	SS	100	(+)
Multiply Halfword	4C	MH	RX	48	
Or Immediate	96	OI	SI	5	
Pack	F2	PACK	SS	40	(+)
Shift and Round Packed	F0	SRP	SS	95	(+)
Store	50	ST	RX	5	
Store Halfword	40	STH	RX	5	
Subtract Register	1B	SR	RR	5	
Subtract	5B	S	RX	9	
Subtract Packed	FB	SP	SS	77	(+)
Subtract Halfword	4B	SH	RX	9	
Translate	DC	TR	SS	80	(+)
Unpack	F3	UNPK	SS	40	(+)
Zero and Add Packed	F8	ZAP	SS	65	(+)

Notes: (++)   In branch instructions, instruction time will differ if the branch is taken. Add 5 to time if branch is taken.

(+)   Indicates that the instruction time increases as the field(s) length increases.

Figure 10.5   Some IBM 370 mainframe instructions and rough estimates of their relative times.

(sections are discussed in Sec. 2.11). This would be useful when you have a rather large paragraph performed many times and the size of the program is a consideration. By placing performed paragraphs in sections of differing priority numbers, storage should be saved.

What may seem surprising is that the concept of copying code to be more efficient when linking from one part of a program to another also applies when linking to nested programs. When a program calls a program contained within it, the optimizer will attempt to place the entire called program in-line in the calling program at the point of the call. Even though I am a strong believer in efficiency, this seems rather absurd to me (to a certain extent so does the entire concept of nested programs).

10.6.2 Library Routine CALLs

The COBOL II compiler does have some instances when it calls fewer COBOL internal library routines, thereby making the code more efficient. In Fig. 10.6, VS COBOL executed two run-time library routine calls for the multiply on line 000050 and four for the multiply on line 000060. In COBOL II, the first multiply is done completely in-line and the second with only one call to a run-time library routine. The efficiency does, however, produce a longer object program.

10.6.3 Arithmetic on COMP-3 Fields

One change from VS COBOL to COBOL II that may seem quite baffling occurs when a constant or another COMP-3 data field is added or subtracted to or from a signed COMP-3 data field. The VS COBOL compiler produced only an Add Packed (AP) or Subtract Packed (SP) instruction. COBOL II still produces the same instruction but then issues a Zero and Add Packed (ZAP) of the resulting field into itself. The ZAP is executed for a very subtle reason. When two negative numbers

```
000010 DATA DIVISION.
000020 WORKING-STORAGE SECTION.
000030 01  WS-SIGNED-COMP-DBLWORD     PIC S9(16) COMP VALUE +100.
000040 PROCEDURE DIVISION.
000050     MULTIPLY +1 BY WS-SIGNED-COMP-DBLWORD.
000060     MULTIPLY WS-SIGNED-COMP-DBLWORD BY WS-SIGNED-COMP-DBLWORD.
```

(a)

	VS COBOL	COBOL II
Line 000050	2	0
Line 000060	4	1

(b)

Figure 10.6 Example showing that the COBOL II compiler generates fewer calls to IBM run-time library routines. (a) Code; (b) number of internal library routine calls generated by compiler.

are added together and an overflow occurs, the overflow flag in the condition code is turned on while the resulting sign is set as if overflow did not occur. This means that if two numbers each defined as PIC S9(3) COMP-3 were added together, and they had values of -1 and -999 before the addition, the resulting field would be zero (the digit that overflowed was truncated) with its sign negative. The ZAP will preserve the sign of all other computations but will change a zero with a negative sign to a zero with a positive sign.

Ensuring a positive sign in a zero result was not necessary in the VS COBOL compiler. This is because the VS COBOL compiler used a Compare Packed (CP) instruction to compare numeric fields. It is interesting that COBOL II now often produces a Compare Logical Character (CLC) instruction to compare numeric fields. While this is a faster instruction than CP (see Fig. 10.5), it requires the same sign value for an equal condition to occur. For example, a CP instruction will find fields with hexadecimal values of '0F' and '0C' equal, while the CLC will not.

The ZAP added to signed arithmetic instructions causes an add to an unsigned field to often be faster than an add to a signed field [the unsigned add will generate an Or Immediate (OI) instruction to strip the sign, an instruction faster than ZAP]. One idiosyncracy of the compiler is that when the ON SIZE ERROR clause is used in the ADD or SUBTRACT statement, the code produced does not contain the ZAP to correct the sign.

10.6.4 Clearing Fields

The code produced to clear short fields to spaces has changed. The VS COBOL compiler moves a space to the first position of the field with a Move Immediate (MVI) instruction, then clears the field by using an overlapping move (overlapping moves are discussed in Sec. 11.4). This did not require any spaces to be stored in the literal pool (the literal pool is the part of a COBOL module where the literals used in the program are stored). The COBOL II compiler stores spaces and clears short fields to spaces with a single move.

10.6.5 Efficiency Differences When Running VS COBOL Programs Under COBOL II

VS COBOL and COBOL II programs may be run together, either with VS COBOL programs calling COBOL II programs or vice versa. The VS COBOL programs do not have to be recompiled. However, some VS COBOL programs may experience quite severe performance degradation when run with the COBOL II libraries. Performance may be improved if the VS COBOL program is converted to COBOL II (without any logic changes—only making those changes necessary so that it will compile under COBOL II). Even after conversion, some programs may still end up taking more than twice as long to run under COBOL II when compared with VS COBOL. In the cases when a program runs much slower under COBOL II, a company's system staff should be called upon to check the COBOL II options in use (compilation and run-time—both those set during COBOL II installation and defaults of the options that can be changed by an applications programmer) and tune the system. This includes checking for static versus dynamic calls (static calls process much faster) and use of the LIBKEEP run-time option (to keep library routines in storage until a task terminates). Regardless of the amount of tuning of COBOL II, VS COBOL programs still may take more than twice as long to run under COBOL II, as shown in Fig. 10.7. The times shown come from a program (PROGRAM1) that only contained a CALL statement to PROGRAM2. The CALL statement was executed 200,000 times through the use of a PERFORM. PROGRAM2 only contained a GOBACK statement as its entire PROCEDURE DIVISION.

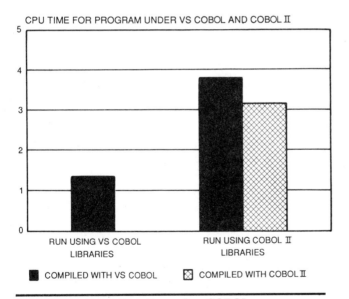

Figure 10.7 Execution time of a COBOL program issuing many CALLs to a second program that immediately returns to the calling program. The programs were run with VS COBOL libraries and with COBOL II libraries.

COBOL II Efficient Coding Techniques

11.1 ARITHMETIC EFFICIENCIES

11.1.1 Types of Arithmetic Fields

The IBM 370 family of mainframe computers does its fixed-point arithmetic using one of two formats, either packed decimal or binary. Packed decimal fields in COBOL II programs are represented as COMP-3 or PACKED-DECIMAL, and binary fields as COMP or BINARY. The alternate format of data definition (PACKED-DECIMAL rather than COMP-3, BINARY rather than COMP) produces the same code as the standard format. While packed decimal arithmetic is done using fields in memory, binary arithmetic always requires at least one register. This means that computations using binary fields usually require more instructions than computations using packed decimal fields. However, binary instructions are faster, which usually more than makes up for the additional instructions. For a packed decimal field, it is more efficient if the field contains no more than 15 digits since multiplication or division of larger numbers will force generation of a call to a COBOL II library routine to do the computation.

A zoned decimal field is defined in COBOL as display numeric (i.e., a numeric field with neither COMP-3, PACKED-DECIMAL, COMP, nor BINARY associated with it). If arithmetic calculations must be performed on the field, the hardware requires that the field be converted to either packed decimal or binary, thus increasing the amount of time necessary for the code to execute.

Arithmetic calculations should be done using fields of a similar type whenever possible, packed decimal to packed decimal or binary to binary. Whenever a calculation is made involving a packed decimal and a binary field, the compiler will be forced to convert one of the fields (to either packed decimal or binary depending upon the exact circumstances), thus using extra computer time. The compiler will usually (but not necessarily) use binary arithmetic for computations in which both fields are less than 10 digits long, either type for arithmetic when at least one field in a computation is from 10 to 18 digits, and packed decimal arithmetic for all computations that will require more than 18 digits. While COBOL only allows numeric fields up to 18 digits, more digits may be required for the intermediate results of a computation. The intermediate results will be placed into temporary storage fields in the COBOL TGT (temporary storage fields are discussed in Sec. 14.6.4).

11.1.2 Compiler Options

For the efficiencies discussed in Sec. 11.1.1 to be realized, the NUMPROC(PFD) and TRUNC(OPT) compiler options should be used. The NUMPROC option affects decimal data items while the TRUNC option affects binary data items. The other choices for the NUMPROC and TRUNC options generate code that may cause run-times inconsistent with what you would expect; arithmetic on COMP fields might take longer than arithmetic on COMP-3 fields and even longer than on DISPLAY fields. If you must choose between the other options, NUMPROC(NOPFD) is more efficient than NUMPROC(MIG) when IS EQUAL TO is used for comparing numeric fields, but NUMPROC(MIG) might save time when using other conditions that involve unsigned fields. TRUNC(STD) and TRUNC(BIN) are both inefficient and should be avoided whenever possible. Always remember that, except in rare cases, efficiency is not the major consideration when choosing compiler options; one option may be the only choice for a program to run properly.

Numeric calculations using packed decimal fields will take longer under COBOL II than under VS COBOL, regardless of the COBOL II compiler options used. This is because after the result of a computation is produced, the compiler issues a Zero and Add Packed (ZAP) instruction of the result into itself (see Sec. 10.6.3).

11.1.3 Number of Decimal Places

An often overlooked efficiency is that calculations are faster if performed on fields that have an equal number of decimal places. It is not very important whether one field is longer than the other (although a computation involving a binary field greater than nine digits will produce less efficient code), only that the number of places to the right of the decimal point be the same. When this is not the case, the compiler has to create code to move one of the fields into a temporary storage area where it will be given the same amount of decimal places as the other field. This may also cause an additional move if the field in the temporary storage area must then be moved into the resulting field.

When calculations are to be performed upon fields of different descriptions or differing number of decimal places, one of the fields can be moved to a WORKING-STORAGE field that matches the description of the other field. This technique will improve the speed of the program if the moved field is then used multiple times. However, it is not useful when a field will be used only once since the COBOL compiler will make the conversion just as efficiently as an added MOVE statement.

11.1.4 Lengths of Arithmetic Fields

An understanding of packed decimal and binary arithmetic on the IBM 370 leads one to analyze the lengths that are best for each type of data. Packed decimal fields allow two digits for each byte except the last, which contains one digit and a sign. Therefore, a packed decimal field will always contain an odd number of digits when acted upon by the object code. If a packed decimal field is defined to COBOL as having an even number of digits, the object code uses an extra digit and then must generate code to strip it off. The inefficiency of the additional code is avoided when a packed decimal field is defined with an odd number of digits.

Binary fields are handled as either halfwords (which can hold any four-digit decimal number) or fullwords (which can hold any nine-digit number). The hardware has different instructions to handle halfword and fullword arithmetic. Fullword arithmetic is done at approximately the same speed as halfword arithmetic [compare the fullword Add (A) instruction with the Add Halfword (AH) instruction in Fig. 10.5]. The difference is so slight that it is of little practical value to care about it. The main fact to consider when choosing between halfwords and fullwords is that fullwords require twice as much storage.

Any binary field larger than 4 bytes (nine decimal digits) must be manipulated by the COBOL compiler to produce proper results since the hardware does not specifically support an instruction for this function. Binary fields with more than nine digits should be used only when absolutely necessary. Although some large binary numbers can be handled efficiently by the compiler, frequently the fields are internally converted to packed decimal. While COBOL allows only 18 digits for a numeric field, the hardware allows 31 for a packed decimal field.

Beware of using large numeric fields, regardless of their internal representation. For instance, if a division is done using two 18-digit fields, with differing numbers of decimal places, a COBOL run-time library routine will be called to do a division similar to the long-hand way it is done on paper. The division may take as long as the rest of the program. There are ways to get around this problem. One way is to use floating-point numbers to produce considerably faster code. Another is to use an IF statement to check how many significant digits actually exist in a numeric field. If a field is defined as 18 digits long but only contains a 5-digit value, you can move the field to a data item defined with fewer digits and then perform the necessary calculations.

11.1.5 Use of Signs

Arithmetic should also be done between fields that are defined with a sign, an S in the data definition. COBOL does all arithmetic as signed whether or not the fields involved are signed. When arithmetic is performed upon fields that are not defined as signed, the compiler must insert an extra object code instruction to remove the sign from the result.

Due to an idiosyncrasy of the COBOL II compiler, adding to an unsigned packed decimal field can actually be more efficient than adding to a signed field (depending upon the compiler options). This goes against what one would expect. It is because of the compiler insertion of a ZAP instruction after an Add Packed (AP) instruction (see Sec. 10.6.3). When the COBOL II compiler strips the sign of an unsigned field, it uses an Or Immediate (OI) instruction, which is faster than the ZAP.

11.1.6 Use of Rounding

Avoid rounding whenever possible (ROUNDED has no effect on floating-point arithmetic since floating-point numbers are always rounded). The code generated to round an answer can take longer than the code to compute the result.

While on the subject of rounding, beware of using the ROUNDED verb on a COMPUTE statement. Many programmers think that the ROUNDED verb only causes rounding after the result of several operations is performed; it actually causes rounding on each intermediate result. In some cases the answer received from a COMPUTE with a ROUNDED can be quite different than when you code the arithmetic statements individually (see Fig. 11.1). The calculations required to determine the number of decimal places in intermediate results are described in App. A of the *VS COBOL II Application Programming Guide.*

11.1.7 COMPUTE Versus Other Arithmetic Statements

In an arithmetic statement involving only one operation (e.g., ADD FIELD1 TO FIELD2), a COMPUTE statement (COMPUTE

```
000010 DATA DIVISION.
000020 WORKING-STORAGE SECTION.
000030 01  A  PIC S9(3)V9(4) COMP-3  VALUE 1.1234.
000040 01  B  PIC S9(3)V9(4) COMP-3  VALUE 1.6789.
000050 01  C  PIC S9(1)V9(8) COMP-3  VALUE 1.23456789.
000060 01  D  PIC S9(3)V9(4) COMP-3.
000070 01  E  PIC S9(3)V9(6) COMP-3.
000080 01  RESULT  PIC S9(5)V9(6) COMP-3.
000090                                              DISPLAY Results
000100 PROCEDURE DIVISION.
000110      COMPUTE RESULT = A / B * C.              00000826084
000120      DISPLAY RESULT.
000130
000140      COMPUTE RESULT ROUNDED = A / B * C.      00000826085
000150      DISPLAY RESULT.
000160
000170      DIVIDE A BY B GIVING D.
000180      MULTIPLY D BY C GIVING RESULT.           00000826049
000190      DISPLAY RESULT.
000200      DIVIDE A BY B GIVING D ROUNDED.
000210      MULTIPLY D BY C GIVING RESULT.           00000826049
000220      DISPLAY RESULT.
000230      DIVIDE A BY B GIVING D.
000240      MULTIPLY D BY C GIVING RESULT ROUNDED.   00000826049
000250      DISPLAY RESULT.
000260      DIVIDE A BY B GIVING D ROUNDED.
000270      MULTIPLY D BY C GIVING RESULT ROUNDED.   00000826049
000280      DISPLAY RESULT.
000290
000300      DIVIDE A BY B GIVING E.
000310      MULTIPLY E BY C GIVING RESULT.           00000826083
000320      DISPLAY RESULT.
000330      DIVIDE A BY B GIVING E ROUNDED.
000340      MULTIPLY E BY C GIVING RESULT.           00000826085
000350      DISPLAY RESULT.
000360      DIVIDE A BY B GIVING E.
000370      MULTIPLY E BY C GIVING RESULT ROUNDED.   00000826084
000380      DISPLAY RESULT.
000390      DIVIDE A BY B GIVING E ROUNDED.
000400      MULTIPLY E BY C GIVING RESULT ROUNDED.   00000826085
000410      DISPLAY RESULT.
```

Figure 11.1 Using a COMPUTE statement with the ROUNDED clause may give you different results than coding the arithmetic statements individually.

FIELD2 = FIELD1 + FIELD2) is no more or less efficient. In arithmetic computations involving many operations (COMPUTE FIELD1 = FIELD2 * FIELD3 / FIELD4 + FIELD5) a COMPUTE statement can be more efficient and is usually easier to understand than a number of separate arithmetic statements. The reason for the efficiency of a COMPUTE is that it can store intermediate results in the most efficient data format. This is not necessarily the format it will use when separate arithmetic statements are coded (in this case the format of the results of each statement is determined by the field definition of the results).

11.1.8 Arithmetic Operations·

Addition and subtraction are the fastest of the arithmetic operations. Multiplication is much slower, and division slower still, sometimes twice as slow as a multiplication. Exponentiation is the slowest of the arithmetic operations and, with very large exponents, goes into a COBOL II library routine that can literally take seconds to execute one statement.

You can often substitute one arithmetic operation for another to increase the efficiency of your program. For instance, MULTIPLY 2 BY FIELD1 can be coded as ADD FIELD1 TO FIELD1, or SUBTRACT FIELD1 FROM ZERO GIVING FIELD1 can be coded rather than MULTIPLY -1 BY FIELD1. Also, avoid multiple constants in a row in computations since they require the program to recompute the expression each time the statement is executed. As an example, "COMPUTE FIELD1 = FIELD2 * (1 + 3 / 4)" will run more than twice as fast when coded as "COMPUTE FIELD1 = FIELD2 * 1.75."

11.2   IF STATEMENTS

Many programmers fail to code the IF statement efficiently. Code runs much faster when it checks for a range of values rather than checking for each value individually (see Fig. 11.2). However, the IF statement requires a certain amount of understanding and finesse to code elegantly. The second segment of code in Fig. 11.2 is an attempt to be faster, yet accomplish the same function as the first segment. If CHECK-FIELD is always numeric, the second version will run much faster and is fine. However, if CHECK-FIELD is not always numeric, while the second segment looks equivalent to the first, it may produce different results. A value of '2M' will not make the first IF statement true but will make the second true.

Alphanumeric rather than numeric compares should be used whenever possible since they are usually faster. (As mentioned earlier,

```
000010 DATA DIVISION.
000020 WORKING-STORAGE SECTION.
000030 01  CHECK-FIELD              PIC XX.
000040     88  CHECK-VALUES         VALUE '19' '20' '21'
000050                                    '22' '23' '24'.
000060
000070 PROCEDURE DIVISION.
000080     ...
000090     IF CHECK-FIELD =  '19' OR '20' OR '21' OR
000100                       '22' OR '23' OR '24'
000110         DISPLAY '***IS EQUAL***'.
```

(a)

```
000010 DATA DIVISION.
000020 WORKING-STORAGE SECTION.
000030 01  CHECK-FIELD              PIC XX.
000040     88  CHECK-VALUES         VALUE '19' THRU   '24'.
000050
000060 PROCEDURE DIVISION.
000070     ...
000080     IF CHECK-FIELD > '18' AND < '25'
000090         DISPLAY '***IS EQUAL***'.
```

(b)

Figure 11.2 Examples of inefficient (*a*) and efficient (*b*) ways
to code an IF statement to check for a range of sequential
values.

COBOL II sometimes does comparisons of numeric fields, such as
checking for numeric equality, by using logical compares rather than
packed decimal compares. This happens most often when the
NUMPROC(PFD) compiler option is used. In these cases, the numeric
compares end up as efficient as alphanumeric compares.) Numeric
compares may also cause ABENDs when invalid data appears in a
field whereas alphanumeric compares will not. Note that signed display numeric fields are the least efficient fields to compare. The compiler must first convert the fields to packed decimal so that a numeric
compare can be done.

11.2.1 Immediate Instructions

One valuable piece of information about 370 hardware is the fact that
"immediate instructions" exist where the operand field is a single
character placed into the instruction itself rather than into the literal
pool in storage. When an IF or MOVE statement operates on a single
literal character in the statement rather than operating on a constant
single character field in WORKING-STORAGE, an immediate

instruction can be generated in the object code. This enables the code to possibly run 3 times as fast. Defining frequently checked indicators as 1-byte fields, with values of 'Y' and 'N' instead of 'YES' and 'NO', should not detract from the clearness of a program but will increase its speed. Whenever possible, define single character fields as alphanumeric rather than numeric. Numeric comparisons may take considerably longer than alphanumeric comparisons.

It should be mentioned that using an 88 level field in an IF statement is neither more nor less efficient than comparing a field to a constant. In either IF statement in Fig. 11.2, code of equivalent speed would have been generated had the program used the 88 level rather than the constant values. In the first case, six comparisons must be done, while in the second only two.

11.2.2   Complex IF Statements

Complex IF statements that contain a number of AND and OR conditions can be speeded up simply by rearranging the order of the condition checks. The rule for efficient comparisons is as follows: in statements with many OR conditions, put the conditions with the greatest chance of truth first; in statements with many AND conditions, put the conditions with the greatest chance of truth last. In an OR condition, the first true condition found will satisfy the IF and the other conditions will not have to be checked. This is why the conditions that will most probably be true should be first. For AND conditions, all conditions must be true to satisfy the IF. Every condition must be checked until a condition is found to be false. If a false condition is quickly hit, the other conditions do not have to be checked.

Avoid repeating a test for the same IF condition more than once. Repeating the checking of a condition will make the code run slower and often can make the logic harder to follow. Figure 11.3 illustrates this situation with two code segments that run at different speeds but produce exactly the same results.

11.3   DATA MOVEMENT

The number of bytes moved in COBOL is dependent upon the size of the receiving field. This means that in each line of code in Fig. 11.4, 3 bytes of data will be moved. Lines 000110, 000120, and 000140 are equally as efficient. They are more efficient than the other MOVE statements in the program. Each of the three statements will move the first (or only) 3 bytes of the sending field to the receiving field. Since FIELD1 and FIELD2 are shorter than the receiving field (FIELD3), the compiler will have to generate extra code to move

```
000010 DATA DIVISION.
000020 WORKING-STORAGE SECTION.
000030 01  WS-SIGNED-COMP         PIC S9(4) COMP.
000040 01  WS-SWITCH              PIC X.
000050
000060 PROCEDURE DIVISION.
000070     ...
000080     IF WS-SIGNED-COMP IS EQUAL TO 1 OR 2 OR 3 OR 4
000090         ADD +1 TO WS-SIGNED-COMP.
000100     IF WS-SIGNED-COMP IS EQUAL TO 1
000110         MOVE 'A' TO WS-SWITCH.
000120     IF WS-SIGNED-COMP IS EQUAL TO 2
000130         MOVE 'C' TO WS-SWITCH.
000140     IF WS-SIGNED-COMP IS EQUAL TO 3
000150         MOVE 'Z' TO WS-SWITCH.
000160     IF WS-SIGNED-COMP IS EQUAL TO 4
000170         MOVE 'B' TO WS-SWITCH.
```

(a)

```
000010 DATA DIVISION.
000020 WORKING-STORAGE SECTION.
000030 01  WS-SIGNED-COMP         PIC S9(4) COMP.
000040 01  WS-SWITCH              PIC X.
000050
000060 PROCEDURE DIVISION.
000070     ...
000080     IF WS-SIGNED-COMP IS EQUAL TO 1
000090         ADD +1 TO WS-SIGNED-COMP
000100         MOVE 'A' TO WS-SWITCH
000110     ELSE
000120     IF WS-SIGNED-COMP IS EQUAL TO 2
000130         ADD +1 TO WS-SIGNED-COMP
000140         MOVE 'C' TO WS-SWITCH
000150     ELSE
000160     IF WS-SIGNED-COMP IS EQUAL TO 3
000170         ADD +1 TO WS-SIGNED-COMP
000180         MOVE 'Z' TO WS-SWITCH
000190     ELSE
000200     IF WS-SIGNED-COMP IS EQUAL TO 4
000210         ADD +1 TO WS-SIGNED-COMP
000220         MOVE 'B' TO WS-SWITCH.
```

(b)

Figure 11.3 Example showing the inefficient (a) and efficient (b) ways to code IF statements that produce more than one result for a given condition. The length of the code does not correspond to its execution time.

```
000010 DATA DIVISION.
000020 WORKING-STORAGE SECTION.
000030 01  FIELD1                PIC X(1).
000040 01  FIELD2                PIC X(2).
000050 01  FIELD3                PIC X(3).
000060 01  FIELD4                PIC X(4).
000070 01  HOLD-DATA             PIC X(3).
000080 PROCEDURE DIVISION.
000090     MOVE FIELD1 TO HOLD-DATA.
000100     MOVE FIELD2 TO HOLD-DATA.
000110     MOVE FIELD3 TO HOLD-DATA.
000120     MOVE FIELD4 TO HOLD-DATA.
000130     MOVE 'A' TO HOLD-DATA.
000140     MOVE 'A  ' TO HOLD-DATA.
```

Figure 11.4 Efficient alphanumeric MOVE statements have the receiving field length less than or equal to the sending field length.

spaces to the remainder of the receiving field. The same concept applies when moving literals. Line 000130 will be almost as inefficient as line 000090 (line 000130 runs faster because the code can generate an "immediate instruction" to move the first byte).

11.4   PERFORM AND GO TO

When I teach that VS COBOL PERFORMs are inefficient and should be avoided where program speed is the overriding concern, it never fails to amaze me when at least one person jumps up and complains that I am attempting to destroy structured programming concepts. One would think that I was a KGB agent that had infiltrated the United States to destroy programming through my teachings.

Take a look at the code in Fig. 11.5. It is not hard to tell which segment of code is easier to read as well as many times faster. Unless a PERFORM is in-line, as can be done in COBOL II, one has to find the performed paragraph, making the code harder to follow. Comparing the in-line PERFORM to the out-of-line PERFORM in Fig. 11.5, the in-line PERFORM is clearer and processes more efficiently. However, the code that clears the table without a PERFORM is considerably faster than the in-line PERFORM and certainly no harder to follow. Since out-of-line PERFORM statements (and even in-line PERFORM statements) may be harder to follow than in-line code, and certainly run slower, avoid them when possible. A basic out-of-line PERFORM statement may take six instructions for the PERFORM and two instructions for the performed paragraph to return; complex PERFORM statements with VARYING clauses will require many more instructions. When a segment of code is performed millions of times, elimi-

```
000010 DATA DIVISION.
000020 WORKING-STORAGE SECTION.
000030 01   TABLE-SUB                        PIC S9(4) COMP.
000040 01   TABLE-OF-VALUES.
000050      05   TABLE-ENTRY OCCURS 3 TIMES PIC S9(3) COMP-3.
000060
000070 PROCEDURE DIVISION.
000080      ...
000090 CLEAR-TABLE.
000100      PERFORM CLEAR-ENTRIES THRU CLEAR-ENTRIES-END
000110           VARYING TABLE-SUB FROM +1 BY +1
000120           UNTIL TABLE-SUB IS GREATER THAN +3.
000130      ...
000140 CLEAR-ENTRIES.
000150      MOVE ZERO TO TABLE-ENTRY (TABLE-SUB).
000160 CLEAR-ENTRIES-END. EXIT.
```

(a)

```
000010 DATA DIVISION.
000020 WORKING-STORAGE SECTION.
000030 01   TABLE-SUB                        PIC S9(4) COMP.
000040 01   TABLE-OF-VALUES.
000050      05   TABLE-ENTRY OCCURS 3 TIMES PIC S9(3) COMP-3.
000060
000070 PROCEDURE DIVISION.
000080      ...
000090      PERFORM
000100           VARYING TABLE-SUB FROM +1 BY +1
000110           UNTIL TABLE-SUB IS GREATER THAN +3
000120        MOVE ZERO TO TABLE-ENTRY (TABLE-SUB)
000130      END-PERFORM.
```

(b)

```
000010 DATA DIVISION.
000020 WORKING-STORAGE SECTION.
000030 01   TABLE-OF-VALUES.
000040      05   TABLE-ENTRY OCCURS 3 TIMES PIC S9(3) COMP-3.
000050
000060 PROCEDURE DIVISION.
000070      ...
000080 CLEAR-TABLE.
000090      MOVE ZERO TO TABLE-ENTRY (1).
000100      MOVE ZERO TO TABLE-ENTRY (2).
000110      MOVE ZERO TO TABLE-ENTRY (3).
```

(c)

Figure 11.5 Segments of code to clear a table shown in increasing order of efficiency. (*a*) Out-of-line PERFORM—inefficient; (*b*) in-line PERFORM—more efficient; (*c*) in-line code—very efficient.

nating the overhead of PERFORMs could be significant. Additionally, out-of-line PERFORM statements may cause extra paging if the performed paragraph is not near the PERFORM statement.

When processing a large table, a PERFORM statement is much more practical than moving data to each table entry with a separate statement. However, there exists another method to clear a table. It is faster than any of the three methods in Fig. 11.5 and much faster than the code generated for an INITIALIZE statement. (For moving fields up to 768 bytes long this method is extremely fast, requiring only one machine language instruction to move each 256 bytes; for moving fields more than 768 bytes long a COBOL II run-time library routine is called to do the move.) This method is shown in Fig. 11.6. When used, it yields the same added bonus as when the INITIALIZE statement is used; you do not have to change table initialization code in the PROCEDURE DIVISION if the number of occurrences in a table is changed. This method was actually a recommended method in some companies many years ago. While it is an excellent coding technique from an efficiency standpoint, it will confuse a programmer who has never seen it. If you decide to use the technique, it might be a good idea to document it.

To explain why this code works, it is better to illustrate it with characters than with packed numbers. The code in Fig. 11.7 sets each TABLE-ENTRY to a value of 'ABC'. There is one basic principle that explains why the code works; when a Move Character (MVC) instruction is executed on IBM 370 hardware, regardless of the number of bytes moved, movement of data is done 1 byte at a time. By the time the hardware attempts to move the fourth byte of the sending field [the first byte of TABLE-ENTRY (1)] to the fourth byte of the receiving field [the first byte of TABLE-ENTRY (2)], the fourth byte of the sending field had previously had an 'A' moved into it. The diagram in Fig. 11.7 illustrates how the data movement works.

When the code in either Fig. 11.6 or 11.7 is executed, the COBOL II compiler issues a warning message—*Data Items "TABLE-INIT" and*

```
000010 DATA DIVISION.
000020 WORKING-STORAGE SECTION.
000030 01   TABLE-INIT.
000040      05   FILLER                   PIC S9(3) COMP-3 VALUE ZERO.
000050      05   TABLE-OF-VALUES.
000060           10   TABLE-ENTRY OCCURS 3 TIMES PIC S9(3) COMP-3.
000070
000080 PROCEDURE DIVISION.
000090      ...
000100      MOVE TABLE-INIT TO TABLE-OF-VALUES.
```

Figure 11.6   Very efficient but possibly confusing way to clear a table.

```
000010 DATA DIVISION.
000020 WORKING-STORAGE SECTION.
000030 01  TABLE-INIT.
000040     05  FILLER                PIC X(3) VALUE 'ABC'.
000050     05  TABLE-OF-VALUES.
000060         10  TABLE-ENTRY OCCURS 3 TIMES PIC X(3).
000070 PROCEDURE DIVISION.
000080     ...
000090     MOVE TABLE-INIT TO TABLE-OF-VALUES.
```

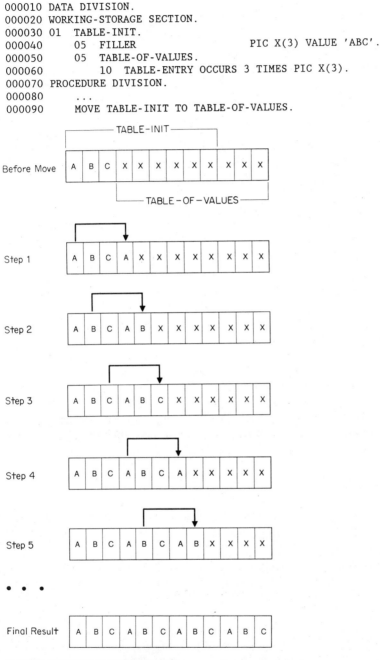

Note: 'X' represents an uninitialized byte.

Figure 11.7 The illustration shows why the code properly initializes all table entries in TABLE-OF-VALUES to 'ABC'. The move is done 1 byte at a time. You can see that Step 4 moves an A, not an X.

"TABLE-OF-VALUES" had overlapping storage. An overlapping move may occur at execution time. The code will still work as intended. Since overlapping moves are often unintended, the COBOL II compiler has been updated to produce this warning. This message did not exist in VS COBOL.

11.4.1 GO TO DEPENDING ON

One rarely used but extremely efficient statement in COBOL is GO TO DEPENDING ON. Regardless of how many possible paragraphs are the object of the GO TO clause, the code never takes more than 10 to 12 instructions to branch to the correct paragraph. This is because COBOL does not generate a list of IF statements but uses a branch table (a list of addresses, one of which is branched to) that uses the DEPENDING ON value as its subscript. When analyzed, there are a number of cases that can use the GO TO DEPENDING ON statement, such as a program that performs 50 different routines depending upon a numeric state code.

I feel that GO TO DEPENDING ON is an easy statement to understand. This fact combined with its extreme efficiency makes it a quite reasonable statement to use in a program. It is not the type of statement that has applicability to a majority of programs, but when it applies, it makes sense to use it. However, its use has fallen out of favor in recent years. It is looked upon as a nonstructured statement. You will have to make your own decision about using it, but its use is so precise (each numerically sequential paragraph name directly corresponds to the value of a data item) that it could only be nonstructured from an extreme true believer's point of view.

11.5 CALLS

In COBOL II, until Release 3, CALLs were either to another load module (dynamic calls) or to another program that had been link-edited into the same load module (static calls). The CALL statement was always quite inefficient. In Release 3, while the CALL can be quite efficient, it rarely is. A CALL executes with the efficiency of a PERFORM when multiple PROCEDURE DIVISIONs are coded within the same program and a CALL exists from one PROCEDURE DIVISION to another (a CALL to a nested program).

When CALLs are made, you should attempt to pass as few parameters as possible (see Fig. 11.8). Each parameter requires a separate BLL cell in the called program. Additional parameters may require additional registers to be used and each certainly requires the loading of a register with its base address. Even when many fields are next to each other and can all use the same BLL cell, as in the code in Fig. 11.8, called COBOL programs can only do this when the calling program has passed the information as a single parameter. Also, it requires more code in the calling program when more parameters are passed to a program. When you pass many fields from one program to another, efficiency is increased if you group the fields together in WORKING-STORAGE and pass them as one parameter.

11.6 TABLE SEARCHING

It is basic knowledge that a binary search (SEARCH ALL) can only be used when a table is in sorted order. It can be much more efficient than a serial search. Each check of an entry during a binary search will either find the entry in question or will cut in half the number of entries left to search. However, many programmers fail to realize that a binary search always calls a COBOL run-time library routine whereas a serial search can be performed in-line. The overhead in setting up a binary search makes it less efficient than a serial search when a small table is being acted upon.

On a table of 10 entries a binary search will take more than twice as long as a serial search. In a table where the possibility of looking for any particular entry in the table is equal, use serial searches on tables of less than 70 entries. For tables over 70 entries binary searches should be used. However, if only a few entries in a large table would

```
000010 DATA DIVISION.
000020 WORKING-STORAGE SECTION.
000030 01  LINK-FIELDS.
000040     05  LINK-FIELD-1      PIC 9(6).
000050     05  LINK-FIELD-2      PIC 9(6).
000060     05  LINK-FIELD-3      PIC 9(6).
000070     05  LINK-FIELD-4      PIC 9(6).
000080     05  LINK-FIELD-5      PIC 9(6).
000090     05  LINK-FIELD-6      PIC 9(6).
000100
000110 PROCEDURE DIVISION.
000120*THE CALLED PROGRAM WILL USE SIX DIFFERENT BLL CELLS
000130     CALL 'PROGRAM2' USING LINK-FIELD-1 LINK-FIELD-2
000140                           LINK-FIELD-3 LINK-FIELD-4
000150                           LINK-FIELD-5 LINK-FIELD-6.
000160
000170*THE CALLED PROGRAM WILL ONLY USE ONE BLL CELL
000180     CALL 'PROGRAM2' USING LINK-FIELDS.
```

Figure 11.8 CALL statements with many parameters in the USING clause will cause less efficient code to be generated in both the calling and called programs than when a single parameter can pass the same information.

be searched for most of the time, it is best to use a serial search and put the table entries in decreasing order of frequency, with the items searched for most frequently at the beginning of the table. This is similar to the efficiency of putting the most probable conditions closer to the beginning of an EVALUATE statement.

The SEARCH verb is among the slowest of the COBOL verbs to execute, so avoid it whenever possible. Figure 10.1 is a practical example of how to avoid using a search when each entry in a table is based upon its sequentially numeric position in the table.

11.6.1 Partitioned Search

When the speed of a search is of critical value, especially in a table of 10 to 50 values, a partitioned search will be considerably faster than either a serial search, a binary search, or sequential IF statements checking for every possible value. A partitioned search works just as its name implies; the information to be searched is partitioned and the code first checks for the partition that data falls into. It then checks for an equal condition only within that partition. By only checking in a specific partition, the number of checks (IFs) is greatly reduced when compared to a string of IF statements alone. The problem with using a partitioned search is that you have to code each IF statement rather than just coding a SEARCH statement in a program.

To search for one of the spelled out words from 'ONE' through 'TEN', the methods that can be used (from least to most efficient) are a binary search, a serial search, a number of sequential IF statements, or a partitioned search. Figure 11.9 shows a list of IF statements and a partitioned search to serve the same function. The partitioned search in the example is the simplest partitioned search possible, breaking the table into only two parts. If the table was larger, lets say 50 entries, you would want to break it into more partitions, perhaps five.

Assume that one of each of the 10 possible values for COMPARE-VALUE were processed by the code in Fig. 11.9. The sequential IF statements would execute 55 IF statements (10 to locate 'TWO', 9 to locate 'THREE', ..., 1 to locate 'EIGHT') while the partitioned search would execute 40 IF statements (2 to locate 'EIGHT' or 'SEVEN', ..., 6 to locate 'ONE' or 'TWO'). The partitioned search in the example saves over 27 percent of the IF statement processing time and will save even more with a larger set of values to check.

11.7 TABLE HANDLING

Optimizer programs can do a great deal to improve the performance of table handling in COBOL II programs. Yet there are a number of

```
000010 DATA DIVISION.
000020 WORKING-STORAGE SECTION.
000030 01   COMPARE-VALUE           PIC X(5).
000040 01   NUM-VALUE               PIC S9(3) COMP-3.
000050 PROCEDURE DIVISION.
000060      ...
000070      IF COMPARE-VALUE IS EQUAL TO 'EIGHT'
000080              MOVE +8 TO NUM-VALUE
000090      ELSE IF COMPARE-VALUE IS EQUAL TO 'FIVE '
000100              MOVE +5 TO NUM-VALUE
000110      ELSE IF COMPARE-VALUE IS EQUAL TO 'FOUR '
000120              MOVE +4 TO NUM-VALUE
000130      ELSE IF COMPARE-VALUE IS EQUAL TO 'NINE '
000140              MOVE +9 TO NUM-VALUE
000150      ELSE IF COMPARE-VALUE IS EQUAL TO 'ONE  '
000160              MOVE +1 TO NUM-VALUE
000170      ELSE IF COMPARE-VALUE IS EQUAL TO 'SEVEN'
000180              MOVE +7 TO NUM-VALUE
000190      ELSE IF COMPARE-VALUE IS EQUAL TO 'SIX  '
000200              MOVE +6 TO NUM-VALUE
000210      ELSE IF COMPARE-VALUE IS EQUAL TO 'TEN  '
000220              MOVE +10 TO NUM-VALUE
000230      ELSE IF COMPARE-VALUE IS EQUAL TO 'THREE'
000240              MOVE +3 TO NUM-VALUE
000250      ELSE IF COMPARE-VALUE IS EQUAL TO 'TWO  '
000260              MOVE +2 TO NUM-VALUE.
```

(a)

```
000010 DATA DIVISION.
000020 WORKING-STORAGE SECTION.
000030 01   COMPARE-VALUE           PIC X(5).
000040 01   NUM-VALUE               PIC S9(3) COMP-3.
000050 PROCEDURE DIVISION.
000060      ...
000070      IF COMPARE-VALUE IS NOT GREATER THAN 'ONE  '
000080          IF COMPARE-VALUE IS EQUAL TO 'EIGHT'
000090                  MOVE +8 TO NUM-VALUE
000100          ELSE IF COMPARE-VALUE IS EQUAL TO 'FIVE '
000110                  MOVE +5 TO NUM-VALUE
000120          ELSE IF COMPARE-VALUE IS EQUAL TO 'FOUR '
000130                  MOVE +4 TO NUM-VALUE
000140          ELSE IF COMPARE-VALUE IS EQUAL TO 'NINE '
000150                  MOVE +9 TO NUM-VALUE
000160          ELSE IF COMPARE-VALUE IS EQUAL TO 'ONE  '
000170                  MOVE +1 TO NUM-VALUE.
000180          ELSE NEXT SENTENCE
000190      ELSE
000200          IF COMPARE-VALUE IS EQUAL TO 'SEVEN'
000210                  MOVE +7 TO NUM-VALUE
000220          ELSE IF COMPARE-VALUE IS EQUAL TO 'SIX  '
000230                  MOVE +6 TO NUM-VALUE
000240          ELSE IF COMPARE-VALUE IS EQUAL TO 'TEN  '
000250                  MOVE +10 TO NUM-VALUE
000260          ELSE IF COMPARE-VALUE IS EQUAL TO 'THREE'
000270                  MOVE +3 TO NUM-VALUE
000280          ELSE IF COMPARE-VALUE IS EQUAL TO 'TWO  '
000290                  MOVE +2 TO NUM-VALUE.
```

(b)

Figure 11.9 Comparison of sequential IF statements
(a) and a partitioned search using IF statements (b).

technical points to consider to increase program speed when process-ing tables, whether or not your program will be optimized. Most COBOL programmers can recite that it is better to use an index than a subscript, mainly because it is a common interview question. What most programmers do not realize is that not only are literal subscripts [subscripts defined as a constant in the statement using it, e.g., MOVE ENTRYX (2) TO ENTRYX (4)] the most efficient form of subscripting but they are more efficient than indexes and no less effi-cient than using a field that is not in a table. When a literal subscript is used, the compiler makes the exact determination of where the field is. At run-time, the object code does not have to perform calculations to locate the field in the table.

Indexes are more efficient than nonliteral subscripts. This is be-cause an index contains a displacement that can directly be used to offset the beginning address of a table. A subscript contains an entry number and must have computations performed upon it to convert it to a displacement. However, many, if not most, programmers do not use indexes often. Perhaps it is because they do not know how to use them properly or how to find them in a dump (Sec. 14.6.1 describes how to find the value of an index in a dump).

When a subscript is used, it is always internally used as a binary integer. Therefore, subscripts should be defined as COMP whenever possible. The more levels of subscripting used in a table, the more time it takes to compute the displacement to access the table entry. Although Release 3 allows up to seven levels in a table, more than three levels should only be used when absolutely necessary.

11.8   FILE PROCESSING

11.8.1   Variable Length Records

Fixed-length records should be used rather than variable length records whenever possible because they can be processed more effi-ciently by I/O routines. When the minimum and maximum record sizes of a variable length file are close (e.g., from 500 to 510 bytes), it should be made into a fixed-length file. However, when the minimum and maximum record sizes are far apart (e.g., from 100 to 1000 bytes), converting the file to fixed-length records of the maximum record size would decrease efficiency. The additional time and storage required to process the additional data would more than offset any advantage of fixed-length processing.

When variable length records with a wide range of lengths are used in an output file, one extremely efficient coding technique is to use an APPLY WRITE-ONLY clause in the I-O-CONTROL paragraph for

ach variable length file. The AWO option of the Release 3 compiler
erves the same purpose and requires no program changes. (It applies
o all variable length output files in a program.) While it may come as
a surprise to many, COBOL often does not fill up a variable length
block before writing it. As an example, take a program that creates a
file containing two record sizes, 100 and 10,000 bytes. Assume that
the block size of the file is 10,008. While it may seem that many 100-
byte records will be placed into a block before it is written, this is normally not the case.

After COBOL puts a variable length record into a block (when the
AWO option and APPLY WRITE-ONLY are not in effect), it checks to
see whether the largest record that may be written by the program
can fit into the current partially filled block. If it cannot, the current
block is written out. In our example, if a 100-byte record is written
into an empty block by a program, COBOL checks to see whether a
10,000-byte record will fit into the partially filled block. It cannot, so
the block is written. If the program continually writes 100-byte
records, each will be placed into its own block.

I/O takes a considerable amount of computer time and when records
are not blocked, the processing time can increase significantly. To prevent this, the APPLY WRITE-ONLY clause (or AWO option) instructs
the compiler to fill a variable length block to its maximum capacity,
waiting until the record length of a WRITE statement is known rather
than checking the space left within a block and determining whether
a WRITE of a maximum size record would be too large to place into
the block. The coding restrictions that were required in VS COBOL
when APPLY WRITE-ONLY was used, such as that the output record
cannot contain any fields that are the object of an OCCURS DEPEND-
ING ON clause or that fields within the output record cannot be modified (other than the 01 record itself), are not in force in COBOL II.

Avoid using the OCCURS DEPENDING ON clause to define variable length COBOL II data items, whether they are record descriptions or WORKING-STORAGE fields. Every time a variable length
data item is used, COBOL takes time to recompute its length. When
there are only two or three possible sizes of a variable length data
item, it is more efficient to separately redefine the data item for each
size and use each definition as is necessary.

11.8.2   Blocking

Efficient blocking and buffering are just as important for fixed-
length files as they are for variable length files. When large blocks
are used, more main storage is required than when smaller blocks
are used, but larger blocks save CPU time and disk space. Addition-

ally, extra buffers may save elapsed time since you will not have to wait for another read or write to complete before your program can continue processing.

The number of buffers for a Queued Sequential Access Method (QSAM) file is specified in the JCL through the BUFNO subparameter of the DCB. When not coded, the default is five buffers. The default is reasonable although you may sometimes want to specify as many as 20 buffers if your program is processing a file sequentially and is I/O intensive. Specifying too many buffers (e.g., BUFNO = 250) decreases rather than increases efficiency. An excessively large number of buffers will increase paging since the buffer in use will constantly change to one not recently used.

For VSAM files, BUFNI and BUFND are specified as subparameters of AMP in the JCL. BUFNI specifies the number of index buffers (the default is one for a KSDS data set) and BUFND the number of data buffers (the default is two). For a file defined with ACCESS MODE IS RANDOM in its SELECT clause, the minimum number of index buffers recommended is one more than the number of index levels while the BUFND default of two is fine. For files defined with ACCESS MODE IS SEQUENTIAL only one index buffer is used, so the default of BUFNI = 1 is sufficient. However, at least five data buffers are usually recommended for sequential access. When a program uses ACCESS MODE IS DYNAMIC, the number of index and data buffers used should be the higher of the numbers required for either random or sequential access.

A word of warning: some programmers fail to realize that when you leave out the BLOCK CONTAINS 0 RECORDS clause for a QSAM file, the program does not end up using the block size specified in the JCL—it assumes that the records are not blocked. Leaving out the phrase is the equivalent of coding BLOCK CONTAINS 1 RECORD. At best, when the clause is not coded, output files in your program will run inefficiently; at worst, input files may ABEND because of an inconsistency between the actual block size of a file and the fact that the program specified that the file was unblocked.

11.8.3 Opening and Closing Files

Opening multiple files using a single OPEN verb (line 000100 in Fig. 11.10) uses more storage but saves time when compared with opening multiple files using multiple OPEN verbs (lines 000030 and 000040). Most files in a program are only opened once, so the savings realized for opening many files with a single OPEN statement may not be significant. Additionally, when a file is opened, it requires storage for buffers. You therefore may not want to open a file until it is necessary.

```
000010 PROCEDURE DIVISION.
000020 SLOW-FILE-OPEN-CLOSE.
000030     OPEN INPUT INPUT-FILE.
000040     OPEN OUTPUT OUTPUT-FILE.
000050     ...
000060     CLOSE INPUT-FILE.
000070     CLOSE OUTPUT-FILE.
000080
000090 FAST-FILE-OPEN-CLOSE.
000100     OPEN INPUT INPUT-FILE OUTPUT OUTPUT-FILE.
000110     ...
000120     CLOSE INPUT-FILE OUTPUT-FILE.
```

Figure 11.10 Less code and resources are used when multiple files are opened or closed in a single statement rather than using separate statements.

This is particularly true for a seldom used file, such as a file that is only used once a month.

11.8.4 READ INTO

It is equally efficient to execute the statement READ IN-FILE INTO FIELD1, when compared to the two statements READ IN-FILE and MOVE IN-REC TO FIELD1. However, there is a controversy among COBOL instructors about whether it is better to code a READ statement to only read a record into a buffer or to read a record and use the INTO clause (or a MOVE statement) to also place the record into WORKING-STORAGE. Placing a copy of a record into WORKING-STORAGE yields the following advantages:

- If an ABEND occurs, the record can be located in WORKING-STORAGE and does not have to be found in the buffer.

- A program will avoid a possible ABEND if it checks a data field in the WORKING-STORAGE copy of a record after an end-of-file occurs. The record would not be available in the buffer (the record definition in the FD).

- At the time of an ABEND, you would be able to look at the actual data in the record read (by locating it in the buffer) as well as having the copy in WORKING-STORAGE that may have been modified.

For these reasons, most instructors feel that each record read should be placed into WORKING-STORAGE. I disagree. It is certainly more efficient when you do not execute the additional code to move a record into WORKING-STORAGE, especially for large records. Does a program really need two copies of the input record? Would it be considered good code if a program had two copies of each field in the WORKING-STORAGE SECTION? Regardless of the method of coding, a programmer should know how to find a record in a buffer (see Chap. 14). When attempting to resolve difficult problems, this can sometimes be necessary. One cannot learn to code quickly simply by avoiding all areas that may cause confusion.

It is true that problems can be caused by using fields of a record in a buffer after an end-of-file condition. However, it is normally a logic problem when this occurs. Defensive coding, using methods that will prevent a program from ABENDing when logic errors exist, has no place in application programming. You are better off with an ABEND since you will then realize that a problem exists and can fix it.

12

Compiler Options

What if someone told you that they might be able to make your COBOL program run faster without changing a line of code? It is fact that programs will run faster or slower depending upon the compiler options chosen. This has nothing to do with a compile taking much longer because options like LIST and XREF, rather than NOCOMPILE, are used on a first compile.

For each specific situation, choosing the incorrect COBOL compiler options can make a program compile slower, run slower, and occasionally run incorrectly. If this is the case, why are so many programmers unaware of the options and their significance? Were the options created to be used on a case by case basis or as a way to customize the compiler for each specific company?

If the options were simply set for each installation, they would all be part of the compiler installation. While there are some installation options, most options are explained in the *VS COBOL II Application Programming Guide,* showing that they are for all programmers, not just systems programmers. It is unfortunate that most programmers have accepted compilation procedures as "canned." Whatever their current project uses as a standard compilation procedure is considered "proper" and changes are not made to it. Programmers often feel there is no need to learn the options since a procedure is already set up. I have worked on COBOL projects where I was forced to use standard compilation procedures even after proving their inefficiencies. While using standard procedures is a reasonable choice in a production environment, using canned procedures is not the prudent choice in the test environment. They can slow down the time of each compile, possibly decreasing the throughput of jobs, as well as forcing options that are not optimal for a programmer's debugging needs.

When using the COBOL compiler options, there are some general rules to follow. Some compiler options must be set depending upon specific programming products used with COBOL II. For instance, CICS requires some options while restricting others, and the IBM interactive debugger requires a specific compiler option. However, many options depend upon subjective factors such as debugging ability (e.g., the programmer can understand a Procedure Map) and debugging methodology (e.g., the programmer reads dumps rather than recompiling a program with TEST and rerunning with a trace). Still others depend upon whether the compilation is being done to find compilation errors or for a completely different purpose such as creating a listing for documentation.

The compiler options are specified in the PARM parameter of the JCL EXEC statement. Each compiler option has a default. Some are set to a value if not specified (e.g., SIZE = MAX); others are set depending upon whether another option is specified (e.g., OFFSET will force NOLIST—see Appendix C for the list of mutually exclusive COBOL II compilation options); some are set to either one specific setting or another (e.g., QUOTE/APOST); others are set depending upon subparameters of the option [TRUNC(STD), TRUNC(OPT), TRUNC(BIN)]; most are either set on or off depending upon whether or not the option is preceded with NO (e.g., MAP/NOMAP).

12.1   COMPILATION TIME

Choosing an efficient set of options can considerably decrease the compilation time of a program (see Fig. 12.1). As you will see when reading this chapter, the saving of compilation time can only be realized in certain situations. However, any saving of CPU processing time and elapsed time will save money and increase throughput.

12.2   OPTIONS GUIDING THE COMPILER

12.2.1   COMPILE/NOCOMPILE

One of the least used and most efficient options (from the point of decreasing compilation time) is NOCOMPILE (the default is COMPILE). It tells the compiler to check for syntactical errors and to not produce object code. This option should always be used when a program is compiled the first time. In the rare case that a program compiles without errors the first time, use of this option will require the program be compiled again without the option. However, it is rare that a programmer writes a significant amount of code without at least one compilation error.

The NOCOMPILE option instructs the compiler not to produce a

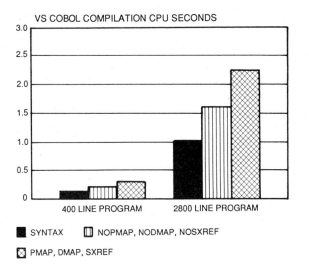

VS COBOL COMPILATION CPU SECONDS

400 LINE PROGRAM   2800 LINE PROGRAM

■ SYNTAX   ▥ NOPMAP, NODMAP, NOSXREF

▨ PMAP, DMAP, SXREF

COBOL II COMPILATION CPU SECONDS

400 LINE PROGRAM   2800 LINE PROGRAM

■ NOCOMPILE   ▥ NOLIST, NOMAP, NOXREF

▨ LIST, MAP, XREF

Figure 12.1   Graph showing the relative compilation times of a VS COBOL program and a
COBOL II program. The time depends upon
the options used in the compilation.

text (object) deck. When NOCOMPILE is in effect, the DECK,
FDUMP, LIST, OBJECT, OFFSET, OPTIMIZE, SSRANGE, and
TEST options may be specified but have no effect. However, they will
be listed in the compilation listing if they are the defaults or are specifically requested.

There are three other options, NOCOMPILE(W), NOCOMPILE(E),

and NOCOMPILE(S). They tell the compiler to proceed as if it were doing a regular compilation but as soon as an error equal to or exceeding the subparameter specified (W, E, or S) is encountered, switch to a NOCOMPILE compile. While NOCOMPILE(S) is not quite as efficient as NOCOMPILE, it is a good choice after a large number of compilation errors have been fixed in a program and you are unsure as to whether or not the compile will be error free.

12.2.2   OBJECT/NOOBJECT and DECK/NODECK

The OBJECT and DECK options often confuse programmers. Both options instruct the compiler to produce an object deck. OBJECT causes the output to go to the data set specified in the SYSLIN DD statement while DECK causes the object deck to be written to the data set defined in the SYSPUNCH DD statement. OBJECT is the default and JCL procedures take the output from the SYSLIN DD statement data set as input to the link-edit step. NODECK is a default since its output is only used when a backup (e.g., a card deck) is required.

12.2.3   SIZE

The SIZE option specifies the amount of storage to be used for the compilation. It can be specified in bytes (SIZE = 655360) or in kilobytes (SIZE = 640K). A larger SIZE is generally more efficient and will usually result in a faster compilation. This is because (1) the buffer space for the compiler work files is increased and (2) increased storage lowers or eliminates I/O for the dictionary created for the names used in the program. In COBOL II the maximum storage size for compilation can be requested with the SIZE(MAX) option, which is the default. In VS COBOL the default was 128K but the COBOL II compiler requires at least 640K. Since for large and/or complex programs, a SIZE larger than the COBOL II minimum requirement of 640K may be necessary, and larger sizes are usually more efficient, SIZE(MAX) should normally be used. [If not enough storage is available for the compiler to process, an unrecoverable error message (level U, return code 16) is produced and the compilation is terminated.] However, in an MVS/XA environment, SIZE(MAX) causes the compiler to use all available user storage above the 16-megabyte line and some storage below the line (for buffers and for compiler modules that cannot run above the line). This may cause extra overhead unless the XA environment is tuned accordingly. For this reason, SIZE(MAX) is not recommended in an MVS/XA environment.

12.2.4 QUOTE and APOST

The QUOTE option indicates that the double quote (") is used to delineate literals and constants within the code while APOST informs the compiler that the apostrophe (') will serve this function. While APOST was the default prior to VS COBOL, the QUOTE option has been the default since. Usually either the QUOTE or APOST option will be set as a standard for a company and should not be overridden except in special cases. Company-wide copy members and database dictionaries will create data in either one format or the other, forcing programmers within a company to be consistent in their usage of this option. An example of a case where the option would have to be used is when a set of COBOL programs is licensed from a vendor and constantly updated by the vendor. In this case it is more advantageous to use the option consistent with the vendor than to change all of the vendor's programs.

COBOL II is much more lenient than VS COBOL when the wrong option (QUOTE or APOST) is used in a compile. VS COBOL took the character that was not specified with this option as an invalid character, which caused various errors throughout a program. COBOL II will allow the alternate character that was not specified in the option but issues an error message (level E) informing you of this.

12.2.5 LIB/NOLIB

The LIB option instructs the compiler to check libraries to resolve COPY or BASIS (which copies an entire source program from a library) statements. It also is required when a REPLACE statement appears in a program. When COPY or REPLACE statements appear in a program, a SYSLIB DD statement must be coded in the JCL to specify the library or libraries (partitioned data sets) that contain the data to be copied. Additionally, a work file (SYSUT5) must be specified in the JCL whenever the LIB option is in effect. The NOLIB default saves compilation time (the library and work file will not have to be opened or accessed) but should only be used when no COPY, REPLACE, or BASIS statements appear in a program.

12.3 COMPILER LISTING DIRECTIVES

12.3.1 LIST/NOLIST and
OFFSET/NOOFFSET

The LIST option (which was called PMAP in VS COBOL) produces an assembler language listing (Procedure Map) of the code produced by the COBOL II compiler. It is usually quite long and takes a considerable amount of compilation time to produce. It makes paper companies very happy when used in a compilation that will be printed. While it is quite valuable for debugging, it should only be requested when there is a chance that it will be used for such a purpose, certainly not in a first compile when many errors occur.

In simple programs, compiling with the OFFSET option (which was called CLIST in VS COBOL) to produce a Condensed Listing, may be the preferred choice over compiling with LIST. It lists each line number, the verb on the line, and the hexadecimal displacement of where the object code for the verb begins. The object code created for each instruction is not listed (sample Procedure Maps and a Condensed Listing are shown in Chap. 13).

The LIST and OFFSET options are mutually exclusive and the default is to produce neither. If a dump occurs and you have an OFFSET listing, while you will not be able to identify the precise machine language instruction that caused the ABEND, you will be able to identify which verb caused the problem. This is done by comparing the program offset computed from the dump with the offsets in the Condensed Listing. For programmers who can understand some assembler code and follow a Procedure Map, the LIST option may be useful; for programmers who will merely want to relate the displacement of an ABEND to the line in the source program that caused it, a Condensed Listing is appropriate.

The LIST option produces all of the following outputs in the order below:

1. An assembler language code listing of the initialization code used by the program.

2. The Program Global Table (PGT). It contains the Literal Pool for System Literals.

3. The Constant Global Table (CGT). It contains the program's Literal Pool in both EBCDIC and hexadecimal.

4. The assembler language listing of the program.

5. The location of internal tables. These tables are used by the COBOL debugger and formatted dump routines and only appear when the TEST or FDUMP compiler options are used.

6. The Task Global Table (TGT) (fully described in Chap. 14).

7. The location and size of I/O control blocks, other control blocks, and WORKING-STORAGE.

8. Information specific to dynamic storage (this information is only

included if the program is reentrant through the use of the RENT compiler option).

12.3.2 MAP/NOMAP

The MAP option (called DMAP in VS COBOL) produces a data description listing. It shows each data field used in the program, its associated base locator cell (BL, BLF, BLW, BLS, BLX, BLV, BLL), its displacement from the beginning of the base locator cell, its size, its usage, and its data attributes. During debugging, the Data Map is extremely useful to locate the data fields in a dump.

Under Release 3 the MAP option also instructs the compiler to produce a nested program map. It shows where each nested program is defined and its attributes (COMMON or INITIAL). Examples of both the data map and the nested program map are shown and fully described in Chap. 13.

12.3.3 XREF/NOXREF

XREF produces a sorted cross-reference of data and procedure names. (In VS COBOL the option was SXREF. The XREF option that produced a nonsorted cross-reference is no longer supported.) In Release 3 it also produces an imbedded cross-reference and a cross-reference of programs. Examples and descriptions of the cross-references are discussed in Sec. 5.2. While quite useful on printed listings, it is usually a waste of time to produce a cross-reference when working online. References to a field can be found more easily by editing a program than by editing the listing and locating the cross-reference.

12.3.4 NUMBER/NONUMBER

Error messages, as well as many portions of a COBOL listing (Procedure Map, Condensed Listing, cross-references) and COBOL output (output from the debugger) contain line numbers. NUMBER (abbreviated NUM) is used when line numbers existing in columns 1 through 6 of the source code are to be used in these instances; NONUM instructs COBOL to use its own generated line numbers. When the numbers in the original source code are used (NUM), it is simple to relate messages given at the end of the listing to the source.

When the compiler-generated numbers are used and the program contains copy members or goes through a precompilation (e.g., CICS, IDMS), you must look at a listing to relate the numbers to the source. Since the length of the source program compiled will depend on the length of the copied code, there is no specific correlation between the relative line number in the original source code and the compiler-generated number. However, while the NUM option resolves this problem, it causes another. A programmer often does not have control of all of the copy members used in a program. Even if a programmer did, copy members still appear at different points in different programs. When the NUM option is in effect and an error occurs within a copy member, the line number within the copy member is used. This may be confusing since the same line number might be used in the program.

12.3.5 SEQUENCE/NOSEQUENCE

When numbers are supplied by the programmer in columns 1 through 6 of the source code, the SEQUENCE option (abbreviated SEQ) indicates that the compiler should check for ascending order of line numbers. If lines are found that are not in ascending sequence, a warning message is printed in the listing. The SEQ option is a carryover from when programs were entered on punch cards. To make sure the punch cards were in order (especially after a programmer attempted to place a dropped deck back in its original statement order), the option was used. The NOSEQ option instructs the compiler not to check ascending sequence of line numbers.

If you do a compilation with the SEQ option and the sequence numbers in a copy member are not coordinated with the sequence numbers in the program at the point of the COPY statement that includes it, an out of sequence condition will arise. The *COBOL II Application Programming Guide* suggests sequence numbers in COPY members and program source statements be coordinated, but I do not think that this can reasonably be accomplished.

12.4 DEBUGGING OPTIONS

12.4.1 TEST/NOTEST

Use of the TEST option allows a program to be debugged using the IBM COBOL II interactive and batch debuggers (see Sec. 4.7). This facility lets a programmer step through a program, examining various data areas during execution; enables the changing of data items; and even allows the path of program execution to be altered. When TEST is used in VS COBOL, the FLOW, STATE, and COUNT options cannot be used. In COBOL II, these options are no longer part of the compiler but their functionality exists as part of the debugger. You therefore only have access to their functions when debugging under COBOL II.

The TEST option lengthens compilation time and yields quite inefficient code. It should only be used if the program will certainly be used with the COBOL II debugger. The TEST option causes the object module to be considerably larger than it would have been with NOTEST. This is because it causes the generation of information for the debugger and places the information into the object module. In VS COBOL this information was placed into a separate file that was located through the SYSUT5 DD statement in the JCL.

The FDUMP option (described next) cannot be used in conjunction with the TEST option. If you want a dump while using the debug facility, you can use the DUMP command. However, it is rare that the DUMP command would be necessary since the whole point of using the debug facility is to interactively or batch debug and avoid dump reading. The TEST option also cannot be used with the OPTIMIZE option. This is reasonable since it certainly would make no sense to spend time optimizing a program that is not tested.

12.4.2 FDUMP/NOFDUMP

FDUMP is used so that a symbolic dump will be generated at the time of an ABEND. The output produced is written to the file defined by the SYSDBOUT DD statement in the JCL. Since the information produced by FDUMP is generated by COBOL II routines, and not general operating system routines, it produces much more detailed information for a COBOL II program. The dump lists the program running when the ABEND occurred, the user or system completion code, the PSW, the contents of the general purpose registers, and the line number and verb number in the source code that caused the abnormal termination [when the COBOL II optimizer (the OPT option of the compiler) is in effect, the hexadecimal offset into the program is listed instead of the line number]. Additionally, a considerable amount of information is listed about the DATA DIVISION. For each program that was running at the time of the ABEND, the name, data type (PICTURE), and value of each data item in the program (including records in an FD) is listed. Informational messages are printed next to some of the data fields. For instance, if a numeric field contains invalid data, the message INVALID DATA FOR THIS DATA TYPE appears, while when an alphanumeric field contains nonprintable hexadecimal data, the message UNPRINTABLE DATA FOR THIS DATA TYPE is received.

A sample FDUMP listing can be seen in Fig. 12.2. COBOL II programs PROGA and PROGB were compiled with the FDUMP option. PROGA called PROGB, and then PROGB ABENDed. Following the listing of the registers, each DATA DIVISION field for PROGA is shown, followed by each DATA DIVISION field for PROGB. For the table at the end of PROGB, the occurrence number and value of each entry (WS-EE-LOCATION) is separately listed.

FDUMP works quite efficiently. It basically does not change the executable code. It works by keeping a table of addresses that indicates where each statement begins and ends. It also keeps track of each data name used by the program. In programs that contain a large number of data names in the DATA DIVISION, this may make the object module considerably larger. However, these tables are only used when the program ABENDs. The efficiency of normal processing is only very slightly affected; the tables used by the FDUMP option take up extra storage and therefore extra paging may occur.

```
              --- VS COBOL II FORMATTED DUMP AT ABEND ---

                         PROGRAM      PROGB
COMPLETION CODE = SOC7        PSW AT ABEND = 078D000082E0848A
LINE NUMBER/VERB NUMBER BEING EXECUTED:   000010/1

                     GP REGISTERS AT ENTRY TO ABEND
REGS 0-3      02E09E1E  00000000  00005BA8  02E00688
REGS 4-7      02E08414  0000A0A8  0000A1A8  00FD32D0
REGS 8-11     80006E14  02E04140  02E08444  000052E4
REGS 12-15    02E08440  0000A1F8  02E0847C  80007FF0

                     DATA DIVISION DUMP OF  PROGA
00006 01 PROGA.WS-RECORDS-READ       S9(5)         INVALID SIGN - POSITIVE VALUE IS
      CMP3    ===>+00000
              HEX>000
                  000

                     DATA DIVISION DUMP OF  PROGB
00006 01 PROGB.ERROR-X               S999          INVALID SIGN - POSITIVE VALUE IS
      CMP3    ===>+000
              HEX>00
                  00
00007 01 PROGB.WS-DAYS               XXX
      DISP    ===>***                              INVALID DATA FOR THIS DATA TYPE
              HEX>000
                  000
00008 01 PROGB.FILLER                AN-GR
00009 02 PROGB.WS-EE-NUM-ENTRY       AN-GR
00010 00 PROGB.EE-LOC-INDEX          IX
           ===>1
00011 03 PROGB.WS-EE-LOCATION        XX
                 SUB(1)
      DISP    ===>54
                 SUB(2)
      DISP    ===>65
              --- END OF VS COBOL II FORMATTED DUMP AT ABEND ---
```

Figure 12.2 Listing of FDUMP output after PROGA called PROGB and PROGB ABENDed.

Despite the advantages of using a formatted dump for debugging, I cannot unequivocally recommend using the FDUMP option. Since all the data fields of each program compiled with FDUMP are listed, the output can be rather large. The alternative would have been for FDUMP to print only those fields that its routines determined were most probably the reason for the error. This is not totally practical since it is nearly impossible for the routines to make an intelligent determination. If only selected DATA DIVISION fields were printed, an entire dump of the DATA DIVISION would be required when the fields listed were not enough to resolve the problem.

Some of the informational messages supplied with each data field seem rather silly. For instance, if a program ABENDs and some fields in the DATA DIVISION were not initialized, these fields will appear as INVALID DATA or INVALID SIGN. I find these messages to be overkill since the determination of whether a field is invalid can easily be made by a programmer by looking at a field's hexadecimal value. Invalid data should only be listed in hexadecimal; FDUMP attempts to print the numeric value of invalid data (e.g., low values in a packed decimal field are listed as a zero with an invalid sign). The message UNPRINTABLE can appear for a data item and is useful for distinguishing unprintable data from invalid data.

12.5   OPTIONS AFFECTING PROGRAM EXECUTION

The options mentioned so far, while changing the information produced in the listing, and acting as debugging aids, will not change the required output of a program's execution. To be specific, if a program was written to generate a report, the report will look the same no matter which previously mentioned options were used. The options I will now discuss can actually change the way a program executes; arithmetic computations may yield different results; a program may ABEND because the compiler did not realize that a called program did not have to be included in the link-edit. All COBOL programmers should make an effort to fully understand these options.

12.5.1   TRUNC

The TRUNC option is one of the most difficult and confusing of the compiler options to understand. It affects binary data fields (COMP and BINARY). Most of the confusion is caused by IBM's implementation of it; there are too many choices, the documentation is inadequate, and the object code produced is lengthy, puzzling, and inefficient. Had I hired IBM to write the compiler for my company and they designed the TRUNC option as it presently exists in Release 3, I would withhold payment until it was changed. It is extremely complex when it really does not have to be. After reading the explanation of the option, I expect that you will agree with me.

12.5.1.1 VS COBOL

Few programmers fully understand the TRUNC and NOTRUNC options used in VS COBOL. The TRUNC option assures that after arithmetic is performed on a binary field (COMP) or when data is moved to a binary field, if the resulting field exceeds the maximum value that the field is defined as, the result will be truncated to the PICTURE size. This is how packed decimal and display numeric fields are handled. Extra machine code is required to truncate binary fields to their PICTURE size, thus increasing execution time. Rarely does a program need to ensure that a binary field exceeding its defined number of digits be truncated to the defined size. The only time that it would make sense to use the TRUNC option is when decimal truncation is required when a program moves a value to a binary receiving field that is defined with fewer significant digits than the sending field (e.g., moving an 11-digit packed decimal field to a 9-digit binary field).

The VS COBOL and COBOL II compilers allocate a halfword (2 bytes) for binary (COMP or BINARY) fields up to four digits long and a fullword (4 bytes) for binary fields from five to nine digits long. A halfword really holds a decimal value up to 32,767 while a fullword holds up to 2,147,483,648. While the PICTURE of a halfword or fullword binary field in COBOL is defined as having a limit of 9999 or 999,999,999, respectively, the actual numbers that may be put into the fields are larger. The NOTRUNC option allows a program with binary fields to hold up to the maximum value that may be put into a halfword or fullword rather than the maximum value determined by the PICTURE clause. A program with binary fields will run faster when compiled with NOTRUNC. Furthermore, depending upon how a program was coded, NOTRUNC may actually be a necessary option for the program to run properly.

12.5.1.2 COBOL II Release 2

In COBOL II through Release 2, although the names of the TRUNC and NOTRUNC options remained the same as in VS COBOL, the functionality has somewhat changed. The TRUNC option produces the same results but is executed using different code. In the VS COBOL compiler, binary data was converted to decimal so that the truncation would occur based on the decimal value. In Release 2 the intermediate result in an arithmetic operation is divided by a power of 10 (e.g., by

10,000 when a four-digit binary field is used) and the remainder is used as the final result.

The Release 2 NOTRUNC option was not written to function in exactly the same way as the VS COBOL NOTRUNC option. It produces somewhat similar, but not precisely the same, results as the VS COBOL NOTRUNC option. The IBM *VS COBOL II Application Programming Guide* warns that you cannot know the exact results it produces unless you actually use it and then run the code. What good is an option if the manual cannot precisely define the results? What the manual means is that the compiler will choose the more efficient method between either truncating the data based upon its PICTURE clause or not truncating the data by allowing the field hold the maximum value in the storage allocated.

In COBOL II Release 2 IBM has made the NOTRUNC and the TRUNC object code quite similar for fullwords and doublewords. The divide instruction used in the TRUNC code is the major difference between the code produced for the two options. Regardless of the differences in processing of the NOTRUNC option between VS COBOL and COBOL II Release 2, the NOTRUNC option should always be used unless a specific program has processing that must ensure that decimal truncation occurs when the defined binary field PICTUREs are exceeded. The results produced from NOTRUNC in Release 2 will be made clearer in the following discussion of TRUNC in Release 3.

12.5.1.3   COBOL II Release 3

Release 3 completely confused the TRUNC issue. The TRUNC option was basically renamed TRUNC(STD). A new option, TRUNC(BIN), has been added. This option produces similar results to the VS COBOL NOTRUNC option but functions much less efficiently. TRUNC(BIN) guarantees that truncation will not occur based upon the PICTURE clause but will only occur based upon the maximum value that can fit into the length of the halfword, fullword, or doubleword. While it is not clearly stated in the IBM manuals, TRUNC(OPT) in Release 3 is the NOTRUNC option as it existed in Release 2 (not exactly the same as the NOTRUNC option that existed in VS COBOL). The TRUNC(OPT) option informs the compiler to choose the optimal TRUNC option for each use of a binary field; in some cases it processes like TRUNC(STD) and in other cases like TRUNC(BIN).

If TRUNC is entered as an option for a Release 3 compile, a warning message is produced that states that the option is not supported but that TRUNC(STD) was put into effect; when NOTRUNC is entered, a warning messages is produced stating that TRUNC(OPT) was put into effect. While this seems to make sense [Release 2 TRUNC is

TRUNC(STD) in Release 3, and Release 2 NOTRUNC is TRUNC(OPT)], a severe error should have occurred instead. Release 2 NOTRUNC is TRUNC(OPT) in Release 3 but VS COBOL NOTRUNC is TRUNC(BIN) in Release 3. The Release 3 compiler assumes that you meant to use the Release 2 NOTRUNC option. It happens to be an assumption that will often be incorrect.

For all practical purposes, the VS COBOL TRUNC and NOTRUNC options met the needs of all applications. (When was the last time someone told you that their program is not working properly because of the processing of TRUNC and NOTRUNC?) Additionally, the NOTRUNC code was extremely efficient, even more so than the code produced from the TRUNC(OPT) option. Now IBM expects you to use the TRUNC(BIN) option whenever the NOTRUNC option was used in VS COBOL.

When the TRUNC(BIN) option is coded (regardless of any other options—the NUMPROC option does not affect binary field processing), although the code it produces works as documented, it is inconsistent with what you would expect for binary data. When two binary fields are added together in Release 3 using the TRUNC(BIN) option, or even when a constant is added to a binary field, the option causes the compiler to do its arithmetic in packed decimal format. The binary fields are converted to packed decimal fields, the arithmetic calculations are performed, and then the packed decimal fields are converted back to binary. This is extremely inefficient (the TRUNC option, the inefficient choice under VS COBOL, did convert numbers to decimal and back but at least did the arithmetic in binary).

When fields are DISPLAYed in programs compiled with the TRUNC(BIN) option, they are DISPLAYed using the full halfword, fullword, or doubleword value of the fields, regardless of their PICTUREs. When fields are DISPLAYed in programs compiled with TRUNC(STD) and TRUNC(OPT), they are DISPLAYed based upon their PICTURE size. This is true for the TRUNC(OPT) option even when the compiler decides to treat fields as if TRUNC(BIN) had been coded rather than TRUNC(STD). If you use DISPLAY statements for debugging, be aware that the values displayed may not be the actual values in the fields.

12.5.1.4 Which TRUNC Option to Use?

It is a common practice for a COBOL program to require that a binary field not be truncated because it is holding an address, as is the case in CICS programs. While many addresses have been converted from COMP or BINARY to POINTER data items in COBOL II, other addresses may still remain as binary. Binary fields should also not be truncated when used as record keys, record lengths, or data fields that interface with products such as IDMS or SHRINK. Programs using DB2 or programs written in FORTRAN or PL1 may also be expected to use the maximum values of binary fields. It is recommended by IBM that VS COBOL programs interfacing with any programs or products just mentioned be compiled with the TRUNC(BIN) option. The problem remains as to whether to take IBM's recommendation or whether it is better to choose one of the other Release 3 TRUNC options.

Regardless of the application in VS COBOL, the NOTRUNC option was the option of choice because it enabled the compiler to generate substantially more efficient code when manipulating binary fields. Since NOTRUNC rather than TRUNC was recommended in VS CO-BOL, we would probably want the corresponding option in COBOL II. In Release 2, the NOTRUNC option, although functioning differently, is the efficient and recommended choice. In Release 3, the recommended choice is certainly not the TRUNC(STD) option, which functions the same as the VS COBOL TRUNC option. Before making the decision of which TRUNC option to choose, we must examine the working of the TRUNC option in more detail. As an example, consider the code in Fig. 12.3 and carefully read the accompanying notes. For instance, the results of the MOVE on line 000100 in the figure may look weird when the resulting field is not truncated. This is because an overflow occurred and sometimes the overflow will set the high-order (sign) bit on, making the result negative.

Remember that truncation of data in lines like 000090 and 000100 in Fig. 12.3 is reasonably easy to understand and prevent. You can see that the constant or data item moved to a field has more significant digits than the receiving field. The best way to avoid problems that may occur when a program is compiled with a TRUNC option other than the one expected is to ensure that the values in binary fields do not exceed their PICTURE definitions.

Each of the TRUNC options has its uses. While the TRUNC(BIN) option prevents truncation, it is so inefficient that I cannot recommend its use for all programs. The TRUNC(OPT) should yield reasonable results and the efficiency obtained seems to more than outweigh the rare case where you would need TRUNC(BIN). It is just as likely that in certain cases you would prefer the TRUNC(OPT) results rather than the results of TRUNC(BIN). The brutally inefficient code produced by TRUNC(BIN) greatly outweighs any advantage of using a binary rather than a packed decimal numeric field. If you do decide to use the TRUNC(BIN) option, I highly recommend that you define as few fields as possible as binary and that these fields be used in as few arithmetic computations as practical.

```
000010 DATA DIVISION.
000020 WORKING-STORAGE SECTION.
000030 01   FIELD-8-BIN              PIC S9(8) COMP.
000040 01   FIELD-9-BIN              PIC S9(9) COMP.
000050 01   FIELD-11-COMP3           PIC S9(11) COMP-3 VALUE +12345678901.
000060
000070 PROCEDURE DIVISION.
000080      MOVE 123456789 TO FIELD-8-BIN.
000090      MOVE 1234567890 TO FIELD-9-BIN.
000100      MOVE FIELD-11-COMP3 TO FIELD-9-BIN.
000110      MOVE 999999998 TO FIELD-9-BIN.
000120      ADD 3 TO FIELD-9-BIN.
```

(a)

Compile done using	Decimal value of FIELD-8-BIN	DISPLAY of FIELD-8-BIN
VS COBOL TRUNC	23456789	23456789
VS COBOL NOTRUNC	123456789	23456789
Release 3 TRUNC(STD)	23456789	23456789
Release 3 TRUNC(OPT)	123456789	23456789
Release 3 TRUNC(BIN)	123456789	123456789

(b)

Compile done using	Decimal value of FIELD-9-BIN	DISPLAY of FIELD-9-BIN
VS COBOL TRUNC	234567890	234567890
VS COBOL NOTRUNC	1234567890	234567890
Release 3 TRUNC(STD)	234567890	234567890
Release 3 TRUNC(OPT)	234567890	234567890
Release 3 TRUNC(BIN)	1234567890	1234567890

(c)

Compile done using	Decimal value of FIELD-9-BIN	DISPLAY of FIELD-9-BIN
VS COBOL TRUNC	345678901	345678901
VS COBOL NOTRUNC	-539222987	53922298P
Release 3 TRUNC(STD)	345678901	345678901
Release 3 TRUNC(OPT)	345678901	345678901
Release 3 TRUNC(BIN)	-539222987	53922298P

(d)

Compile done using	Decimal value of FIELD-9-BIN	DISPLAY of FIELD-9-BIN
VS COBOL TRUNC	1	1
VS COBOL NOTRUNC	1000000001	1
Release 3 TRUNC(STD)	1	1
Release 3 TRUNC(OPT)	1000000001	1
Release 3 TRUNC(BIN)	1000000001	1000000001

(e)

Figure 12.3   The values of FIELD-8-BIN and FIELD-9-BIN will depend upon the TRUNC option used during compilation. (a) Code; (b) output from line 000080; (c) output from line 000090; (d) output from line 000100; (e) output from line 000120.

Notes: 1. The code on line 110 produces the obvious results with any of the TRUNC options.
2. When the VS COBOL TRUNC option was used, the compiler produced the cautionary message 'CONSTANT INTERMEDIATE FIELD HAD TO HAVE ITS HIGH ORDER DIGIT POSITION TRUNCATED' for lines 000080 and 000090.
3. When the VS COBOL TRUNC option was used, the compiler produced the warning message 'AN INTERMEDIATE RESULT OR A SENDING FIELD MIGHT HAVE ITS HIGH ORDER DIGIT POSITION TRUNCATED' for lines 000100 and 000120.
4. When the COBOL II TRUNC(OPT) (or NOTRUNC in Release 2) option was used, the compiler produced the warning message 'THERE IS A POTENTIAL DIFFERENCE OF RESULTS FOR THIS STATEMENT BETWEEN OS/VS COBOL AND COBOL II. SEE THE APPLICATION PROGRAMMING GUIDE DESCRIPTION OF THE "NOTRUNC" COMPILER FOR A MORE COMPLETE EXPLANATION.' for lines 000090 and 000100.
5. The negative numbers from line 000100 appear when the overflow in the fullword happens to set the high-order bit on. This bit is the sign bit. The DISPLAY of this field is signed with a D, so the last byte (D7) is listed as a P. (When a DISPLAY statement is used on a signed numeric field, the last digit sometimes appears as a nonnumeric character. This is why many programmers prefer to first move signed numeric fields to numeric-edited fields and then DISPLAY them.)

Figure 12.3   *(Continued)*

As you have likely concluded, it is difficult to determine which option would be required in a particular case, so why not choose the efficient one that produces quite reasonable results. Release 2 programs were forced to use NOTRUNC [the equivalent option to TRUNC(OPT)] when they did not want truncation. It seems to have been working well enough. If IBM thought that the TRUNC(BIN) option was so important, why did they make TRUNC(STD) the default? The TRUNC(OPT) option is clearly the best choice as the default for all compiles.

12.5.2   DYNAM/NODYNAM

Dynamic calls allow a called program to be loaded at the time of its invocation rather than forcing it to be statically link-edited into the same load module as the calling program. The DYNAM option makes all CALLs in a program into dynamic calls. While CALLs to a program whose name is defined as a data field in a CALL statement are automatically considered dynamic, CALLs that have the program name coded as a literal are static unless the DYNAM option is used. Figure 12.4 shows how static calls and dynamic calls can both exist within the same program.

For static calls, the copy of the called program to use is determined at link-edit time. If a statically called program is updated and the calling program is not re-link-edited, the old copy of the called program

```
000010 DATA DIVISION.
000020 WORKING-STORAGE SECTION.
000030 01  PROGRAM2                PIC X(8) VALUE 'PROGRAM2'.
000040
000050 PROCEDURE DIVISION.
000060*THE FOLLOWING CALL WILL BE STATIC IF THE NODYNAM OPTION IS USED
000070     CALL 'PROGRAM1'.
000080
000090*THE FOLLOWING CALL WILL ALWAYS BE DYNAMIC REGARDLESS OF THE
000100*COMPILER OPTIONS USED
000110     CALL PROGRAM2.
```

Figure 12.4 Static calls and dynamic calls can both exist in the same program if the program is compiled with the NODYNAM compiler option.

will still be used. This problem would not occur if the program was dynamically called since the copy of a dynamically called program to use is determined at run-time, not link-edit time. Be careful not to call a program dynamically from one program and to call the same program statically from another program. This can result in two copies of the called program being placed into storage and may result in an ABEND or other unexpected outcome.

When a program will definitely be called, a static call to the program will use less storage and execute faster than a dynamic call to the program. However, large statically called programs that are used infrequently waste memory. These programs can be dynamically called and the overhead of the module would only occur when the module was used. Even though the system uses more storage to process a dynamically called program, in reality less storage may be used. This is because infrequently used programs need never be brought into memory and programs that have completed processing may be taken out of memory with a CANCEL statement. If a dump is produced after a CANCEL statement is issued for a program, the program will not appear in the dump.

If the name of a called program is not known until the calling program is run, you have no choice but to use a dynamic call. Dynamic calls must also be used if you wish a COBOL II program running in 31-bit addressing mode to call or be called by a program link-edited as AMODE(24). Until CICS Release 1.7, CICS programs required NODYNAM since only static calls were allowed. Release 1.7 allows dynamic calls to programs that do not request CICS services while dynamic calls to programs that contain CICS requests are allowed in CICS Release 2.1.

12.5.2.1 Converting Static Calls to Dynamic Calls

Static calls contained in VS COBOL and COBOL II programs can be changed into dynamic calls without recompiling the programs. This is accomplished through the use of the IGZBRDGE assembler macro available under COBOL II Release 3. Use of the macro saves recompiling the programs and would be the only method to change calls to dynamic when the source code for the programs is not available. The macro can only be used with COBOL programs.

There are cases when changing a program call from static to dynamic would be required. If a called program had been run below the 16-megabyte line and was then recompiled with the RENT option and link-edited to run either above or below the 16-megabyte line, the program would have to be called dynamically.

The IGZBRDGE macro contains the names of the program or programs to be dynamically called, not the names of the calling programs. Suppose PROGRAM1 statically calls PROGRAM2, which dynamically calls PROGRAM3, which statically calls PROGRAM4. PROGRAM1 and PROGRAM3 could make use of the IGZBRDGE macro by assembling one IGZBRDGE macro specifying the names of PROGRAM2 and PROGRAM4 and including the object module stub generated in the link-edit of PROGRAM1. A more cumbersome but equally effective method would be to code one IGZBRDGE macro for PROGRAM2 and include the stub created in the PROGRAM1 link-edit and code another IGZBRDGE macro for PROGRAM4 and include this stub in the link-edit of PROGRAM3. Make sure to always INCLUDE the IGZBRDGE object module stub before including the statically called program. The format of the two choices for coding the macros appears below.

```
STATDYN  IGZBRDGE  ENTNAMES = ( PROGRAM2 , PROGRAM4 )
```

or

```
STATDYN1 IGZBRDGE  ENTNAMES = ( PROGRAM2 )
STATDYN2 IGZBRDGE  ENTNAMES = ( PROGRAM4 )
```

12.5.2.2 Register Save Areas with Dynamic Calls

Analyzing a calling chain (the sequential list of called programs that are presently active) using the register save areas in a dump can get rather confusing when dynamic calls are used under COBOL II. When a static call is made from PROGRAM1 to PROGRAM2, the register save area of PROGRAM2 directly follows the register save area of PROGRAM1. When a standard dynamic call (not using IGZBRDGE) is made from PROGRAM1 to PROGRAM2, the register save area of IGZCLNK (the COBOL II run-time library routine that handles CALL and CANCEL processing) appears between the register save areas of PROGRAM1 and PROGRAM2. Figure 12.5 shows the register save areas in a dump where PROGRAM2 ABENDed after being called statically and in a dump where PROGRAM2 ABENDed after being

```
SAVE AREA TRACE
COMBINED WAS ENTERED VIA LINK        AT EP PROGRAM1....C2.1.2.0.08.16.89.16.15.20
SA  00005FA8  WD1 00000000  HSA 00000000  LSA 00009E88  RET 80FD3320  EPA 82E00EC0  R0  FD00000D
              R1  00005FF0  R2  00000040  R3  008EC7C4  R4  008EC7A0  R5  008FB7A8  R6  008C5FF8
              R7  FD000000  R8  008FBA58  R9  808BC360  R10 00000000  R11 008FB7A8  R12 00DFDABA
COMBINED WAS ENTERED VIA CALL        AT EP PROGRAM2....C2.1.2.0.08.16.89.16.00.02
SA  00009E88  WD1 00108001  HSA 00005FA8  LSA 0000A0F8  RET 82E00FC6  EPA 02E033C0  R0  00009FE0
              R1  00000000  R2  82E00FBC  R3  008EC7C4  R4  02E00F14  R5  00009CC8  R6  008C5FF8
              R7  FD000000  R8  80006E14  R9  02E06028  R10 02E00F48  R11 00000000  R12 02E00F40
SA  0000A0F8  WD1 00108001  HSA 00009E88  LSA 00000000  RET 00000000  EPA 00000000  R0  00000000
              R1  00000000  R2  00000000  R3  00000000  R4  00000000  R5  00000000  R6  00000000
              R7  00000000  R8  00000000  R9  00000000  R10 00000000  R11 00000000  R12 00000000


INTERRUPT AT 82E0348A

PROCEEDING BACK VIA REG 13
SA  0000A0F8  WD1 00108001  HSA 00009E88  LSA 00000000  RET 00000000  EPA 00000000  R0  00000000
              R1  00000000  R2  00000000  R3  00000000  R4  00000000  R5  00000000  R6  00000000
              R7  00000000  R8  00000000  R9  00000000  R10 00000000  R11 00000000  R12 00000000
COMBINED WAS ENTERED VIA CALL        AT EP PROGRAM2....C2.1.2.0.08.16.89.16.00.02
SA  00009E88  WD1 00108001  HSA 00005FA8  LSA 0000A0F8  RET 82E00FC6  EPA 02E033C0  R0  00009FE0
              R1  00000000  R2  82E00FBC  R3  008EC7C4  R4  02E00F14  R5  00009CC8  R6  008C5FF8
              R7  FD000000  R8  80006E14  R9  02E06028  R10 02E00F48  R11 00000000  R12 02E00F40
```

(a)

```
SAVE AREA TRACE
PROGRAM1 WAS ENTERED VIA LINK        AT EP PROGRAM1....C2.1.2.0.08.16.89.16.06.43
SA  00005FA8  WD1 00000000  HSA 00000000  LSA 00009E88  RET 80FD3320  EPA 82E00688  R0  FD00000D

              R1  00005FF0  R2  00000040  R3  008EC7C4  R4  008EC7A0  R5  008FB7A8  R6  008C4FF8
              R7  FD000000  R8  008FBA50  R9  808FB508  R10 00000000  R11 008FB7A8  R12 00DFDABA
IGZCLNK  WAS ENTERED VIA CALL        AT EP .IGZCLNK...C22.005.04.88.09.35...N.....
SA  00009E88  WD1 00108001  HSA 00005FA8  LSA 0000A0A8  RET 82E00798  EPA 80007500  R0  82E02DBE
              R1  02E0076E  R2  000052E4  R3  008EC7C4  R4  02E006DC  R5  00009CC8  R6  008C4FF8
              R7  FD000000  R8  80006E14  R9  02E04028  R10 02E00710  R11 00000000  R12 02E00708
PROGRAM2 WAS ENTERED VIA CALL        AT EP PROGRAM2....C2.1.2.0.08.16.89.16.00.02
SA  0000A0A8  WD1 00102401  HSA 00009E88  LSA 0000A1F8  RET 80007A3A  EPA 82E083C0  R0  00000000
              R1  00000000  R2  80006E14  R3  02E00688  R4  02E0076E  R5  0000A1A8  R6  0000A1A8
              R7  00000007  R8  80007A3C  R9  00009E88  R10 00009CC8  R11 00000000  R12 80007532
SA  0000A1F8  WD1 00108001  HSA 0000A0A8  LSA 00000000  RET 00000000  EPA 00000000  R0  00000000
              R1  00000000  R2  00000000  R3  00000000  R4  00000000  R5  00000000  R6  00000000
              R7  00000000  R8  00000000  R9  00000000  R10 00000000  R11 00000000  R12 00000000


INTERRUPT AT 82E0848A

PROCEEDING BACK VIA REG 13
SA  0000A1F8  WD1 00108001  HSA 0000A0A8  LSA 00000000  RET 00000000  EPA 00000000  R0  00000000
              R1  00000000  R2  00000000  R3  00000000  R4  00000000  R5  00000000  R6  00000000
              R7  00000000  R8  00000000  R9  00000000  R10 00000000  R11 00000000  R12 00000000
PROGRAM2 WAS ENTERED VIA CALL        AT EP PROGRAM2....C2.1.2.0.08.16.89.16.00.02
SA  0000A0A8  WD1 00102401  HSA 00009E88  LSA 0000A1F8  RET 80007A3A  EPA 82E083C0  R0  00000000
              R1  00000000  R2  80006E14  R3  02E00688  R4  02E0076E  R5  0000A1A8  R6  0000A1A8
              R7  00000007  R8  80007A3C  R9  00009E88  R10 00009CC8  R11 00000000  R12 80007532
```

(b)

Figure 12.5 Program save areas when PROGRAM2 ABENDs after it was statically called and after it was dynamically called. (*a*) Save area trace after a static call from PROGRAM1 to PROGRAM2; (*b*) save area trace after a dynamic call from PROGRAM1 to PROGRAM2.

called dynamically. The static call was made after PROGRAM1 and PROGRAM2 had been link-edited together into a module named COMBINED.

Two other factors can further confuse a person analyzing a save area trace. First, an installation may define a COBPACK module that contains a collection of COBOL II library modules link-edited together. The COBPACK module is created for efficiency reasons since it allows many COBOL II library routines to be loaded with a single LOAD operation. When COBPACK is used and a dynamic call occurs, the COBPACK module (IGZCPAC) will appear as the program called while IGZCLNK appears as the entry point.

The second factor confusing the issue is that the IGZBRDGE macro may be used to convert a static to a dynamic call. In this case, if PROGRAM1 calls PROGRAM2, the actual call proceeds as follows:

1. PROGRAM1 calls the bridge module stub, which was link-edited with PROGRAM1.

2. The bridge stub calls bridge module IGZEBRG.

3. IGZEBRG calls the dynamic call processor, IGZCLNK.

4. IGZCLNK dynamically calls PROGRAM2.

With this knowledge you should be able to follow a save area trace produced from any COBOL II program, even when the IGZBRDGE macro was used to convert static calls to dynamic calls.

12.5.3 RESIDENT/NORESIDENT

Library routines are used by COBOL programs during execution to perform functions such as I/O processing, floating-point arithmetic, and binary searches. The RESIDENT option (abbreviated RES) makes calls to the COBOL library routines dynamic. It can be used with or without the DYNAM option. However, when dynamic calls exist in a program, the RESIDENT option is automatically in effect. Dynamic calls exist either when the DYNAM option is used for the program compilation or when the program contains calls that define the calling program with a DATA DIVISION field rather than a literal.

NORESIDENT means that calls to the library routines will be static, requiring the routines to be made part of the program load module. The size of a load module will be increased when NORESIDENT is in effect since the library routines are link-edited with the program using them. Note that COBOL II modules compiled with NORESIDENT will generally be larger than VS COBOL modules compiled in this manner since many of the COBOL II library routines are larger than their equivalent VS COBOL counterparts.

NORENT and NODYNAM must be in effect when NORESIDENT is used.

Until Release 3 of COBOL II, use of either the RESIDENT or NORESIDENT option for program compilations had to be consistent among all COBOL programs that called each other. This included calls to or from VS COBOL programs. VS COBOL programs may have been compiled with the NORESIDENT option. This caused a problem if companies using COBOL II Release 2 wanted any of these programs run with COBOL II programs compiled with the RESIDENT option (the RESIDENT option is often used in COBOL II since it is required when the RENT option is in effect). In Release 3, IBM now allows VS COBOL programs and COBOL II programs compiled with the RESIDENT and NORESIDENT options to call one another. The option to do so is named MIXRES but is not specified when a compilation is done. It is implemented through the use of assembler macros IGZOPD and IGZOPT. The module produced from these macros must be INCLUDEd in the link-edit with the main program, and it must also be INCLUDEd with every other load module to be executed that contains a program compiled with the NORESIDENT option.

12.5.4 ADV/NOADV

ADV tells the compiler that when the WRITE...ADVANCING clause is used, the carriage control character (first byte of the record) will not be specified in the program but is to be added automatically by COBOL. With NOADV the carriage control byte is defined in the program's record definition. For example, if a program writes a record with 132 bytes of data and the ADV option is used, the output record would be defined as PIC X(132); with NOADV it would be defined as PIC X(133) and the first byte would be left unused in the program. In either case, COBOL II will set the carriage control character and write out a 133-byte record.

12.5.5 OPTIMIZE/NOOPTIMIZE

OPTIMIZE (abbreviated OPT) instructs the compiler to perform object code optimization. The compilation will take longer when this function is requested. OPT cannot be used in conjunction with the TEST option, which activates the IBM debugger. This does not matter since there would be no advantage to using this option during testing and it actually would be a disadvantage. Since tests often run fairly quickly (or often do not even get to the end), the extra time used in compilation would often outweigh the time saved for the run.

The object code in an optimized compiler listing is harder to follow

```
000010 DATA DIVISION.
000020 WORKING-STORAGE SECTION.
000030 01   FIELD1                    PIC S9(5) COMP-3.
000040 01   FIELD2                    PIC S9(3) COMP-3.
000050
000060 PROCEDURE DIVISION.
000070      ADD FIELD2 TO FIELD1.
000080      GO TO PARA2.
000090 PARA1.
000100      STOP RUN.
000110 PARA2.
000120      MULTIPLY 5 BY FIELD1.
000130      GO TO PARA1.
```

Figure 12.6 Example of "spaghetti code" that gets optimized well when the OPTIMIZE option of the COBOL II compiler is used.

than in a nonoptimized listing. Debugging may therefore be more difficult with an optimized listing. Although the optimization does make the program process faster, non-IBM products such as CA-OPTIMIZER/II for COBOL II may produce faster and shorter code. However, CA-OPTIMIZER/II has to run as a separate step and compilation takes much longer than using the OPT option of the COBOL II compiler.

The IBM optimizer uses many different methods to assist in making a program run faster. It eliminates or improves upon branches in a program. This includes branches that the IBM COBOL II compiler created. (The compiler normally will not create the most efficient code for branching unless the OPT compiler option is used.) Figure 12.6 shows source code in which the optimizer will not create any object code for the GO TO statements. The PROCEDURE DIVISION object code simply ends up as line 000070, followed by line 000120, followed by line 000100. The optimizer also attempts to save time when subscripts are used by checking to see whether the subscript had recently been used and its value still available. Additionally, it will eliminate nonexecutable code (e.g., code that cannot be reached because execution does not fall into it and it is never performed).

Optimized PERFORMs and CALLs to nested programs can be done quite efficiently, on some occasions only two instructions are used to make the branch. When moves occur (1) that move from fields that are contiguous in memory, (2) that move to fields that are contiguous and in the same order in memory as the sending fields, and (3) where the sending and receiving fields are the same length, the optimizer will attempt to move the data with one rather than several moves. While this can sometimes optimize a number of continuous MOVE statements, it often adds to the efficiency of a MOVE CORRESPONDING statement.

The optimizer attempts to do arithmetic computations involving constants at compilation time rather than execution time. For instance, in the statement

```
COMPUTE FIELD1 = 20 * 3.14 / 12 * FIELD2.
```

the computation of 20 times 3.14 divided by 12 will be done during compilation and the result used in the executable module. Normally, it is better for programmers to do the computation of constants and just place the result into the code itself. This ensures that code will run efficiently regardless of the compiler used. However, the trade-off is that it may sometimes be clearer to show each numeric value used in a computation.

Note that the optimizer is not extremely intelligent in determining constants. Had the code above been written as:

```
COMPUTE FIELD1 = FIELD2 * 20 * 3.14 / 12.
```

it would not be optimized as containing constants. However, the constant computations in the following statement would be optimized:

```
COMPUTE FIELD1 = FIELD2 * (20 * 3.14 / 12).
```

The general rule is that the optimizer can locate constant expressions that are to the left of other expressions or can locate constant expressions that are contained within parentheses. Duplicate computations can also be optimized and follow the same rule as constant expressions; they are recognized when on the left side of an expression or when in parentheses. In the following two lines of code, the expression FIELD2 * FIELD3 will be evaluated only once:

```
COMPUTE ANSWER1 = FIELD2 * FIELD3 * FIELD4.
COMPUTE ANSWER2 = FIELD1 * (FIELD2 * FIELD3).
```

while in the code below the compiler will not recognize it as a duplicate computation and will analyze it twice:

```
COMPUTE ANSWER1 = FIELD2 * FIELD3 * FIELD4.
COMPUTE ANSWER2 = FIELD1 * FIELD2 * FIELD3.
```

In some cases, the IBM optimizer is intelligent enough to recognize that a data item is a constant and is never modified in a program. It can therefore generate code that would be as efficient as if a literal was coded each time the data item is used. Be aware that when a parameter is passed to another program BY REFERENCE (the default) rather than BY CONTENT, the compiler is forced to make the assumption that the data item gets modified in the called program.

EXTERNAL data items are never considered constants since they may be modified in other programs.

12.5.6   OUTDD

The OUTDD option is used to send the output of DISPLAY statements to a file defined in the JCL with a DDNAME other that SYSOUT. It is coded as OUTDD(ddname) where "ddname" is the DDNAME that appears on a DD statement. The default is OUTDD(SYSOUT).

It may seem like this option is overkill. However, it does have practical uses. Sometimes a COBOL II program may call another program (not necessarily written in COBOL) that uses SYSOUT as an output file and defines SYSOUT with different DCB information than would be required for the DISPLAY output. An internal sort also uses the SYSOUT data set. In the case of internal sort output interfering with DISPLAY output, there is another way to resolve the conflict than by using the OUTDD option. You can either move the DDNAME for sort messages to special register SORT-MESSAGE or you can code MSGDDN = ddname on the OPTION control statement in the file that contains the sort control statements (the DDNAME for the sort control file can be specified by moving it to the SORT-CONTROL special register). When the DDNAME for sort messages is specified in both the MSGDDN option and the SORT-MESSAGE special register, the MSGDDN is used.

12.6   RUN-TIME OPTIONS

The COBOL II compiler has a number of options that can be turned on and off at the time the program is executed. This is accomplished by coding a PARM parameter on the EXEC statement in your run-time JCL and including the execution parameters in the PARM following a slash (e.g., PARM = '05/01/90/NOSSRANGE' passes 05/01/90 as a parameter to the program and specifies the NOSSRANGE run-time option). COBOL searches backward through the parameter list and if it finds a slash, it assumes that all information after the slash consists of run-time parameters. You must therefore code a slash at the end of a user parameter list that contains a slash, even if run-time parameters are not used (e.g., PARM = '05/01/90' must be coded as '05/01/90/'). Otherwise the part of your parameters after the last slash will be accepted as run-time parameters. Other than the slash, there is no distinction between where the user parameter data ends and the run-time options begin. While many of the run-time options are not frequently overridden, it is important to conform to exact syntax requirements when a slash is passed as part of a user parameter.

The run-time options are not included in the length of the user parameter data passed to the program. While some run-time options are specified in execution JCL, others can only be set at installation time. Following is a brief description of some of the run-time options that can be specified in the JCL. None of the run-time options that can only be set at installation time are discussed.

12.6.1 SSRANGE/NOSSRANGE

NOSSRANGE will disable subscript range checking if the program being executed had been compiled with the SSRANGE option (see Sec. 4.3). It will increase the processing efficiency of a program compiled with the SSRANGE option but not to the point of having compiled the program with the NOSSRANGE option. SSRANGE is the default at execution time and has no effect unless the program had been compiled with the SSRANGE option.

12.6.2 STAE/NOSTAE

The STAE run-time option, which is the default, informs COBOL II to intercept ABENDs and perform standard COBOL II ABEND processing. This includes producing a formatted dump if it was requested with the compiler option FDUMP. When NOSTAE is specified and

```
--- VS COBOL II ABEND Information ---

Completion code = 'SOC7' PSW at ABEND = '0000000D60F174CA'
The GP registers at entry to ABEND were
    Regs  0 - 3  - 'B0020646  0002D28C  0002D5BC  00020186'
    Regs  4 - 7  - '00020054  0002D258  80F129E8  00000868'
    Regs  8 - 11 - '0002086C  0002D5B8  00020094  00020110'
    Regs 12 - 15 - '00020080  0002D418  00020140  00000000'

Program = 'PROGRAM1' compiled on '08/09/89' at '16:03:17'
    TGT = '0002D418'

No files were used in this program.
Contents of base locators for working storage are:
    0-0002D5B8
Contents of base locators for the linkage section are:
    0-00000000
No variably located areas were used in this program.
No EXTERNAL data was used in this program.
No indexes were used in this program.

--- End of VS COBOL II ABEND Information ---
```

Figure 12.7 Sample SYSABOUT output from an ABEND which occurred under CMS.

VS COBOL programs are running together with COBOL II programs, the VS COBOL options of COUNT, STATE, FLOW, SYMDUMP, and TEST are supported. However, when NOSTAE is in effect, COBOL II will not produce any diagnostic messages at the time of an ABEND nor will it process its normal clean-up routines (the partition clean-up, thread clean-up, run-unit clean-up, and program clean-up).

When the STAE option is in effect, and you include a SYSABOUT DD statement in your job step, a SNAP dump and ABEND information will be written out at the time of an ABEND (see Fig. 12.7). The information is produced regardless of the options used in the program's compilation; neither FDUMP nor TEST had to be used. If a SYSABOUT DD statement is not included in the JCL, you will not receive the additional information from COBOL II at the time of an ABEND. Unless your company has a debugging product that includes all of the information output to the SYSABOUT data set, the SYSABOUT DD statement should always be included since, with almost no overhead or setup, you are possibly getting valuable debugging information.

When the SYSABOUT file is specified, the following information is produced:

1. The current PSW at the time of the ABEND (in CMS only).

2. The contents of the general purpose registers at the time of the ABEND (in CMS only).

3. The contents of the floating-point registers at the time of the ABEND (in CMS only).

4. The name of all of the COBOL II programs that were running at the time of the ABEND.

5. The date and time that each COBOL II program was compiled.

6. The address of the TGT of the current program in execution at the time of the ABEND.

7. The contents of the base locator cells for files (specified as BLF in the Data Map) in use by the current program.

8. The contents of the base locator cells for WORKING-STORAGE (specified as BLW in the Data Map) in use by the current program.

9. The contents of the base locator cells for the LINKAGE SECTION (specified as BLL in the Data Map) in use by the current program.

10. The contents of the base locator cells for variably located data fields (specified as BLV in the Data Map) in use by the current

program. These cells are created for data items defined with the OCCURS DEPENDING ON clause.

11. The contents of the base locator cells for EXTERNAL data fields (specified as BLX in the Data Map) in use by the current program. EXTERNAL data items did not exist until Release 3.

12. The contents (hexadecimal value) of each index used in the current program. The names of indexes do not appear. They do appear in the formatted dump output when the FDUMP compiler option is used.

12.6.3 AIXBLD/NOAIXBLD

The AIXBLD option requests COBOL II to call Access Method Services (AMS) with a BLDINDEX command to build alternate indexes for a Key Sequenced Data Set (KSDS) or Relative Record Data Set (RRDS) loaded by the program. The SYSPRINT DD statement in the JCL will be used by AMS to write its messages. AMS may use considerable resources to create the index, and performance degradation will occur when this option is used. The default is NOAIXBLD. This option was supported under VS COBOL but was not supported under CMS until COBOL II Release 3.1.

Part 4

Debugging Techniques

Debugging ability is often the characteristic that separates the good programmer from the superb programmer. Two programmers might be able to code a program at the same speed. However, when a problem develops, one of them might know how to debug it 3 times as fast. If one programmer takes 5 days to write a program and 3 days to test, while another programmer needs 5 days to write code but only 1 day to test, a 25 percent increase in productivity has been realized.

Additionally, debugging ability is a very visible attribute of a programmer. Resolving difficult production ABENDs can be among the most critical tasks that a programmer must perform. Most of all, programmers who have an intimate knowledge of debugging will understand the intricacies of a language. This understanding will enable them to write clearer and more efficient code.

COBOL II gives you the option to produce a Procedure Map, listing the object code produced for your program, and a Data Map containing the displacements of all data items defined in a program. These two maps are immensely helpful in aiding in the resolution of a program exception and are discussed in Chap. 13. Chapter 14 describes the Task Global Table (TGT), the most important debugging control block specific to COBOL. The IBM VS COBOL II Application Programming: Debugging *manual does not describe its fields in enough detail, and the* VS COBOL II Diagnosis Reference *manual, containing a full listing of all its fields, is normally not available to applications programmers.*

Understanding the differences between System ABENDs, User ABENDs, and program exceptions is discussed in Chap. 15. Specifics of the methodology to resolve each of these is examined.

Chapter 13

Reading Data, Program, and Procedure Maps

13.1 READING A COBOL II DATA MAP

A Data Division Map is produced in the listing of a COBOL II compilation when the MAP option is specified. In VS COBOL the equivalent option was DMAP. The Data Map enables you to find data items from the program when analyzing a dump. The IBM debugger allows you to work on the source level and FDUMP lists source level fields and their values at the time of an ABEND. When these are used, knowledge of using a Data Map may not be necessary. However, production programs rarely run using these options.

Any debugging product that does not work on the source level, that simply gets control at the point of an ABEND or program exception, has no additional information other than data in memory. They can only print out memory in general sections, such as program code and WORKING-STORAGE. Even with most state-of-the-art debugging tools, an example being Abend-AID by Compuware (when used without the COBOL source language debugging option, which is how it is usually implemented), knowledge of the Data Division Map is still required. The debugging tools can locate the TGT and WORKING-STORAGE but not each individual field in the TGT and WORKING-STORAGE. Debugging tools certainly cannot determine the names that you have given to fields.

When a dump occurs, knowing the values of fields is usually a prerequisite for solving the dump. Even if a debugging product can precisely find and display each field used by the ABENDing instruction, you often want to check other fields to determine how other processing is proceeding, and you may find other problems at the same time. It is therefore extremely important for a programmer to learn to read a

```
000007 DATA DIVISION.
000008 FILE SECTION.
000009 FD  INPUT-FILE
000010     BLOCK CONTAINS 0 RECORDS
000011     LABEL RECORDS ARE STANDARD.
000012 01  INPUT-RECORD.
000013     05  IN-NAME              PIC X(20).
000014     05  IN-ADDRESS.
000015         10  IN-ADDRESS1      PIC X(35).
000016         10  IN-ADDRESS2      PIC X(35).
000017         10  IN-ZIP           PIC X(5).
000018     05  IN-SSN               PIC 9(9).
000019
000020 WORKING-STORAGE SECTION.
000021 77  WS-NAME                  PIC X(20) VALUE SPACES.
000022 01  FILLER REDEFINES WS-NAME.
000023     05  NAME-LET OCCURS 20 TIMES
000024             INDEXED BY NAME-INDEX   PIC X.
000025 01  RECORD-COUNT             PIC S9(7) COMP-3 EXTERNAL.
000026 01  ADDRESS-PTR              USAGE IS POINTER.
000027 01  SAVE-INDEX               USAGE IS INDEX.
000028 01  FLOAT-NUMBER             COMP-2.
000029 01  TOTAL-DOLLARS            PIC S9(5)V99 COMP-3 VALUE ZERO.
000030 01  COUNTRY-LEVEL.
000031     05  NUM-OF-ENTS          PIC S9(3) PACKED-DECIMAL.
000032     05  STATE-LEVEL.
000033         10  CITY-LEVEL OCCURS 10 TIMES PIC X(10).
000034 01  SUB1                     PIC S9(4) BINARY.
000035 01  TAB-LENGTH               PIC S9(4) COMP.
000036 01  TABLE1.
000037     05. ENTRY-X OCCURS 5 TO 50 TIMES
000038             DEPENDING ON TAB-LENGTH PIC X.
000039 01  OUT-DOLLARS              PIC Z(7).99-.
```

(a)

Figure 13.1   COBOL II program (*a*) and its associated
Data Division Map (*b*).

Data Division Map. It is actually fairly simple. While reading the following discussion, refer to the Data Division Map in Fig. 13.1 and the explanation of abbreviations used in a data map listed in Fig. 13.2.

The first column in the Data Division Map is the source line ID. This enables you to easily reference each line to the associated field in the source listing. The second column contains "normalized" level numbers. Level numbers of 01, 66, 77, and 88 appear as coded. Other level numbers coded below a group 01 level appear in sequential numeric order. (This is not normally how the level numbers are coded. Most programmers leave gaps between level numbers in a group so that the addition of a new level will not require renumbering all lower levels.) For instance, in Fig. 13.1, STATE-LEVEL is listed as level 02 in the Data Division Map rather than the 05 level that was coded in the source code; CITY-LEVEL is listed as level 03 rather than 10.

Immediately to the right of the level number is the data item name used in the source code. Following this is the Base Locator cell (BLF for files, BLW for the WORKING-STORAGE SECTION, BLL for the LINKAGE SECTION, etc.) used for addressability to the data item. The base locator in conjunction with the hexadecimal displace-

```
PP 5668-958 IBM VS COBOL II Release 3.0 09/13/88
Data Division Map
Data Definition Attribute codes (rightmost column) have the following meanings:
D = Object of OCCURS DEPENDING   G = GLOBAL                         S = Spanned file
E = EXTERNAL                     O = Has OCCURS clause              U = Undefined format file
F = Fixed length file            OG= Group has own length definition V = Variable length file
FB= Fixed length blocked file    R = REDEFINES                     VB= Variable length
                                                                       blocked file
Source  Hierarchy and        Base      Hex-Displacement Asmblr Data              Data Def
LineID  Data Name            Locator   Blk  Structure   Definition Data Type     Attributes
    2   PROGRAM-ID PROGRAM1 -------------------------------------------------------------------*
    9   FD INPUT-FILE. . . . .         001                                QSAM        FB
   12   01 INPUT-RECORD. . . . BLF=0000 000                   DS 0CL104    Group
   13     02 IN-NAME . . . . . BLF=0000 000   0 000 000       DS 20C       Display
   14     02 IN-ADDRESS. . . . BLF=0000 014   0 000 014       DS 0CL75     Group
   15       03 IN-ADDRESS1 . . BLF=0000 014   0 000 014       DS 35C       Display
   16       03 IN-ADDRESS2 . . BLF=0000 037   0 000 037       DS 35C       Display
   17       03 IN-ZIP. . . . . BLF=0000 05A   0 000 05A       DS 5C        Display
   18     02 IN-SSN. . . . . . BLF=0000 05F   0 000 05F       DS 9C        Disp-Num
   21   77 WS-NAME . . . . . . BLW=0000 000                   DS 20C       Display
   22   01 FILLER. . . . . . . BLW=0000 000                   DS 0CL20     Group       R
   23     02 NAME-LET. . . . . BLW=0000 000   0 000 000       DS 1C        Display     O
   24       NAME-INDEX. . . . IDX=0001 000                                 Index-Name
   25   01 RECORD-COUNT. . . . BLX=0000 000                   DS 4P        Packed-Dec  E
   26   01 ADDRESS-PTR . . . . BLW=0000 018                   DS 4C        Pointer
   27   01 SAVE-INDEX. . . . . BLW=0000 020                   DS 4C        Index
   28   01 FLOAT-NUMBER. . . . BLW=0000 028                   DS 8C        Comp-2
   29   01 TOTAL-DOLLARS . . . BLW=0000 030                   DS 4P        Packed-Dec
   30   01 COUNTRY-LEVEL . . . BLW=0000 038                   DS 0CL102    Group
   31     02 NUM-OF-ENTS . . . BLW=0000 038   0 000 000       DS 2P        Packed-Dec
   32     02 STATE-LEVEL . . . BLW=0000 03A   0 000 002       DS 0CL100    Group
   33       03 CITY-LEVEL. . . BLW=0000 03A   0 000 002       DS 10C       Display     O
   34   01 SUB1. . . . . . . . BLW=0000 0A0                   DS 2C        Binary
   35   01 TAB-LENGTH. . . . . BLW=0000 0A8                   DS 2C        Binary      D
   36   01 TABLE1. . . . . . . BLW=0000 0B0                   DS 0CL50     Grp-VarLen
   37     02 ENTRY-X . . . . . BLW=0000 0B0   0 000 000       DS 1C        Display     O
   39   01 OUT-DOLLARS . . . . BLW=0000 0E8                   DS 11C       Num-Edit
```

(b)

Figure 13.1 *(Continued)*

ment from the beginning of the base locator (the next column in the Data Division Map) enable a programmer to locate a data item in a dump. Directions on how to find the Base Locator cells are found in the TGT chapter in Secs. 14.6.2 and 14.6.3.

A nice enhancement to the Data Division Map produced by VS COBOL is the Displacement/Structure column, which has the hexadecimal displacement relative to the structure in which the data item appears (e.g., STATE-LEVEL begins at a displacement of 03A from the beginning of BLW zero, but at a displacement of 002 from the beginning of group/structure COUNTRY-LEVEL). A structure is simply a fancy name given to a group data item and its elementary fields.

The next two columns in the Data Division Map are the Assembler Data Definition and the Data Type. The possible values appear in the table in Fig. 13.2. The Assembler Data Definition is an equivalent assembler language description of the COBOL II data item; other methods of defining each data item could have been used if the field was used in an Assembler Language program.

The final column is the Data Definition Attributes. In Release 3 a

Usage	Assembler data definition	Description
GROUP	DS 0CLn	
GRP-VARLEN	DS VLC=x	x is the Variable Length Cell number used in the TGT
DISPLAY	DS nC	Alphanumeric field
DISP-NUM	DS nC	External (unpacked) decimal field
DBCS	DS nC	DBCS Characters (DISPLAY-1)
DBCS-EDIT	DS nC	DBCS edited field
ALPHABETIC	DS nC	Alphabetic field
ALPHA-EDIT	DS nC	Alphabetic edited field
AN-EDIT	DS nC	Alphanumeric edited field
NUM-EDIT	DS nC	Numeric edited field
BINARY	DS xC	x is equal to 2 for COMP fields of up to 4 digits, 4 for COMP fields from 5 to 9 digits and 8 for COMP fields from 10 to 18 digits. The Data Map in Release 2 lists these fields as COMP rather than BINARY.
BINARY	DS 1H, 1F, 2F	This format is used for binary fields that have the SYNCHRONIZED option specified. 1H is used for COMP fields of up to 4 digits, 1F for COMP fields from 5 to 9 digits and 2F for COMP fields from 10 to 18 digits.
COMP-1	DS 4C	Internal floating-point field (single precision)
COMP-2	DS 8C	Internal floating-point field (double precision)
PACKED-DEC	DS nP	Internal (packed) decimal field. These fields were referred to as COMP-3 in Release 2.
INDEX-NAME	not applicable	Index-name
POINTER	not applicable	Pointer field
QSAM	not applicable	Used to indicate a QSAM FD
VSAM	not applicable	Used to indicate a VSAM FD

Figure 13.2 Table giving descriptions of the USAGE (based upon Release 3) and Assembler Data Definitions used in Data Division Maps. Note: n is the number of bytes in an entry.

glossary of the possible values in this column appears at the beginning of the Data Division Map.

13.2 READING A NESTED PROGRAM MAP

When the MAP compiler option is used in Release 3, a Nested Program Map is created in the listing (see Fig. 13.3). This map should not be confused with the Cross-Reference of Programs that is created when the XREF option is used (refer to Sec. 5.2.4). The Nested Program Map shows where in the source code each program is defined as well as the nesting level of the program (a space appears as the nesting level of the main program since it is not nested). Additionally, it lists the program attributes, whether a PROGRAM contains the INITIAL or COMMON attribute on the PROGRAM-ID, and whether

```
Nested Program Map

Program Attribute codes (rightmost column) have the following meanings:
    C = COMMON
    I = INITIAL
    U = PROCEDURE DIVISION USING...

Source  Nesting                                                   Program
LineID  Level    Program Name from PROGRAM-ID paragraph          Attributes
    5            PROGRAM1. . . . . . . . . . . . . . . . . . . .
   10     1        PROGRAM2. . . . . . . . . . . . . . . . . . . . I
   17     2          PROGRAM3. . . . . . . . . . . . . . . . . . .
   25     2          PROGRAM4. . . . . . . . . . . . . . . . . . . I,C
   30     3            PROGRAM5. . . . . . . . . . . . . . . . . .
   38     2          PROGRAM6. . . . . . . . . . . . . . . . . . . C
```

Figure 13.3   Nested Program Map that is produced in Release 3.

the program contains the USING clause on the PROCEDURE DIVISION statement.

13.3   READING A COBOL II PROCEDURE MAP

A Procedure Map is generated when a COBOL II compile is done using the LIST option. It lists the assembler code produced for the COBOL II source statements. Each paragraph or section name appears on a line by itself and is preceded with an asterisk (*). Each statement in the source code normally produces at least two lines in the Procedure Map. The first line contains the source line number and the COBOL verb. Lines that follow show the object code produced (see Fig. 13.5). The object code lines contain the hexadecimal displacement where the generated assembler language statement begins, the actual machine language instruction, any compiler-generated names, the actual assembler language instruction, and specific descriptions of the fields used in the statement. In VS COBOL the source line number and COBOL verb appeared on the same line as the other information just mentioned. However, in COBOL II actual field names rather than compiler-generated field names are used. The actual field names are much easier to follow but are longer, thereby forcing the new format.

The following sections describe the fields in a Procedure Map in more detail. Their purpose is not to teach assembler language. It is to give a COBOL programmer an idea of what is contained in the Procedure Map and its practical use. Each section contains lines of code from COBOL II programs followed by the associated Procedure Maps produced. As you read the code in each section, refer to Fig. 13.4 for an

Symbol	Explanation
BL=n	Base locator for special registers.
BLF=n	Base locator for files.
BLL=n	Base locator for LINKAGE SECTION.
BLS=n	Base locator for sort items (Release 3 only).
BLV=n	Base locator for variably located data.
BLW=n	Base locator for WORKING-STORAGE SECTION.
BLX=n	Base locator for EXTERNAL data (Release 3 only).
CBL=n	Base locator for the Constant Global Table (CGT).
CLLE@=	Load list entry address in TGT.
EVALUATE=n	EVALUATE boolean cell in the TGT.
FCB=n	File Control Block (FCB) address.
GN=n(h)	Generated procedure name including its offset from the program beginning in hexadecimal (h).
IDX=n	Index cell number.
ODOSAVE=n	A save cell used for OCCURS DEPENDING ON.
OPT=d	A temporary storage cell used by the optimization option (OPT) of the COBOL II compiler.
PBL=n	Base locator cell for PROCEDURE DIVISION code.
PFM=n	A cell used when a PERFORM...x TIMES is coded.
PGMLIT AT +d	The field in use is a program literal and is located at a decimal displacement of d from the beginning of the Literal Pool (the Literal Pool is located in the CGT).
PSV=n	A PERFORM save cell.
RBKST=n	A backstore cell for symbolic registers.
SYSLIT AT +d	The field in use is a system literal and is located at a decimal displacement of d from the beginning of the System Literal Pool (the System Literal Pool is located in the PGT). System literals differ from program literals in that program literals are literals that are coded in the program and then used, whereas system literals are literals that are deemed necessary by the compiler even though they do not appear in the source code.
TGT FDMP TEST INFO AREA +d	Information Area used when the FDUMP and TEST COBOL II options are in effect.
TGTFIXD +d	The field is at a displacement of d bytes, in decimal, from the beginning of the fixed portion of the TGT.
TOV=n	A TGT overflow cell is in use.
TS1=d	The field in use is in the TEMPORARY STORAGE-1 area.
TS2=d	The field in use is in the TEMPORARY STORAGE-2 area.
TS3=d	The field in use is in the TEMPORARY STORAGE-3 area.
TS4=d	The field in use is in the TEMPORARY STORAGE-4 area.
V(routine)	IBM 370 Assembler syntax of a V-type constant is used when a program branches to an external routine.
VLC=n	A Variable Length Cell is in use. They are used to hold the lengths of fields described with the OCCURS DEPENDING ON clause.
VN=n	Variable Name procedure cell. The addresses in these cells can change based upon PERFORMs and ALTERs.
VNI=n	Variable Name Initialization.
WHEN=n	Evaluate WHEN cell number in the TGT.

Figure 13.4 Description of the symbols used in a Procedure Map. Note: n is the entry number and d is the offset, in decimal, from the beginning of the entry.

explanation of the abbreviations used in Procedure Maps. The exact instructions produced in each Procedure Map can vary drastically depending upon the options used in the compile [e.g., TRUNC(STD), NUMPROC(PFD), OPTIMIZE]. I will only mention the differences based upon the options when it is absolutely necessary for the discussion.

13.3.1 Procedure Map When Using COMP-3 Fields

In the example in Fig. 13.5, the object code for line 000008 is different from the object code for line 000009. This is because line 000008 adds to a signed field and line 000009 to an unsigned field. Line 000008 can cause an overflow condition, leaving a negative zero as the result. A negative zero would not compare as equal to zero when COBOL II

```
000002 DATA DIVISION.
000003 WORKING-STORAGE SECTION.
000004 01  FIELD1              PIC S9(3) COMP-3 VALUE +5.
000005 01  FIELD2              PIC 9(3) COMP-3 VALUE 5.
000006 PROCEDURE DIVISION.
000007 PARAGRAPH-1.
000008     ADD +1 TO FIELD1.
000009     ADD 1 TO FIELD2.
000010     ADD FIELD1 TO FIELD2.
```

(a)

```
┌─(t)─┐ ┌─────(u)──────┐
000007  *PARAGRAPH-1
000008   ADD
   000188  FA10 9000 A020    AP   0(2,9),32(1,10)   FIELD1      PGMLIT AT +28
   00018E  F811 9000 9000    ZAP  0(2,9),0(2,9)     FIELD1      FIELD1
000009   ADD
   000194  FA10 9008 A020    AP   8(2,9),32(1,10)   FIELD2      PGMLIT AT +28
   00019A  960F 9009         OI   9(9),X'0F'        FIELD2+1
000010   ADD
   00019E  FA11 9008 9000    AP   8(2,9),0(2,9)     FIELD2      FIELD1
   0001A4  960F 9009         OI   9(9),X'0F'        FIELD2+1
   └─(v)─┘ └────(w)──────┘ └(x)┘ └───────(y)──────┘ └────────(z)─────────┘
```

(b)

Figure 13.5 COBOL II code containing ADD statements to signed and unsigned packed decimal fields (a) and the associated Procedure Map (b). (t) Source line number; (u) verb, paragraph, or section name; (v) hexadecimal displacement; (w) machine language instruction; (x) compiler-generated name (does not actually occur in this example); (y) Assembler language instruction; (z) specific descriptions of fields used.

issues a logical character compare rather than an arithmetic compare instruction. COBOL II therefore ensures a preferred sign in arithmetic computations (this was not necessary for the object code produced by the VS COBOL compiler, which did arithmetic compares of numeric numbers). A Zero and Add Packed (ZAP) instruction (at 00018E in the Procedure Map) adds the result to zero. It does not change the numeric value of the result and when executed preserves the sign of the field, except that a negative zero becomes a positive zero. Line 000009 adds to an unsigned field so the result has to be unsigned. To ensure this the compiler removes the sign (makes the sign positive with an F) using an Or Immediate (OI) instruction (at 00019A).

In an ADD instruction, the names in the specific description columns show the field being added to, followed by the field being added. On both lines 000008 and 000009, the name of the field being added to is listed followed by PGMLIT AT, indicating that a literal constant is being added. This is easy to understand since we are adding a constant 1 in each case. For the code on line 000010, the to and from fields used in the ADD statement are listed in the description columns.

The instructions at displacements 19A and 1A4 have FIELD2+1 listed in the specific description column. These instructions are forcing the sign to be positive. The sign is in the second byte of FIELD2, so the code lists the field being changed as FIELD2+1 (+1 is the second byte since the displacements listed are relative to zero).

13.3.2 Procedure Map When Using DISPLAY Fields

Figure 13.6 shows the object code that gets generated when DISPLAY numeric fields are used in arithmetic. The 370 hardware does not have any instructions that do arithmetic on DISPLAY fields. Object code uses the PACK instruction to convert the fields to packed decimal. Since the converted packed decimal field used is not defined in your program, COBOL puts it into a temporary storage field. Temporary storage is actually four separate areas in the TGT, each area usually containing many temporary storage fields (see Sec. 14.6.4). The area names are abbreviated as TS1, TS2, TS3, and TS4 in the Procedure Map. Since many fields within a temporary storage area may be used, the compiler differentiates between them by giving the decimal displacement of the temporary storage field in the Procedure Map. This number is shown after an equal sign. (TS2 = 14 in Fig. 13.6 indicates that it begins on the fifteenth byte of the temporary storage area. The number is relative to zero.) After the result is computed, an Unpack (UNPK) instruction converts the number back to its DISPLAY format.

Note that if a decimal data exception (0C7) occurs when doing arithmetic on a DISPLAY numeric field, the field that actually causes the 0C7 will not be the field defined in your WORKING-STORAGE but will be the temporary storage field in the TGT. Also note that because data format conversions are required when computations are done for DISPLAY numeric fields, more instructions are generated for an ADD statement using DISPLAY numeric fields (Fig. 13.6) than for an ADD statement using COMP-3 numeric fields (Fig. 13.5). For this reason arithmetic operations using DISPLAY fields are less efficient than arithmetic operations using COMP-3 fields.

13.3.3 Procedure Map When Using Data in the LINKAGE SECTION

When a line of code using fields in the LINKAGE SECTION is executed, the registers are not normally already set up to have addressability to the field (unless the field or a field near it had been used just above it in the code, or the WORKING-STORAGE SECTION is small and registers normally assigned to it can be assigned to the LINKAGE SECTION instead). The compiler must therefore load the address of each LINKAGE SECTION 01 level field into a register [this is the purpose of the Load (L) instructions for BLL = 2 and BLL = 1 in Fig. 13.7]. These addresses are loaded from the BLL cells located in the TGT (see Sec. 14.6.3). After the addressability is established, processing continues in the same manner as if the fields had been defined in WORKING-STORAGE.

```
000003 DATA DIVISION.
000004 WORKING-STORAGE SECTION.
000005 01   FIELD1              PIC S9(3) VALUE +5.
000006 01   FIELD2              PIC S9(3) VALUE +5.
000007 PROCEDURE DIVISION.
000008     ADD FIELD1 TO FIELD2.
```

(a)

```
000008   ADD
   000184   F212 D14E 9008    PACK  334(2,13),8(3,9)      TS2=6     FIELD2
   00018A   F212 D156 9000    PACK  342(2,13),0(3,9)      TS2=14    FIELD1
   000190   FA11 D14E D156    AP    334(2,13),342(2,13)   TS2=6     TS2=14
   000196   F811 D14E D14E    ZAP   334(2,13),334(2,13)   TS2=6     TS2=6
   00019C   F321 9008 D14E    UNPK  8(3,9),334(2,13)      FIELD2    TS2=6
```

(b)

Figure 13.6 COBOL II ADD of two display numeric fields and the associated Procedure Map (b).

```
000004 DATA DIVISION.
000005 WORKING-STORAGE SECTION.
000006 ...
000007 LINKAGE SECTION.
000008 01   FIELD1                        PIC S9(3) COMP-3.
000009 01   FIELD2                        PIC S9(3) COMP-3.
000010
000011 PROCEDURE DIVISION.
000012      ...
000029      ADD FIELD1 TO FIELD2.
```

(a)

```
000029  ADD
    00028E  5830 D140        L    3,320(0,13)      BLL=2
    000292  5840 D13C        L    4,316(0,13)      BLL=1
    000296  FA22 3000 4000   AP   0(3,3),0(3,4)    FIELD2      FIELD1
    00029C  F822 3000 3000   ZAP  0(3,3),0(3,3)    FIELD2      FIELD2
```

(b)

Figure 13.7 Procedure Map (b) for two fields in the LINKAGE SECTION that are added together.

13.3.4 Procedure Map for an IF Statement

When the assembler code for an IF statement is generated, it requires branches to points within and after the IF statement. These points are not named in the program and the compiler is forced to create its own paragraph names where it deems necessary. The paragraph names are called Generated Names (GN) and are sequentially numbered within the Procedure Map (see Fig. 13.8). When you see GN = x (where x is the number assigned by the COBOL II compiler to make each generated name unique) in the description column on a line that contains a Branch on Condition (BC) instruction, the name shows the point to which a branch may be taken depending upon the outcome of a condition (BC 15,... is an unconditional branch, BC 8,... is a branch if equal, BC 7,... is a branch if not equal). The point to which a BC instruction may branch is indicated with GN = x (where x matches the number of the generated name in the statement that branched) in the generated name column of the Procedure Map. For example, if the branch at displacement 000196 in Fig. 13.8 is taken, it will branch to GN = 3 at displacement 0001B6. Line 000012 of the program would be the next statement to execute.

The way a Generated Name (GN) is listed in the description column is an improvement over the way it was listed in the VS COBOL Procedure Map. In COBOL II the displacement where the generated name is defined is listed after it. This is helpful since a generated

```
000003 DATA DIVISION.
000004 WORKING-STORAGE SECTION.
000005 01  FIELD1              PIC X(3) VALUE 'ABC'.
000006 01  FIELD2              PIC X(3) VALUE 'XYZ'.
000007 PROCEDURE DIVISION.
000008     IF  FIELD1 NOT = FIELD2
000009         IF FIELD1 = 'XYZ'
000010             MOVE FIELD1 TO FIELD2
000011         ELSE NEXT SENTENCE
000012     ELSE MOVE SPACES TO FIELD1.
```

(a)

```
000008  IF
   00018C  D502 9000 9008        CLC  0(3,9),8(9)      FIELD1       FIELD2
   000192  58B0 C008             L    11,8(0,12)       PBL=1
   000196  4780 B0B6             BC   8,182(0,11)      GN=3(0001B6)
000009  IF
   00019A  D502 9000 A01C        CLC  0(3,9),28(10)    FIELD1       PGMLIT AT +8
   0001A0  4770 B0AE             BC   7,174(0,11)      GN=4(0001AE)
000010  MOVE
   0001A4  D202 9008 9000        MVC  8(3,9),0(9)      FIELD2       FIELD1
   0001AA  47F0 B0B2             BC   15,178(0,11)     GN=5(0001B2)
   0001AE            GN=4        EQU  *
   0001AE  47F0 B0BC             BC   15,188(0,11)     GN=6(0001BC)
   0001B2            GN=5        EQU  *
   0001B2  47F0 B0BC             BC   15,188(0,11)     GN=7(0001BC)
   0001B6            GN=3        EQU  *
000012  MOVE
   0001B6  D202 9000 C000        MVC  0(3,9),0(12)     FIELD1       SYSLIT AT +0
   0001BC            GN=7        EQU  *
   0001BC            GN=6        EQU  *
```

(b)

Figure 13.8 Procedure Map (*b*) produced for nested IF statements.

name might be pages away in a listing and is otherwise difficult to locate.

13.3.5 Procedure Map for an OPEN

Figure 13.9 illustrates a Procedure Map produced for the opening of a QSAM file. First the address of the File Control Block (FCB) is loaded into a register. The FCB (described in Sec. 14.6.7) is a COBOL II-generated control block that contains various information about a specific file used in the program. When used in conjunction with the Data Division Map, the FCB number can be used to distinguish a specific file. Indicators representing the open options (INPUT, OUTPUT, etc.) are then moved to the FCB from the program literals (PGMLIT) in the Constant Global Table (CGT). Next, the file status (STATUS-INFO) is initialized to zero. At hexadecimal displacement 00054C a register is

```
000001 ENVIRONMENT DIVISION.
000002 INPUT-OUTPUT SECTION.
000003 FILE-CONTROL.
000004     SELECT FILE1 ASSIGN TO S-INFILE
000005          FILE STATUS IS STATUS-INFO.
000006
000007 DATA DIVISION.
000008 FILE SECTION.
000009 FD  INPUT-FILE
000010      BLOCK CONTAINS O RECORDS
000011      LABEL RECORDS ARE STANDARD.
000012 01  IN-REC1                PIC X(80).
000013 WORKING-STORAGE SECTION.
000014 ...
000015 01  STATUS-INFO            PIC XX.
000016
000017 PROCEDURE DIVISION.
000018      OPEN FILE1.
```

(a)

```
000018  OPEN
   00053C  5850 D180     L    5,384(0,13)        FCB=1
   000540  D202 5034 A08D MVC  52(3,5),141(10)    (FCB=1)+52    PGMLIT AT +15
   000546  D201 9020 C007 MVC  32(2,9),7(12)      STATUS-INFO   SYSLIT AT +77
   00054C  5840 D05C     L    4,92(0,13)         TGTFIXD+92
   000550  58F0 41E4     L    15,484(0,4)        V(IGZEQOC )
   000554  4110 A131     LA   1,305(0,10)        PGMLIT AT +97
   000558  05EF          BALR 14,15
   00055A  5880 D144     L    8,324(0,13)        BLF=0
```

(b)

Figure 13.9 Procedure Map (*b*) produced when an OPEN statement is coded under COBOL II.

loaded with the address beginning in the ninety-second (hexadecimal 5C) byte into the fixed portion of the TGT (in this case, the pointer to COBVEC, a table containing the addresses of the COBOL library routines). Then the address of the COBOL OPEN/CLOSE routine IGZEQOC is loaded. The routine is used to open QSAM (non-VSAM sequential) files. Whenever COBOL calls a routine whose code does not exist in your program, this is indicated by having the routine name enclosed in parentheses and the left parenthesis preceded by a V [e.g., V(IGZEQOC)]. This is standard Assembly language format for external, V-type address constants.

The Procedure Map instruction at displacement 000554 shows that a parameter list is set up (parameter lists normally use register 1) in the program literal pool (PGMLIT). The following BALR instruction is the actual call to the OPEN routine. Finally, when control returns from the OPEN routine, the address of the input buffer is loaded from the base locator for the file (BLF) to a register so that the COBOL program has addressability to the buffer.

13.3.6 Procedure Map for the EVALUATE Statement

In many EVALUATE statements, usually those that do not simply check the values of a single field, the code generated in the Procedure Map is rather confusing. This is due to the use of EVALUATE cells. They are usually set at the beginning of the EVALUATE statement and then either checked or set and checked in each WHEN clause. The object code produced could have been shorter and considerably easier to read.

Figure 13.10 shows two EVALUATE statements and the object code generated. The first EVALUATE statement produces code that is similar to the code that would have been generated by coding IF statements instead. The second EVALUATE uses a COBOL II EVALUATE cell. The cell is set to a hexadecimal zero (00) when a condition is found to be false and a hexadecimal one (01) when a condition is found to be true. Within each WHEN condition, the code first checks a condition and sets the EVALUATE cell to the appropriate value (0 or 1). It then checks the value of the EVALUATE cell and executes the code in the WHEN condition when true (equal to 1). In this example using the EVALUATE cells is inefficient, confusing, and unnecessary. There are other cases where IBM's use of EVALUATE cells makes sense and reduces the number of times a complex condition would have to be evaluated.

13.3.7 Procedure Map When Comparing Display Numeric Fields

The object code produced for comparisons and computations of packed and display decimal fields is dependent upon the NUMPROC option used in a compilation. When nonsigned display decimal fields are compared, the NUMPROC(PFD) and NUMPROC(NOPFD) options generate a Compare Logical Character (CLC) instruction to do a character comparison of the fields while the NUMPROC(MIG) option generates a Compare Packed (CP) instruction to do an arithmetic comparison (see Fig. 13.11). The CP instruction processes packed decimal fields and can get a decimal data exception (0C7) when executed. This means that a program may run successfully when compiled with one NUMPROC option but ABEND if the program is recompiled with another NUMPROC option. The code in Fig. 13.11 can only get an 0C7 if compiled with the NUMPROC(MIG) option.

```
000006 DATA DIVISION.
000007 WORKING-STORAGE SECTION.
000008 01   CITY-CODE              PIC X(2).
000009      88   CITY-NY           VALUE '01'.
000010      88   CITY-ALBANY       VALUE '02'.
000011      88   CITY-BUFFALO      VALUE '03'.
000012 01   CITY-NAME              PIC X(8).
000013
000014 PROCEDURE DIVISION.
000015      EVALUATE CITY-CODE
000016        WHEN '01'
000017          MOVE 'NEW YORK' TO CITY-NAME
000018        WHEN '02'
000019          MOVE 'ALBANY' TO CITY-NAME
000020        WHEN '03'
000021          MOVE 'BUFFALO' TO CITY-NAME
000022        WHEN OTHER
000023          MOVE 'UNKNOWN' TO CITY-NAME
000024      END-EVALUATE.
000025
000026      EVALUATE TRUE
000027        WHEN CITY-NY
000028          MOVE 'NEW YORK' TO CITY-NAME
000029        WHEN CITY-ALBANY
000030          MOVE 'ALBANY' TO CITY-NAME
000031        WHEN CITY-BUFFALO
000032          MOVE 'BUFFALO' TO CITY-NAME
000033        WHEN OTHER
000034          MOVE 'UNKNOWN' TO CITY-NAME
000035      END-EVALUATE.
```

(a)

Figure 13.10 Two EVALUATE statements and the drastic differences that can occur in the Procedure Map (b).

13.3.8 Procedure Map When Using BINARY (COMP) Fields

The Procedure Map created for BINARY (or COMP) fields is highly dependent upon the TRUNC option (described in detail in Sec. 12.5.1) used in a compilation. Figure 13.12 shows the differences in object code produced for a simple ADD statement when the various TRUNC options are used under VS COBOL and COBOL II. The Convert to Decimal (CVD) instructions change a binary number to packed decimal format and the Convert to Binary (CVB) instruction converts the packed decimal number back to binary. The CVD and CVB instructions are also used when a binary (COMP) field is used in a computation with a packed decimal (COMP-3) field. If the vast differences in the code produced for the various TRUNC options seems quite incongruous to you, you are in good company. Had FIELD1 in Fig. 13.12 been defined as COMP-3 rather than COMP, VS COBOL would only

```
000015      EVALUATE
000016   WHEN
   0001B8   D501 9018 A03C        CLC   24(2,9),60(10)        CITY-CODE      PGMLIT AT +56
   0001BE   58B0 C008             L     11,8(0,12)            PBL=1
   0001C2   4770 B0A4             BC    7,164(0,11)           GN=19(0001D0)
000017   MOVE
   0001C6   D207 9020 A00C        MVC   32(8,9),12(10)        CITY-NAME      PGMLIT AT +8
000018   WHEN
   0001CC   47F0 B0E0             BC    15,224(0,11)          GN=18(00020C)
   0001D0             GN=19       EQU   *
   0001D0   D501 9018 A03A        CLC   24(2,9),58(10)        CITY-CODE      PGMLIT AT +54
   0001D6   4770 B0BE             BC    7,190(0,11)           GN=20(0001EA)
......
000026   EVALUATE
   00020C   9200 D144             MVI   324(13),X'00'         EVALUATE=0
   000210   9201 D144             MVI   324(13),X'01'         EVALUATE=0
000027   WHEN
   000214   9200 D145             MVI   325(13),X'00'         WHEN=0
   000218   D501 9018 A03C        CLC   24(2,9),60(10)        CITY-CODE      PGMLIT AT +56
   00021E   4770 B0FA             BC    7,250(0,11)           GN=9(000226)
   000222   9201 D145             MVI   325(13),X'01'         WHEN=0
   000226             GN=9        EQU   *
   000226   D500 D144 D145        CLC   324(1,13),325(13)     EVALUATE=0     WHEN=0
   00022C   4770 B10E             BC    7,270(0,11)           GN=24(00023A)
000028   MOVE
   000230   D207 9020 A00C        MVC   32(8,9),12(10)        CITY-NAME      PGMLIT AT +8
000029   WHEN
   000236   47F0 B16E             BC    15,366(0,11)          GN=23(00029A)
   00023A             GN=24       EQU   *
   00023A   9200 D145             MVI   325(13),X'00'         WHEN=0
   00023E   D501 9018 A03A        CLC   24(2,9),58(10)        CITY-CODE      PGMLIT AT +54
   000244   4770 B120             BC    7,288(0,11)           GN=11(00024C)
   000248   9201 D145             MVI   325(13),X'01'         WHEN=0
   00024C             GN=11       EQU   *
   00024C   D500 D144 D145        CLC   324(1,13),325(13)     EVALUATE=0     WHEN=0
   000252   4770 B13A             BC    7,314(0,11)           GN=25(000266)
......
000033   WHEN
   00028C   47F0 B16E             BC    15,366(0,11)          GN=23(00029A)
   000290             GN=26       EQU   *
000034   MOVE
   000290   D206 9020 A024        MVC   32(7,9),36(10)        CITY-NAME      PGMLIT AT +32
   000296   9240 9027             MVI   39(9),X'40'           CITY-NAME+7
   00029A             GN=23       EQU   *
```

(b)

Figure 13.10 *(Continued)*

have generated one object code instruction for line 000008 while COBOL II would have generated two instructions.

13.3.9 Initialization of WORKING-STORAGE

At the beginning of every Procedure Map you will see data being moved to each field that contains a VALUE clause in the WORKING-

```
000003 DATA DIVISION.
000004 WORKING-STORAGE SECTION.
000005 01   FIELD1                  PIC 9(3).
000006 01   FIELD2                  PIC 9(3).
000007
000008 PROCEDURE DIVISION.
000009     IF FIELD1 > FIELD2
000010        ...
```

(a)

```
000009  IF
        00018C   D502 9000 9008    CLC   0(3,9),8(9)         FIELD1            FIELD2
        000192   47D0 B0B6         BC    13,182(0,11)        GN=3(0001B6)
```

(b)

```
000009  IF
        00018C   F212 D14E 9000    PACK  334(2,13),0(3,9)    TS2=6            FIELD1
        000192   960F D14F         OI    335,X'0F'           TS2=7
        000196   F212 D156 9008    PACK  342(2,13),8(3,9)    TS2=14           FIELD2
        00019C   960F D157         OI    343,X'0F'           TS2=15
        0001A0   D501 D14E D156    CLC   334(2,13),342(13)   TS2=6            TS2=14
        0001A6   47D0 B0E0         BC    13,224(0,11)        GN=3(0001DC)
```

(c)

```
000009  IF
        00018C   F212 D14E 9000    PACK  334(2,13),0(3,9)    TS2=6            FIELD1
        000192   F212 D156 9008    PACK  342(2,13),8(3,9)    TS2=14           FIELD2
        000198   F911 D14E D156    CP    334(2,13),342(13)   TS2=6            TS2=14
        00019E   47D0 B0D0         BC    13,208(0,11)        GN=3(0001CC)
```

(d)

Figure 13.11 COBOL II code and its associated Procedure Map when display numeric fields are compared. Object code produced is dependent upon the NUMPROC option chosen. (a) Code; (b) Procedure Map when compiled with NUMPROC(PFD); (c) Procedure Map when compiled with NUMPROC(NOPFD); (d) Procedure Map when compiled with NUMPROC(MIG).

STORAGE SECTION. This code enables COBOL II to initialize a dynamic WORKING-STORAGE area obtained for programs compiled with the RENT option. The code also is executed to reinitialize data on each entry to programs defined with the INITIAL attribute (see Sec. 8.3). In the first two instructions in Fig. 13.13, FIELD1 and a FILLER field are initialized. Some of the COBOL II special registers (e.g., SORT-CORE-SIZE and TALLY) are also initialized. The data initialization code is located after the program initialization code (see Sec.

```
000001 IDENTIFICATION DIVISION.
000002 PROGRAM-ID. BINARY1.
000003 DATA DIVISION.
000004 WORKING-STORAGE SECTION.
000005 01  FIELD1              PIC S9(9) COMP.
000006
000007 PROCEDURE DIVISION.
000008     ADD 1 TO FIELD1.
```

(a)

```
8    ADD    0002EC  48 30 C 020           LH    3,020(0,12)           LIT+0
            0002F0  5A 30 6 000           A     3,000(0,6)            DNM=1-32
            0002F4  50 30 6 000           ST    3,000(0,6)            DNM=1-32
```

(b)

```
8    ADD    0002F4  48 30 C 020           LH    3,020(0,12)           LIT+0
            0002F8  5A 30 6 000           A     3,000(0,6)            DNM=1-32
            0002FC  4E 30 D 208           CVD   3,208(0,13)           TS=01
            000300  D7 02 D 208 D 208     XC    208(3,13),208(13)     TS=01    TS=01
            000306  4F 30 D 208           CVB   3,208(0,13)           TS=01
            00030A  50 30 6 000           ST    3,000(0,6)            DNM=1-32
```

(c)

```
000008 ADD
    00017C  4820 A006           LH    2,6(0,10)            PGMLIT AT +2
    000180  8E20 0020           SRDA  2,32(0)
    000184  5840 9000           L     4,0(0,9)             FIELD1
    000188  8E40 0020           SRDA  4,32(0)
    00018C  1A42                AR    4,2
    00018E  1E53                ALR   5,3
    000190  58B0 C00C           L     11,12(0,12)          PBL=1
    000194  47C0 B0A0           BC    12,160(0,11)         GN=8(00019C)
    000198  5A40 C004           A     4,4(0,12)            SYSLIT AT +4
    00019C              GN=8    EQU   *
    00019C  5D40 C000           D     4,0(0,12)            SYSLIT AT +0
    0001A0  5040 9000           ST    4,0(0,9)             FIELD1
```

(d)

Figure 13.12 Code produced for a single ADD statement in a COBOL
program that was compiled with the various TRUNC options under VS
COBOL and COBOL II. (a) COBOL program; (b) compiled with VS
COBOL NOTRUNC; (c) compiled with VS COBOL TRUNC; (d) compiled
with COBOL II TRUNC(STD); (e) compiled with COBOL II
TRUNC(OPT); (f) compiled with COBOL II TRUNC(BIN).

5.3.2) that begins at displacement zero and before the beginning of the
PROCEDURE DIVISION object code.

This data initialization code includes the initialization of tables that
contain VALUE clauses, the new feature added in Release 3. The compiler generates what is ·equivalent to an INITIALIZE statement for

```
000008  ADD
   000178  4820 A006              LH    2,6(0,10)        PGMLIT AT +2
   00017C  8E20 0020              SRDA  2,32(0)
   000180  5840 9000              L     4,0(0,9)         FIELD1
   000184  8E40 0020              SRDA  4,32(0)
   000188  1A42                   AR    4,2
   00018A  1E53                   ALR   5,3
   00018C  58B0 C008              L     11,8(0,12)       PBL-1
   000190  47C0 B0A0              BC    12,160(0,11)     GN=8(000198)
   000194  5A40 C000              A     4,0(0,12)        SYSLIT AT +0
   000198           GN=8          EQU   *
   000198  5050 9000              ST    5,0(0,9)         FIELD1

                            (e)


000008  ADD
   000184  5820 9000              L     2,0(0,9)         FIELD1
   000188  4E20 D168              CVD   2,360(0,13)      TS2=0
   00018C  FA50 D16A A01C         AP    362(6,13),28(1,10)   TS2=2      PGMLIT AT +8
   000192  F895 D186 D16A         ZAP   390(10,13),362(6,13) TS2=30     TS2=2
   000198  D202 D178 C008         MVC   376(3,13),8(12)      TS2=16     SYSLIT AT +8
   00019E  D204 D17B D18B         MVC   379(5,13),395(13)    TS2=19     TS2=35
   0001A4  4F20 D178              CVB   2,376(0,13)          TS2=16
   0001A8  F144 D17B D186         MVO   379(5,13),390(5,13)  TS2=19     TS2=30
   0001AE  4F50 D178              CVB   5,376(0,13)          TS2=16
   0001B2  5C40 C004              M     4,4(0,12)            SYSLIT AT +4
   0001B6  1E52                   ALR   5,2
   0001B8  58B0 C010              L     11,16(0,12)          PBL-1
   0001BC  47C0 B0C0              BC    12,192(0,11)         GN=8(0001C4)
   0001C0  5A40 C000              A     4,0(0,12)            SYSLIT AT +0
   0001C4           GN=8          EQU   *
   0001C4  1222                   LTR   2,2
   0001C6  47B0 B0CA              BC    11,202(0,11)         GN=9(0001CE)
   0001CA  5B40 C000              S     4,0(0,12)            SYSLIT AT +0
   0001CE           GN=9          EQU   *
   0001CE  5050 9000              ST    5,0(0,9)             FIELD1

                            (f)
```

Figure 13.12   *(Continued)*

each WORKING-STORAGE field with a VALUE clause, except that FILLER data items are initialized in the initialization code but would not be if an INITIALIZE statement was executed.

13.4   READING A CONDENSED LISTING

A Condensed Listing is usually less than one-tenth the size of a Procedure Map. As seen in Fig. 13.14, a Condensed Listing lists the line number of each line that contains a verb, the name of the verb, and the beginning hexadecimal displacement of the object code for the verb (HEXLOC). The object code itself is not shown. After an ABEND is analyzed and the displacement of the ABENDing instruction from the program beginning is known, the Condensed Listing enables a

```
00012C                    GN=2   EQU  *
00012C   D209 9000 A03E    MVC   0(10,9),62(10)     FIELD1         PGMLIT AT +58
000132   D207 9010 A048    MVC   16(8,9),72(10)     *FILLER        PGMLIT AT +68
000138   5820 D120         L     2,288(0,13)        BL=1
00013C   D203 2000 A008    MVC   0(4,2),8(10)       SORT-CORE-SIZE PGMLIT AT +4
000142   D203 2008 A008    MVC   8(4,2),8(10)       SORT-FILE-SIZE PGMLIT AT +4
000148   D203 2010 A008    MVC   16(4,2),8(10)      SORT-MODE-SIZE PGMLIT AT +4
00014E   D207 2018 A01C    MVC   24(8,2),28(10)     SORT-MESSAGE   PGMLIT AT +24
000154   D203 2020 A008    MVC   32(4,2),8(10)      TALLY          PGMLIT AT +4
00015A   920E 2028         MVI   40(2),X'0E'        SHIFT-OUT
00015E   920F 2030         MVI   48(2),X'0F'        SHIFT-IN
000162   5830 D12C         L     3,300(0,13)        VN=1
000166   07F3              BCR   15,3
```

Figure 13.13   Code that initializes each WORKING-STORAGE field that contains a VALUE clause is produced in Release 3 programs.

LINE #	HEXLOC	VERB	LINE #	HEXLOC	VERB	LINE #	HEXLOC	VERB
000513	002150	DISPLAY	000514	002162	PERFORM	000515	00217A	CALL
000516	0021A0	CALL	000517	0021C2	MOVE	000518	0021E8	CALL
000519	00220E	DISPLAY	000520	002220	STOP	000527	00222A	ACCEPT
000528	00223E	ACCEPT	000529	00224E	PERFORM	000530	00225E	MOVE
000531	002274	MOVE	000532	002286	ADD	000586	002328	USE
000589	002328	MOVE	000590	00232E	MOVE	000591	00233A	MOVE
000592	002344	CALL	000595	00237A	USE	000597	00237A	MOVE
000598	002384	SUBTRACT	000599	002390	MOVE	000600	00239A	CALL
000614	002416	MOVE	000615	00241C	INITIALIZE	000616	002426	OPEN
000618	002448	OPEN	000620	00246C	READ	000622	0024BC	MOVE
000624	0024C4	ADD	000625	0024D0	PERFORM	000626	0024DC	CALL
000627	0024FA	IF	000628	002506	CALL	000629	002528	CALL
000631	00254E	MOVE	000632	002552	READ	000634	0025A2	MOVE
000636	0025AA	ADD	000641	0025BE	DISPLAY	000644	0025D0	CLOSE
000646	0025EA	EXIT						

Figure 13.14   A Condensed Listing produced from the OFFSET compiler option.

programmer to find the line of source code where the ABEND occurred. For example, if the program whose Condensed Listing is shown in Fig. 13.14 ABENDed at a hexadecimal displacement of 21C8, the ABEND occurred during execution of the MOVE statement on line 000517. This is often enough information to solve most dumps.

Chapter 14

The COBOL Task
Global Table (TGT)

Every COBOL II program contains a Task Global Table (TGT) which can be considered a control block or a data area. It is unfortunate that in our "fourth-generation" society, "control block" and "data area" are terms that a COBOL programmer is not expected to know. The explanation of the TGT in the IBM manuals does not encourage the reader to explore further. In VS COBOL, other than a complete field by field description in the appendix of the *IBM OS/VS COBOL Compiler and Library Programmer's Guide,* the manual describes the TGT as "consisting of switches, addresses, and work areas whose information changes during execution of the program" and "being used to record and save information needed during execution of the object program."

IBM has changed its documentation of the TGT in COBOL II. In the *VS COBOL II Application Programming: Debugging* manual, it now explains how to find the TGT and the use of a few of its fields. Unfortunately, the manual does not have a field by field description. A complete listing of these fields (without descriptions) is now located in the *VS COBOL II Diagnosis Reference* manual. This manual is one in the "LY" series of IBM manuals (the same series as the program logic manuals), usually unavailable to applications programmers.

14.1 WHY UNDERSTANDING THE TGT IS IMPORTANT

Without some sort of education or experience to show otherwise, the description in the manuals may lead one to believe that the TGT is not an area worth studying. While some fields in the TGT are of no use to an applications programmer, others are of considerable importance. The Task Global Table contains a wealth of information about a program, and the information is available nowhere else. Knowledge of this information aids a programmer in other areas of COBOL understanding, such as in reading a Procedure Map (described in Sec. 13.3).

Consider the processing needs of a major bank. If their overnight processing ABENDs and fails to transfer funds to the government, over a million dollars in interest can be lost. A bank does not want to play debugging roulette when one of its programs is not working at 3 A.M. Even problems of a much smaller magnitude are critical to companies. If a problem occurs during a production job that must run, you often do not have enough time in the day, or computer processing time, to guess at solutions and hope they work. Remember that a dump may occur after many hours of CPU processing or in a program that runs just before daybreak. Knowledge and understanding of COBOL, including use of the TGT, is sometimes the only chance to resolve the problem in the necessary time frame.

Although the TGT is not an area used by a programmer on a daily basis, it often contains the key, the vital information, in debugging. Its proper use can make the difference between solving and not solving a problem. Understanding of the TGT and its intricacies can literally save a programmer many weeks of time during his or her programming career. Take for instance the problem of finding the value of an index at the time that a COBOL program ABENDs. The index values (other than those explicitly defined as data fields in a program) only exist in the TGT. From my personal experience, most COBOL programmers do not know how to find an index in a dump. After a dump occurs, a programmer will often rerun a program with a DISPLAY of any index that is in question. This method of debugging will take many times as long as simply analyzing a dump to find the value of the indexes.

It is absurd that a programmer will make use of a subscript value in a dump simply because it is located by using the Data Division Map of a COBOL program but not make use of index value because it is found in a "less convenient" place, the TGT. With the proper understanding, the value of an index in a dump can be located in about the same time it takes to locate the value of any other data item. Other fields in the TGT can be located just as easily.

14.2   FORMAT OF THE TGT

The TGT is composed of two parts. At the beginning is a fixed-length portion which contains a number of fields that always appears in every program (such as the register save area). Following this is a variable length portion containing fields of varying lengths. The variable fields exist or not depending upon specific program requirements determined by the COBOL II compiler for each program.

In COBOL II, fields in the variable portion of the TGT that are not used are not shown in the listing. (This is clearer than the listing of the TGT in VS COBOL where all fields in the variable portion are shown even if they did not exist in the specific program.)

14.3   THE TGT IN A COMPILATION LISTING

The TGT is included in a VS COBOL listing whenever a program is compiled with the PMAP, CLIST, or DMAP options. COBOL II produces a listing of the TGT when the LIST or OFFSET options are used. The displacement of each field from the beginning of the TGT (TGTLOC) is shown directly to the left of the field in the TGT listing.

Figure 14.1 shows a TGT from a COBOL II program compiled with the RENT option, and a TGT from a COBOL II program compiled with the NORENT option. You may want to refer to them throughout the rest of the chapter. The TGT from the compilation with the NORENT option in Fig. 14.1 is considerably larger than the TGT from the RENT compilation. This has nothing to do with the RENT/NORENT compiler options. The size difference is simply because one TGT is from a more complex program that required more information.

14.4   HOW THE RENT AND NORENT
OPTIONS AFFECT THE TGT

In COBOL II the TGT appears near the end of a compilation listing. When the NORENT option (RENT and NORENT are discussed in Sec. 4.4) is used in a compilation, the TGT in use by the program will physically exist as part of the load module, located after the program code and before WORKING-STORAGE. (The order of the various parts of a COBOL program have been rearranged in COBOL II. In a VS COBOL load module the TGT was located after WORKING-STORAGE but before the program code.) The hexadecimal displacement of each field from the beginning of the program (PGMLOC) as well as the relative hexadecimal displacement from the beginning of the TGT (TGTLOC) is shown to the left of each field.

When the RENT option is used to compile a COBOL II program (making a program reentrant so that it can be shared by many users, a requirement for COBOL II programs run under CICS), the TGT (as well as the WORKING-STORAGE) exists in a GETMAINed area (i.e., they are not physically contiguous with the program code in memory). The displacement of each field relative to the beginning of the TGT is

```
*** TGT MEMORY MAP ***
TGTLOC

000000   72 BYTE SAVE AREA
000048   TGT IDENTIFIER
000050   TGT LEVEL INDICATOR
000051   RESERVED - 3 SINGLE BYTE FIELDS
000054   32 BIT SWITCH
000058   POINTER TO RUNCOM
00005C   POINTER TO COBVEC
000060   POINTER TO PROGRAM DYNAMIC BLOCK TABLE
000064   NUMBER OF FCB'S
000068   WORKING STORAGE LENGTH
00006C   POINTER TO PREVIOUS TGT IN TGT CHAIN
000070   ADDRESS OF IGZESMG WORK AREA
000074   ADDRESS OF 1ST GETMAIN BLOCK (SPACE MGR)
000078   FULLWORD RETURN CODE
00007A   RETURN CODE SPECIAL REGISTER
00007C   SORT-RETURN SPECIAL REGISTER
00007E   MERGE FILE NUMBER
000080   RESERVED - 4 HALF WORD FIELDS
000088   PROGRAM MASK OF CALLER OF THIS PROGRAM
000089   PROGRAM MASK USED BY THIS PROGRAM
00008A   RESERVED - 2 SINGLE BYTE FIELDS
00008C   NUMBER OF SECONDARY FCB CELLS
000090   LENGTH OF THE VN(VNI) VECTOR
000094   ADDRESS OF IGZEBST TERMINATION ROUTINE
000098   DDNAME FOR DISPLAY OUTPUT
0000A0   SORT-CONTROL SPECIAL REGISTER
0000A8   POINTER TO COM-REG SPECIAL REGISTER
0000AC   CALC ROUTINE REGISTER SAVE AREA
0000E0   ALTERNATE COLLATING SEQUENCE TABLE PTR.
0000E4   ADDRESS OF SORT G.N. ADDRESS BLOCK
0000E8   ADDRESS OF IGZCLNK DYNAMIC WORK AREA
0000EC   CURRENT INTERNAL PROGRAM NUMBER
0000F0   POINTER TO 1ST IPCB
0000F4   RESERVED
0000F8   POINTER TO ABEND INFORMATION TABLE
0000FC   POINTER TO FDMP/TEST FIELDS IN THE TGT
000100   ADDRESS OF START OF COBOL PROGRAM
000104   POINTER TO VN'S IN CGT
000108   POINTER TO VN'S IN TGT
00010C   POINTER TO FIRST PBL IN THE PGT
000110   POINTER TO FIRST FCB CELL
000114   WORKING STORAGE ADDRESS
000118   POINTER TO FIRST SECONDARY FCB CELL

*** VARIABLE PORTION OF TGT ***

00011C   BASE LOCATORS FOR SPECIAL REGISTERS
000124   BASE LOCATORS FOR WORKING-STORAGE
000128   BASE LOCATORS FOR LINKAGE-SECTION
00012C   VARIABLE NAME (VN) CELLS
000130   PERFORM SAVE CELLS
000134   INTERNAL PROGRAM CONTROL BLOCKS
000148   TEMPORARY STORAGE-1
000158   TEMPORARY STORAGE-2

TGT       WILL BE ALLOCATED FOR 000001A8 BYTES
WRK-STOR  WILL BE ALLOCATED FOR 0000005A BYTES
SPEC-REG  WILL BE ALLOCATED FOR 00000031 BYTES
```

(a)

Figure 14.1 Example TGTs showing the differences based upon source code and compiler options. TGT from a COBOL program compiled with the RENT option (*a*) and the NORENT option (*b*).

```
            *** TGT MEMORY MAP ***
PGMLOC   TGTLOC

0072D8   000000   72 BYTE SAVE AREA
007320   000048   TGT IDENTIFIER
007328   000050   TGT LEVEL INDICATOR
007329   000051   RESERVED - 3 SINGLE BYTE FIELDS
00732C   000054   32 BIT SWITCH
007330   000058   POINTER TO RUNCOM
007334   00005C   POINTER TO COBVEC
007338   000060   POINTER TO PROGRAM DYNAMIC BLOCK TABLE
00733C   000064   NUMBER OF FCB'S
007340   000068   WORKING STORAGE LENGTH
007344   00006C   POINTER TO PREVIOUS TGT IN TGT CHAIN
007348   000070   ADDRESS OF IGZESMG WORK AREA
00734C   000074   ADDRESS OF 1ST GETMAIN BLOCK (SPACE MGR)
007350   000078   FULLWORD RETURN CODE
007352   00007A   RETURN CODE SPECIAL REGISTER
007354   00007C   SORT-RETURN SPECIAL REGISTER
007356   00007E   MERGE FILE NUMBER
007358   000080   RESERVED - 4 HALF WORD FIELDS
007360   000088   PROGRAM MASK OF CALLER OF THIS PROGRAM
007361   000089   PROGRAM MASK USED BY THIS PROGRAM
007362   00008A   RESERVED - 2 SINGLE BYTE FIELDS
007364   00008C   NUMBER OF SECONDARY FCB CELLS
007368   000090   LENGTH OF THE VN(VNI) VECTOR
00736C   000094   ADDRESS OF IGZEBST TERMINATION ROUTINE
007370   000098   DDNAME FOR DISPLAY OUTPUT
007378   0000A0   SORT-CONTROL SPECIAL REGISTER
007380   0000A8   POINTER TO COM-REG SPECIAL REGISTER
007384   0000AC   CALC ROUTINE REGISTER SAVE AREA
0073B8   0000E0   ALTERNATE COLLATING SEQUENCE TABLE PTR.
0073BC   0000E4   ADDRESS OF SORT G.N. ADDRESS BLOCK
0073C0   0000E8   ADDRESS OF IGZCLNK DYNAMIC WORK AREA
0073C4   0000EC   CURRENT INTERNAL PROGRAM NUMBER
0073C8   0000F0   POINTER TO 1ST IPCB
0073CC   0000F4   RESERVED
0073D0   0000F8   POINTER TO ABEND INFORMATION TABLE
0073D4   0000FC   POINTER TO FDMP/TEST FIELDS IN THE TGT
0073D8   000100   ADDRESS OF START OF COBOL PROGRAM
0073DC   000104   POINTER TO VN'S IN CGT
0073E0   000108   POINTER TO VN'S IN TGT
0073E4   00010C   POINTER TO FIRST PBL IN THE PGT
0073E8   000110   POINTER TO FIRST FCB CELL
0073EC   000114   WORKING STORAGE ADDRESS
0073F0   000118   POINTER TO FIRST SECONDARY FCB CELL


*** VARIABLE PORTION OF TGT ***

0073F4   00011C   BACKSTORE CELL FOR SYMBOLIC REGISTERS
00743C   000164   BASE LOCATORS FOR SPECIAL REGISTERS
007444   00016C   BASE LOCATORS FOR WORKING-STORAGE
007490   0001B8   BASE LOCATORS FOR LINKAGE-SECTION
0074BC   0001E4   BASE LOCATORS FOR FILES
```

Figure 14.1 *(Continued)*

```
0074D0   0001F8   BASE LOCATORS FOR VARIABLY LOCATED DATA
0074D4   0001FC   BASE LOCATORS FOR EXTERNAL DATA
0074D8   000200   CLLE ADDR. CELLS FOR CALL LIT. SUB-PGMS.
0074DC   000204   VARIABLE NAME (VN) CELLS
0075CC   0002F4   INDEX CELLS
0075D8   000300   PERFORM SAVE CELLS
0077D0   0004F8   VARIABLE LENGTH CELLS
0077EC   000514   ODO SAVE CELLS
007804   00052C   FCB CELLS
007818   000540   LOCAL FCB CELLS FOR EXTERNAL FILES
007824   00054C   INTERNAL PROGRAM CONTROL BLOCKS
0078E4   00060C   AREA FOR EVALUATE BOOLEAN VALUES
0078E7   00060F   AREA FOR EVALUATE WHEN VALUES
0078F0   000618   TEMPORARY STORAGE-1
007920   000648   TEMPORARY STORAGE-2
```

```
TGT        LOCATED AT 0072D8 FOR 00000798 BYTES
DCB00001   LOCATED AT 007A70 FOR 00000060 BYTES
FCB00001   LOCATED AT 007AD0 FOR 00000100 BYTES
DCB00002   LOCATED AT 007BD0 FOR 00000060 BYTES
FCB00002   LOCATED AT 007C30 FOR 00000100 BYTES
DCB00003   LOCATED AT 007D30 FOR 00000060 BYTES
FCB00003   LOCATED AT 007D90 FOR 00000100 BYTES
DCB00004   LOCATED AT 007E90 FOR 00000060 BYTES
FCB00004   LOCATED AT 007EF0 FOR 00000100 BYTES
DCB00005   LOCATED AT 007FF0 FOR 00000060 BYTES
FCB00005   LOCATED AT 008050 FOR 00000100 BYTES
GDT00001   LOCATED AT 008150 FOR 00000050 BYTES
GDT00002   LOCATED AT 0081A0 FOR 00000050 BYTES
FSD00002   LOCATED AT 0081F0 FOR 00000030 BYTES
GDT00003   LOCATED AT 008220 FOR 00000050 BYTES
FSD00003   LOCATED AT 008270 FOR 00000030 BYTES
GDT00004   LOCATED AT 0082A0 FOR 00000050 BYTES
WRK-STOR   LOCATED AT 0082F0 FOR 00012374 BYTES
SPEC-REG   LOCATED AT 01A668 FOR 00000031 BYTES
```

(b)

Figure 14.1   (*Continued*)

shown before each field in the listing (the displacement relative to the
program beginning cannot be shown since the TGT is not located ad-
jacent to the program code).

14.5   LOCATING THE TGT

Once the physical beginning address of a COBOL II program compiled
with the NORENT option is located in a dump, the address is added to
the displacement of any specific field in the TGT (relative to the beginning of the program—PGMLOC column in listing) to locate the
field. For example, if you wished to locate the INDEX CELLS in the
TGT (for the program compiled with the NORENT option) in Fig.
14.1, you would add hexadecimal '75CC' to the address at which the
program physically begins in memory.

The TGT will be located in storage outside the load module when the RENT option is used to compile a COBOL II program. You therefore have to use the registers to find it. When a COBOL II program is executing, register 13 normally points to the TGT. If a COBOL II run-time library routine is running at the time of an ABEND, register 9 usually points to the TGT. When you think you have located a TGT, you can verify this fact since the TGT always starts with a hexadecimal '00108001' and contains the alphabetic constant C2TGT+48 at a hexadecimal offset of '48'. It is even easier to find fields in the TGT when an installation has COBOL II debugging tools that format the TGT whenever a dump is produced.

14.6   SPECIFIC FIELDS IN THE TGT

The following is a discussion of the major fields that can be found in the TGT.

14.6.1   INDEX CELLS

Each implicitly defined index in a COBOL program (e.g., INDEXED BY INDEX1) takes up a fullword (4 bytes) in the INDEX CELLS. COBOL stores an index cell in binary as if it were defined as a PIC S9(9) COMP in the program. Indexes are stored as displacements into the table upon which they function. For a one-dimensional table, to determine which occurrence number in the table an index is pointing to at the time of an ABEND, divide the value of the INDEX CELL by the length of the table entry and add 1. As an example, suppose that a table contained entries of 10 bytes each. If the INDEX CELL used for the table contained a hexadecimal value of 00000032 (decimal 50), the index would be pointing to the sixth entry in the table (50 / 10 + 1).

The index cells appear in the same order that indexes are defined in the program; the first fullword is for the first implicit index defined, the second fullword is for the second implicit index defined, etc. Explicitly defined indexes (e.g., a WORKING-STORAGE field defined as '01 INDEX1 USAGE IS INDEX.') are located in WORKING-STORAGE and therefore do not exist in the TGT.

The indexes in a program are numbered in the Data Division Map. For each field in the Data Division Map that has a usage of INDEX-NAME, the BASE column of the Data Division Map lists each index sequentially as IDX=0001, IDX=0002, etc. You no longer have to count the index cells yourself as was required in VS COBOL (VS COBOL did not number the indexes). The displacement into the index cells where the index value begins can be calculated by subtracting 1 from the sequential index number and multiplying by 4.

14.6.2 BASE LOCATORS

Base Locator cells exist for WORKING-STORAGE, files, special registers, variably located data, external data, and linkage (the Base Locators for linkage will be discussed in the next section). This is in contrast to VS COBOL where there were only Base Locator cells for linkage, WORKING-STORAGE, and files, and there was no distinction made in the TGT between the BL cells for files and the BL cells for WORKING-STORAGE. Each Base Locator cell is a fullword that contains an address. Base Locator cells for files are indicated in the Data Division Map as BLF; WORKING-STORAGE cells, as BLW; special register cells, as BLS; variable located data cells, as BLV; and external data cells, as BLX. The pointers to records (BLF) appear first. Following them is one BLW cell for each 4096 bytes of WORKING-STORAGE that the program contains.

To find any data field at the time of an ABEND, locate the field in question in the Data Division Map and find its Base Locator cell listed next to it. Find the appropriate Base Locator cell in the TGT (remembering that each Base Locator cell takes up 4 bytes). Add its value to the displacement of the field listed in the Data Division Map.

It is a common misconception that the registers at the time of the ABEND always point to the DATA DIVISION field or fields that caused the problem. While the registers often point to the DATA DIVISION fields causing the ABEND (but not always since fields are sometimes moved into work areas—see TEMPORARY STORAGE in Sec. 14.6.4), they certainly do not always point to all the various fields in the WORKING-STORAGE and FILE sections that a programmer might have to examine. The Base Locator cells can be used to find any data field in question.

14.6.3 BASE LOCATORS FOR LINKAGE SECTION

The BLL cells are similar to the other Base Locator cells. Each is a fullword address. The major difference is that while the other Base Locator cells refer to WORKING-STORAGE, file areas, external data, and special registers, BLL cells refer to areas in the LINKAGE SECTION. The first BLL cell is reserved for COBOL II's internal use (in VS COBOL the first two are reserved for internal use). The first BLL cell used in the program will therefore be referred to as

BLL=0001 (relative to zero) in the Data Division Map. In VS COBOL Command Level CICS, BLL 3 points to the EIB, BLL 4 to the COMMAREA, and BLL 5 points to itself. CICS command level under COBOL II uses BLL=0001 (the second BLL cell) to point to the EIB, BLL=0002 to point to the COMMAREA, and has no self-pointing BLL cell.

Using BLL cells to locate LINKAGE SECTION fields is done in the same manner as using the other Base Locator cells. The appropriate BLL cell is located in the TGT and its value is added to the displacement of a field you want to find. A BLL cell with a value of zero indicates a parameter that had not been passed to the program (in batch) or a cell that had not been initialized (in CICS). When fields referred to in a program use a BLL cell that has a value of zero, an 0C4 program exception will likely occur. In VS COBOL CICS, defining and setting BLL cells was the responsibility of the programmer, and improper values in the BLL cells frequently caused storage violations and 0C4s. Defining BLL cells is no longer the responsibility of the programmer in COBOL II CICS. They are set either by using the SET...TO ADDRESS OF... COBOL II statement or the SET option of CICS commands.

14.6.4   TEMPORARY STORAGE Fields

There are four temporary storage areas used by COBOL II as internal work areas to hold and manipulate data (TEMPORARY STORAGE-1, TEMPORARY STORAGE-2, TEMPORARY STORAGE-3, TEMPORARY STORAGE-4). Each area is variable in size (or nonexistent) depending upon the specific data definitions and COBOL II verbs used in a program. TEMPORARY STORAGE-2 is used for arithmetic calculations (these calculations were done in TEMP STORAGE and/or TEMP STORAGE-2 in VS COBOL). Some examples of TEMPORARY STORAGE-2 use are when two fields with different numbers of decimal places are added together, when calculations are done with fields that have different usage modes (COMP and COMP-3), or when calculations are done using display numeric fields.

TEMPORARY STORAGE-2 is also used to hold the parameters that are passed in a CALL BY CONTENT statement. In VS COBOL, if a called program incorrectly defined a data parameter and made the length of the parameter too large, the section of the calling program's WORKING-STORAGE after the parameter could have been overlaid. This would have produced a difficult problem to debug. When a similar situation occurs using a CALL BY CONTENT, a part of the TGT rather than WORKING-STORAGE will be overlaid. This may yield more obscure ABENDs than the similar situation in a VS COBOL program. However, data passed BY CONTENT is normally not modified.

TEMPORARY STORAGE-1 is used for SEARCH ALL processing. TEMPORARY STORAGE-3 is now used to hold the parameter addresses when a CALL is executed. The parameter addresses had been placed in the VS COBOL TGT PARAM CELLS, which do not exist in COBOL II.

When a dump occurs, the failing instruction may have been using values in temporary storage. For instance, if fields defined as display numeric are added together, and one is not numeric, the 0C7 program exception that occurs will not point to the nonnumeric field in the DATA DIVISION. The fields will have been PACKed into temporary storage (PACK never causes a decimal data exception). A temporary storage field will be in use at the time that the fields are added together and the ABEND occurs.

Knowledge of the way temporary storage fields are used enables a programmer to more easily follow a Procedure Map and resolve the problems causing an ABEND. In the Procedure Map temporary storage fields are indicated as TS1=x, TS2=x, TS3=x, and TS4=x, where x is the displacement (relative to 0) into the temporary storage area.

14.6.5   VARIABLE LENGTH CELLS

Fields in the DATA DIVISION that are defined with the OCCURS DEPENDING ON clause are variable in length. At the time of an ABEND it may be of value to determine the current length of one of these fields. Each Variable Length cell is a fullword and contains the length (not the number of occurrences) of one variable length field in a program (a field may be up to 16MB). When Variable Length cells are used in a Procedure Map, they are listed as VLC=x, where x is the cell number (relative to 1).

14.6.6   72 BYTE SAVE AREA

Although COBOL's save area can often be found elsewhere in a dump, and COBOL programmers normally are not concerned with it, it should be noted that the SAVE AREA is the first field in the TGT. The TGT was the first field after WORKING-STORAGE in VS COBOL. When a VS COBOL program had invalid subscripts that caused a move to a data area to exceed the WORKING-STORAGE boundary, the SAVE AREA was the first field to be overlaid. The TGT no longer

directly follows WORKING-STORAGE in COBOL II and the chance of
the Save Area being overlaid is very slight.

14.6.7 FCB CELLS

In COBOL II, a File Control Block (FCB) and a File Information Block
(FIB) exist for each VSAM and non-VSAM file (these control blocks do
not exist for files used in CICS or when databases such as DB2 or
IDMS are used). In the listing of the fixed portion of the TGT you can
find the NUMBER OF FCB'S (at hexadecimal displacement '733C' in
the TGT from a NORENT compilation in Fig. 14.1) and the POINTER
TO FIRST FCB CELL (at displacement '73E8'). The number of FCBs
is self-explanatory and the pointer to the first FCB cell indirectly
points to the FCBs in use by the program; it points to a list of 4-byte
addresses, one address pointing to each FCB. Each FCB begins with
the constant "FCB" and is followed by 2 bytes (alphanumeric) indicating
the number of the FCB.

Each FIB begins with the constant "FIB". At a displacement of 6 bytes
it contains the DDNAME of the file to which it pertains. The address
of the FIB is in its associated FCB at a hexadecimal displacement of
'A4'.

The FCB has extremely valuable information concerning VSAM errors in a COBOL program. At hexadecimal displacement 'B3' is the
file status code from the last I/O whether or not a program requested
the file status with a FILE STATUS clause in the SELECT. However,
the status code in the FCB is a 1-byte hexadecimal field, not in the
same format but containing the same value as the 2-byte alphanumeric file status used in a COBOL II program. Additional VSAM error
information, other than the standard file status code, was only available in the FCB under VS COBOL. In COBOL II it is now available in
the extended VSAM feedback area in the file status. In addition to the
2-byte file status that VS COBOL used, an additional 6-byte VSAM
status is available (see Sec. 2.1). Whether or not the extended VSAM
status information was requested in a program, it can be found in the
FCB. At displacements 'B5', 'B6', and 'B7' the binary values of the
VSAM return code, function code, and feedback code, respectively, can
be found. (The binary values are the same as those returned to the
program in the extended VSAM feedback status codes. Since all
VSAM status codes are less than 255, they can be represented in only
1 byte. COBOL, however, requires at least 2 bytes to represent a binary
field.)

The specific information about a particular VSAM I/O request is
contained in the VSAM Request Parameter List (RPL). In the rare

case that all the detailed information of the VSAM RPL is needed, the FCB (at hexadecimal displacement 'A8') points to a work area called GMAREA. GMAREA contains the address of two RPLs (at displacements '1A' and '1E'). The first RPL is used for read/write access while the second RPL is used for read/only access.

14.7   DCB AND FCB LOCATIONS LISTED AFTER THE TGT

Directly after the TGT in a COBOL II listing is the storage map of I/O control blocks and of WORKING-STORAGE (in the TGT from a NORENT compilation in Fig. 14.1, the map begins after TEMPORARY STORAGE-2 located at hexadecimal displacement '7920'). It lists displacements from the program beginning and lengths of various areas including all DCBs, FCBs, WORKING-STORAGE, and special registers. [In VS COBOL the Data Control Block (DCB) addresses were located through the Program Global Table (PGT), another control block like the TGT.] The displacements of these areas are not listed if the program is compiled with the RENT option. In any case the DCB (for non-VSAM files) or the Access Method Control Block (ACB—for VSAM files) can be located by using its address located at hexadecimal displacement '78' in the FCB. When information relating to a non-VSAM file is required, the DCB contains important information such as the record format, record length, block size, and number of buffers. It can also be used to determine whether the file is open and to locate the address of the current record. For VSAM files, the information that can be found in the ACB includes the number of buffers and the type of processing allowed for the file (e.g., sequential or keyed).

The current record can also be found using the BLF cells. Additionally, the address of the current record for either VSAM or non-VSAM files also can be found in the FCB at a hexadecimal displacement of 'AC'. You often do not have to worry about finding the current record since many debugging products exist that will display the current record and often the prior record as well. One advantage to finding the record in the buffer is that the buffer will often contain other records; you will be able to see a number of records previously read or written.

Within the control blocks at the end of the listing you may also notice FSD (File Specific Declarative table) and GDT (Generic Declarative Table) entries based upon the number of nested programs. These control blocks are not of practical value for the debugging needs of COBOL II applications programmers.

Chapter 15

Understanding ABENDs and Program Exceptions

15.1 COMPARISON OF ABENDS AND PROGRAM EXCEPTIONS

Most COBOL programmers categorize program exceptions (program interrupts, e.g., an 0C7) under the general topic of ABENDs. Although the lack of differentiation between a program exception and an ABEND is acceptable to many programmers, there is a big difference between the two. Program exceptions are detected by hardware, while ABEND conditions are detected by software, usually the operating system. To further confuse the issue, some programmers do not understand the differences between processes handled by the hardware and processes handled by the operating system.

When a program attempts to add two packed decimal numbers together on IBM 370 hardware, regardless of the programming language used, it will execute an Add Packed (AP) instruction. If one of the fields does not contain a valid packed decimal number, the hardware generates a program interrupt. This is an exception condition and is distinct from an error such as attempting to open a nonexistent file. An OPEN verb in COBOL II generates a Supervisor Call (SVC) instruction. This passes control to the operating system (MVS, VSE, etc.). If the operating system software detects a problem while attempting to open the file, it may decide to issue an ABEND instruction. This is a true software-generated ABEND.

The basic difference between an ABEND and a program exception is that while an ABEND is always done on purpose by the program issuing it (either the operating system or the user program), a program exception will occur unexpectedly by a program (except in rare cases when a program interrupt is used in place of an ABEND or for special reasons in very sophisticated code).

15.2 SYSTEM AND USER ABENDS

To more finely define ABENDs, the system breaks them into two different types, System ABENDs and User ABENDs. System ABENDs occur when the operating system issues an ABEND macro with the SYSTEM parameter; User ABENDs occur when a user program issues the ABEND macro with the USER parameter. Any COBOL II program can request a User ABEND by calling run-time library routine ILBOABN0 (see Sec. 9.5). The number assigned to a User ABEND must be less than 4096 and is specified in the ABENDing program. ABENDs that occur in programs written by software vendors are not operating system ABENDs. For instance if SyncSort or IDMS software decides to issue an ABEND, the ABEND will be a user ABEND. Obviously, if SyncSort or IDMS requests a service from the operating system (such as to open a file) and the request fails, a System ABEND may occur.

A list of the System ABENDs can be found in *MVS Message Library: System Codes*. User ABENDs can be found in the documentation describing a programming product, such as the *VS COBOL II: Application Programming Debugging* manual, or by examining the program causing the user ABEND. Figure 15.1 shows part of an MVS/XA job log after a System ABEND, a User ABEND, and a program exception. The job log shows System ABENDs as SYSTEM = *xxx* or ABEND = S*xxx* where *xxx* is the ABEND number; User ABENDs are shown as USER = *xxxx* or U*xxxx* where *xxxx* is the ABEND number; program exceptions are shown as SYSTEM = 0C*x* or ABEND = S0C*x* where *x* is the exception number. Note that the job log lists a program exception as a System ABEND.

All User ABENDs produced by COBOL II (not to be confused with other User ABENDs that may occur when a COBOL II program executes) have an accompanying error message [except for two User ABENDs (U1090 and U1091) that are produced by COBOL II only under CICS]. The COBOL II User ABENDs are between 1000 and 1999 and in the format U1*nnn*. The *nnn* in the ABEND number is used to locate message IGZ*nnn*I in the debugging manual, the manual in which the errors are explained.

15.3 PROGRAM EXCEPTIONS

One of the reasons that programmers have trouble understanding dumps is that they do not realize what they represent. I once tried to

```
10.14.17 JOB 1544   IEA995I  SYSTEM DUMP OUTPUT
                    ABEND CODE SYSTEM=806  TIME=10.14.16
                    ....
10.14.24 JOB 1544   IEF450I TSTJOB1 GO - ABEND=S806 U0000 REASON=00000000
```

(a)

```
11.09.04 JOB 1126   IEA995I  SYSTEM DUMP OUTPUT
                    ABEND CODE USER=1037    TIME=10.14.16
                    ....
11.09.11 JOB 1126   IEF450I TSTJOB2 GO - ABEND=S000 U1037 REASON=00000000
```

(b)

```
12.45.33 JOB 1971   IEA995I  SYSTEM DUMP OUTPUT
                    ABEND CODE SYSTEM=0C7  TIME=10.14.16
                    ....
12.45.40 JOB 1971   IEF450I TSTJOB3 GO - ABEND=S0C7 U0000 REASON=00000000
```

(c)

Figure 15.1 Part of a job log created when an 806 System ABEND (*a*), a 1037 User ABEND (*b*), and an 0C7 program exception (*c*) occurs.

explain to a colleague that many programmers do not know what an 0C1 program exception is. He quickly answered that most programmers do know, that it is a branch to a program that was not included in the link-edit. He had given a specific instance of when an 0C1 program exception can occur, not described what it was. His answer was similar to responding "DB2" to the question of "What is a database?"

15.3.1 Operation Exception (0C1)

An 0C1 program exception is an operation exception. It indicates that the CPU attempted to execute an instruction that was invalid for the hardware. On the IBM 370 hardware the operation code of a machine language instruction is 1 byte long (excluding a few privileged instructions that are 2 bytes long), allowing 256 different values. Less than 256 instructions exist, so not all of the possible values are valid. When a COBOL II program issues a static call (or when an assembly language program calls another program), the reference is through a V-type address constant that gets resolved at link-edit time. If the V-type constant is not resolved, it is set to zero. When the program then uses the V-type constant as an address to branch to, a branch to address zero in memory follows. This area in memory does not contain a valid operation code and an operation exception occurs.

A program branch using an uninitialized address (such as using the value in a register that had not been properly set) may cause an 0C1. Actually, it is to your advantage if an unexpected value at the target location of a bad branch does cause an operation exception. Otherwise, if the uninitialized address happens to point to executable code, you may end up executing a piece of code unexpectedly. This would be an extremely difficult problem to debug since it is conceivable that you might not even know a certain piece of code was executed. This is an important point to remember: When a program gets a program exception or ABENDs, you are probably lucky. Rather than forcing you to spend hours or days to find where a problem is occurring, the ABEND code can be used to reference the reason for the problem, or the Program Status Word (PSW) will point to the next sequential instruction following the instruction causing the program exception. The PSW is generally of little value when a System or User ABEND occurs since it merely points to the ABEND macro that cancelled the job step.

If an Assembly language program attempts to do I/O before a data set is opened, an 0C1 can occur. The address of the access method to perform the read or write is located in a control block (e.g., the DCB). This address is filled in when the data set is opened. If the data set is never opened, the address will contain a zero and an I/O operation will cause a branch to address zero in memory. This same problem can occur in a COBOL II program. A program may open a file, but the OPEN may fail. If a FILE STATUS clause was coded for the file, CO-BOL II will not ABEND the program. When the FILE STATUS clause is coded for a file, it becomes the responsibility of the program to determine whether or not processing is to continue after an error condition. In this case, if a program continues after a severe I/O error (such as a file failing to open), a READ or WRITE statement to the unopened file may cause an 0C1.

The 0C1 dumps that are usually the hardest to solve are the ones that occur because of a storage overlay. It is easy to find out why the 0C1 occurred but may not be easy to find why the storage overlay occurred. For instance, if 100 bytes in the middle of a program's object code were overlaid with a person's name and that area had been executing, you will probably get an 0C1. In this case you know to look where the person's name is moved and try to find where an invalid subscript or index may have been used. However, if a piece of code had been overlaid with 2 bytes of hexadecimal zeros, it would be a completely different matter. It may not be easy to determine where in the code the move of the bad data had been executed.

Be aware that overlays of data can exist in a program and may not become known until the program is updated. If code overlays an area that is not used in the rest of the program, the overlay will be unnoticed. If the program is then modified to use a field in the overlaid area, an ABEND may occur. The person maintaining the program may at first think that the new code has caused the generation of the invalid data rather than realizing a coding error that previously existed was producing the invalid data.

15.3.2 Privileged Operation (0C2) and Execute (0C3) Exceptions

An 0C2 program exception occurs when a program in the problem state (as opposed to supervisor state) attempts to execute a privileged instruction. Applications almost always run in the problem state. They are not allowed to issue privileged instructions (e.g., those that change the PSW, set the system clock, or modify storage keys). Since an uninitialized address may cause a branch to an area of memory which contains the value of a privileged instruction, a program in the problem state may attempt to issue a privileged instruction that was not coded in it (COBOL II never generates any privileged instructions in the object code). Attempts to READ or WRITE to unopened files may also get a privileged exception (these may also cause an 0C1, as discussed in the previous section).

An 0C3 is among the rarest of events on a 370 machine. It can only occur when a program issues an Execute (EX) instruction that has another Execute instruction as its target. I have never heard of an instance when one occurred in a COBOL program.

15.3.3 Protection Exception (0C4) and Addressing Exception (0C5)

One of the most common program exceptions is an 0C4. It occurs when a program attempts to store data in an area of memory (or fetch data from an area of memory for some instructions) that it is not permitted to use. The specific technical reasons for the interrupt can get complex (the hardware recognizes key-controlled protection when the access key is not equal to the storage key, low-address protection in the first 512 bytes of memory, and segment protection). Basically a protection exception indicates that although the storage requested for use exists (either in real or virtual storage, depending on the program executing), the hardware and operating system are not allowing the program to use it.

An 0C4 should not be confused with an 0C5, which is an addressing exception. An 0C5 addressing exception occurs when the address used by an instruction does not exist in the hardware configuration. An 0C5 was more common before virtual storage operating systems like

MVS. Programs used to run in real storage and, although addresses of up to 16 megabytes were valid in the hardware, most machines had a considerably smaller amount of memory. With virtual storage, a program usually has access to the maximum range of addresses allowed in a 370 instruction and 0C5s rarely occur. When invalid addresses are used, the address will usually exist but will not be valid for use by the problem program. This will cause an 0C4.

The most common reason for a COBOL II program to get an 0C4 is that a subscript or index exceeded its maximum value. However, there is a greater chance that parts of the program's data or code will be overlaid than that an 0C4 will occur. The 0C4 will only occur if the index or subscript has a positive or negative value large enough to exceed the boundaries of the program (for standard COBOL II programs), exceeds the size of the WORKING-STORAGE and TGT (for COBOL II CICS programs and COBOL II programs compiled with the RENT option), or exceeds the length of a GETMAINed area. In all of these cases the 0C4 may not occur if the area referenced happens by chance to fall into another program or another storage area within the job step.

An 0C4 can also occur when variable length data items are used in a COBOL II program. When the length of an OCCURS DEPENDING ON field is incorrect, data moved to this variable length field may exceed the maximum length given to it by the COBOL II compiler. This will either cause other fields to be overlaid or will cause an 0C4.

Another frequent cause of an 0C4 is when the USING clause in a CALL statement does not match the USING clause in the PROCEDURE DIVISION statement of the called program. This can cause the address of a data item to be missing or can cause a passed field in the calling program to mismatch its definition in the called program. In either case, the called program code may attempt to use an area not properly allocated to it and an 0C4 may ensue.

You should realize that when an 0C4 occurs, the instruction causing the protection exception may have already been partially executed. For example, if a Move Character Long (MVCL) instruction [used to move fields longer than the 256-byte limit of the Move Character (MVC) instruction] is executed, the protection exception may not occur until a multiple of 256 bytes had already been moved. This means that the registers pointing to the sending and receiving fields, as well as the length of the data to be moved, may not contain the values which they contained when the instruction began to execute.

15.3.4 Specification Exception (0C6)

An 0C6 program interrupt is a specification exception that occurs when certain machine language instructions are specified incorrectly for execution. Examples are a branch instruction attempting to branch to an odd numbered address, an odd numbered register specified in an instruction that requires an even numbered register, or an invalid floating-point register being used.

An 0C6 rarely occurs in COBOL II programs. With 360 hardware they occurred more frequently. Instructions like Load Halfword (LH) and Load (L) fullword required the operands to be respectively on halfword and fullword boundaries. When COMP fields were used and slack bytes were not properly defined, 0C6s sometimes occurred.

15.3.5 Decimal Data Exception (0C7)

The 0C7 is the most common of all of the program exceptions. It is a decimal data exception and occurs when data is in an invalid format for the instruction referencing it; specifically, the numeric digits are not in the range of 0 through 9, or the sign is not one of the valid values of A, B, C, D, E, or F. They most often occur when a program attempts to use a field that had not been initialized.

Although many 0C7s occur through oversights, some occur through lack of knowledge. Possible problems when moving numeric data are discussed in Sec. 9.1.2. Frequent situations that may cause decimal data exceptions are:

- Failure to initialize a field.

- A COMP-3 field is initialized at a group level rather than at the elementary field level. The data will therefore be in display numeric rather than in packed numeric format.

- A COMP-3 field is moved to the group level of a display numeric field. The data format is not converted and the numeric data not in display numeric format.

15.3.6 Program Exceptions 0C8 through 0CB

I will now briefly mention other program exceptions. An 0C8 is a fixed-point overflow exception, which occurs when a fixed-point signed binary arithmetic instruction or an instruction which shifts a signed number left, causes an overflow. An 0CA is a decimal overflow exception and is similar to an 0C8, except that an 0CA applies to decimal rather than binary numbers. It occurs when at least one nonzero digit is lost during the processing of a decimal instruction. Both of these exceptions may occur when you divide by a very small number or multiply by a very large number. When either a decimal overflow or a fixed-point overflow occurs, execution of the instruction that caused the problem is completed. Even though the program exception occurs, the result is correct except for the fact that the information that over-flowed is lost.

An 0C9 is a fixed-point divide exception which is caused when a divide by zero occurs in a binary arithmetic operation or when a Convert to Binary (CVB) instruction causes a result that exceeds the 32-bit register size. A decimal divide exception (0CB) occurs when a zero is used as the divisor in a decimal divide instruction or when the quotient is greater than the size of the receiving field. When the quotient is greater than the size of the receiving field, a COBOL II program will not get an 0CB. This is because the compiler can use temporary storage fields to perform the computation and then move the result to your receiving field. When this occurs, you may lose significant digits in the result.

When numbers with many significant digits (e.g., packed decimal fields with more than 15 digits) are processed under COBOL II, arithmetic calculations are performed in a COBOL II run-time library routine rather than being performed by the in-line object code. A program may pass numbers that would normally cause a divide by zero within the library routine. If a divide by zero actually occurred in the routine, it would be hard for a programmer to debug. Furthermore, you would have to determine if the error was caused by the numeric values you passed to it or by an actual bug in the routine. For these reasons, the library routines do not allow an 0CB to occur. They check to see if your code has requested a division by zero. If so, message IGZ061I is produced and a User ABEND of U1061 follows.

15.3.7   Program Exceptions 0CC through 0CF

Program exceptions 0CC through 0CF only apply to floating-point operations. They rarely occur in COBOL II programs. 0CC and 0CD are, respectively, exponent overflow and exponent underflow exceptions. An overflow exception occurs when a result of a numeric operation is so large that it cannot be accurately represented by the floating-point numbers allowed by the hardware (the characteristic is greater than 127); an underflow exception occurs when the result of a floating-point numeric operation is too small (the characteristic is less than zero).

A significance exception (0CE) occurs when an addition or subtraction results in a floating-point fraction of absolute zero. When a program executes a floating-point division by zero, an 0CF follows.

15.4   ANALYZING AN ABEND

The first step that is required to read a dump is to understand why the dump was produced. It is often needless to analyze the detailed data in a dump because the reason for the ABEND is quite explicit. For instance, if a program gets a User ABEND of 200, and it is clearly known through documentation that this error indicated a control card was missing from a file in the JCL, there is no reason to spend time analyzing the data in the dump. If the control card in question was present and the error still occurred, only then would it be necessary to investigate the dump.

Programmers must understand the differences between program exceptions, System ABENDs, and User ABENDs. Additionally, programmers must learn to properly use the IBM debugging reference manuals. Too often a programmer attempts to find the reason for a User ABEND by searching through *MVS Message Library: System Codes* (which only contains System ABENDs and program exceptions) or by searching through *MVS System Messages*. The popular expression, "I do not have to memorize it, I can look it up in the manual" is only true if you are looking in the proper manual. Experience has shown that many programmers do not understand the purpose of what should be the most commonly used manuals. Knowledge will make the difference between fumbling through a dump page after page and effectively analyzing the information in it.

15.4.1 Identifying Messages in a Job Log

It is important to know which part of the system placed an error message in the job log. The first three letters in an error message identifies the origin of the message. Figure 15.2 shows the most common error message prefixes that could be encountered by a COBOL II programmer. For example, you can tell that message IGZ061I is produced from a COBOL II run-time routine.

Error message prefix	Source of error message	Described in publication
DFH	CICS/VS	*CICS/VS Messages and Codes*
DFS	IMS/VS	*IMS/VS Messages and Codes*
DSN	DB2	*IBM DataBase 2 Messages and Codes*
ICE	Sort program	*OS/VS Sort Merge Programmers Guide*
IDA	VSAM	*MVS System Messages*
IDC	Access Method Services	*MVS System Messages*
IEA	MVS supervisor, I/O supervisor	*MVS System Messages*
IEC	Data management	*MVS System Messages*
IEF	Job scheduler	*MVS System Messages*
IEW	Linkage-editor and loader	*MVS System Messages*
IGZ	COBOL II run-time routine	*VS COBOL II Application Program Debugging*
IKF	VS COBOL run-time routine	*IBM OS/VS COBOL Compiler and Library Programmers Guide*
IOS	I/O supervisor	*MVS System Messages*
WER	SyncSort	*A Programmer's Guide to SyncSort*

Figure 15.2 Error message prefixes, the sources of the messages, and the publication in which the messages are described. Note that the exact publication titles may vary between different versions of the operating system (e.g., *MVS/XA System Messages*, *MVS/ESA System Messages*).

Epilogue

Where do all of the COBOL II differences leave us? I personally find many of the new changes fascinating and complex. Had I designed specifications for COBOL II, I certainly would have included more useful options than allowing code to be written in lowercase characters and allowing fields in which FILLER does not have to be coded. Regardless, I enjoy being a technician and will have fun with the new features and their idiosyncrasies. However, from the standpoint of the hype that claims that COBOL II will "improve programmer productivity, improve efficiency, and ease maintenance," I am not impressed. Complexity and additional features leave more for a programmer to understand, making it harder for a programmer to maintain code. There is now a greater possibility that a programmer will not be familiar with the subset of COBOL features that another programmer has decided to use. As always, judicious choices from the available coding options will produce more efficient, easily maintained code while, as always, injudicious choices will send the program in the opposite direction.

The compilation time of a program is certainly slower. The difference in speed is considerable enough that you can literally feel the difference in time when you do an online compile. What about the speed of program execution? IBM claims that programs will now run considerably faster. From the people I know who have done minimal studies in execution time comparisons, one company claims that the COBOL II programs run between 5 percent slower and 5 percent faster when compared with VS COBOL, while another company says that they run from slightly slower to about the same speed. My own experience has shown that while some programs run slightly faster, others will take more than 3 times as long to execute. Also, choosing a poor set of compiler options usually will have a more detrimental effect in COBOL II than it would have had in VS COBOL.

Regardless of whether or not COBOL II is easier to use and maintain, and more efficient, it is here to stay. IBM has created a product that companies will be converting to, whether we like it or not. What I cannot understand is why it takes a company like IBM three releases of a compiler to realize that it needs something as fundamental as compatible numeric processing so that programs can be easily migrated.

Element Differences
Between COBOL Versions

COBOL element	Features	Section references
ACCEPT MESSAGE-COUNT	A	1.2
ACCEPT DAY-OF-WEEK	G	1.8
ACTUAL KEY	A	1.2
ADD	K	3.1
ADD...TO...GIVING	B,C,H	7.19
ADDRESS OF	F	6.1.4
ALPHABET keyword in SPECIAL-NAMES	G	
ALPHABETIC class	E	7.2
ALPHABETIC-LOWER	G	7.2
ALPHABETIC-UPPER	G	7.2
ALTER	I	7.20.2
ASSIGN nonnumeric literal	H	
AUTHOR	I	7.20.3
CALL	K	3.1
CALL BY REFERENCE, BY CONTENT	F	2.5
CALL BY CONTENT with data items	G	2.5
CALL...ON EXCEPTION	G	7.5
CALL...ON OVERFLOW	E	7.5
CALL USING procedure name	A	2.5
CLOSE...REEL/UNIT, ...FOR REMOVAL, with single reel files	G	
COMMON	G	8.2.1
COMMUNICATION SECTION	A	1.2
Comparisons of fields with PICTURE P	E	
COMPUTE	K	3.1
CONTINUE	F	3.2
COPY, lowercase allowed	E	2.10
COPY, nested	F	2.10
CURRENCY SIGN IS clause can use letter L	H	
CURRENT-DATE	A	1.8
DATA DIVISION is optional	G	8.2
DATE-WRITTEN	I	7.20.3
DATE-COMPILED	I	7.20.3
DAY-OF-WEEK (see ACCEPT)		
De-editing	G	7.13
DBCS	F	3.7
DEBUG-ITEM	I	7.20.4
DELETE	K	3.1
DISABLE	A	1.2
DISPLAY enhancements	B	
DISPLAY...NO ADVANCING, with DBCS operands	G	1.7
DIVIDE	K	3.1
EBCDIC as an ALPHABET	G	
ENABLE	A	1.2
END PROGRAM	G	8.2

A—The element was available in VS COBOL but is eliminated in COBOL II.
B—The VS COBOL element was updated when implemented in Release 2.
C—The VS COBOL element was updated when implemented in Release 3.
D—The Release 2 element was updated when implemented under Release 3.
E—The Release 2 element may produce different results in execution when used under Release 3.

COBOL element	Features	Section references
ENTER	I	
ENVIRONMENT DIVISION is optional	G	8.2
EVALUATE	F,K	3.4, 3.1
EXAMINE	A	1.6
EXHIBIT	A	1.7
EXIT	C	7.6
EXIT PROGRAM not the only statement in a paragraph	H	7.7
EXIT PROGRAM state	E	7.8.1
Explicit Scope Terminators	F	3.1
EXTERNAL	G	8.1
FILE STATUS codes	B,E	2.1, 7.9
FILLER is optional	G	7.12
Floating-point	B	2.3
GENERATE	A	1.2
GLOBAL	G	8.2.2
GOBACK state	E	7.8.1
GREATER OR EQUAL, > =	G	7.17
Hexadecimal literals	H	7.16
IF	K	3.1
IF...OTHERWISE	A	3.4.1
Indexing and subscripting (seven levels)	H	7.10.1
INITIAL	G	8.3
INITIATE	A	1.2
INITIALIZE	F	3.3
INITIALIZE with multiple REPLACING	H	3.3.1
INSPECT enhancement	G	1.6
INSTALLATION	I	7.20.3
IS keyword is optional	G	7.2
KANJI	F	3.7.1
LABEL RECORDS is optional	H,I	7.20.1
LABEL RECORDS...TOTALING AREA	A	7.20.1
LENGTH OF	F	6.1.8
LESS OR EQUAL, < =	G	7.17
LINE-COUNTER	A	1.2
Lowercase letters in code	G	7.15
MERGE WITH multiple GIVING clauses	D	7.11
Mixed indexes and subscripting	H	7.10.1
MOVE (see De-editing, CURRENT-DATE, TIME-OF-DAY)		
MULTIPLY	K	3.1
Nested programs	G	8.2
NOMINAL KEY	A	1.2
Nonnumeric literals of 160 characters	H	7.16
NOT phrase (additional support)	G	7.23, 7.24
NOTE	A	1.9

F—The element is a new feature in Release 1 or 2 and still exists in Release 3.
G—The new element in Release 3 only functions under the NOCMPR2 option.
H—The new element in Release 3 will function even with the CMPR2 option.
I—Obsolete element to be removed from next ANSI standard.
J—Does not affect program execution in whichever compiler that allows element.
K—Element allows an explicit scope terminator in COBOL II.

COBOL element	Features	Section references
OBJECT COMPUTER, MEMORY-SIZE	I	
OBJECT COMPUTER, SEGMENT-LIMIT	A	2.11
OCCURS...DEPENDING ON execution	B,E	2.2, 7.3
OCCURS, seven levels	H	7.10.1
ON	A	1.5
ON EXCEPTION (see CALL)		
ON OVERFLOW (see CALL)		
ON SIZE ERROR	E	7.18
OPEN EXTEND for relative files	G	
OPEN, obsolete options	A	2
ORGANIZATION not required	G	7.21
PADDING CHARACTER	G,J	
PAGE-COUNTER	A	1.2
PERFORM	B,K	2.6, 3.1
PERFORM VARYING	E	7.8.2
PICTURE A and B	E	7.2
PICTURE continuation, ends with comma	H	
PROCEDURE DIVISION is optional	G	8.2
PROCESSING MODE	A,J	
PROGRAM COLLATING SEQUENCE	E	7.25
PROGRAM-ID (see COMMON and INITIAL)		
READ	K	3.1
READ...INTO	E	7.3, 7.4.2
READY TRACE	A	1.4, 4.7.3
RECEIVE	A	1.2
RECORD CONTAINS	E	7.4
RECORD DELIMITER	G,J	
RECORD IS VARYING	G	7.4
Reference modification	G	8.4
Relative subscripting	H	7.10.1
REMARKS	A	1.9
REPLACE	G	8.5
REPORT	A	1.2
REPORT SECTION	A	1.2
RERUN	I	7.20.4
RERUN, checkpoint on first record	A,I	7.20.4
RESERVE ALTERNATE AREA(S)	B	2
RESET TRACE	A	1.4
RETURN	K	3.1
RETURN...INTO	E	7.3, 7.4.2
REWRITE	K	3.1
SEARCH	B,K	1.3, 3.1

A—The element was available in VS COBOL but is eliminated in COBOL II.
B—The VS COBOL element was updated when implemented in Release 2.
C—The VS COBOL element was updated when implemented in Release 3.
D—The Release 2 element was updated when implemented under Release 3.
E—The Release 2 element may produce different results in execution when used under Release 3.

COBOL element	Features	Section references
SECURITY	I	7.20.3
SEEK	A,J	
SELECT OPTIONAL for all VSAM files	G	7.9
SEND	A	1.2
SET...ON/OFF	G	
SET pointer	F	6.1.3
SET...TO TRUE	E,F	3.5
SHIFT-IN	F	3.7
SHIFT-OUT	F	3.7
SIGN (multiple clauses in hierarchy)	H	
SORT with multiple GIVING clauses	G	7.11
SORT...WITH DUPLICATES	G	7.11
SORT-CONTROL	F	12.5.6
SORT-CORE-SIZE, SORT-FILE-SIZE, SORT-MESSAGE, and SORT-MODE-SIZE may be overridden by SORT-CONTROL file	B	12.5.6
SPECIAL NAMES	B	
STANDARD-2 as an ALPHABET	G	
START	K	3.1
START...USING	A	
STRING	K	3.1
STRING INTO a group	B,H	7.22
SUBTRACT	K	3.1
SYMBOLIC CHARACTERS	G	
TERMINATE	A	1.2
TIME-OF-DAY	A	1.8
TITLE	F	3.6
TRACK-AREA	A	1.2
TRACK-LIMIT	A	1.2
TRANSFORM	A	1.6
UNSTRING into numeric-edited field	A	2
UNSTRING	E,K	7.22, 3.1
UPSI switches	E	
USAGE BINARY	G	7.14
USAGE DISPLAY-1	F	3.7
USAGE PACKED-DECIMAL	G	7.14
USAGE POINTER	F	6.1.3
USE BEFORE REPORTING	A	1.2
VALUE IS NULL	F	6.1.6
VALUE with OCCURS	G	7.10.2
WHEN-COMPILED	B	2.12
WRITE	K	3.1
WRITE...AFTER POSITIONING	A	2

F—The element is a new feature in Release 1 or 2 and still exists in Release 3.
G—The new element in Release 3 only functions under the NOCMPR2 option.
H—The new element in Release 3 will function even with the CMPR2 option.
I—Obsolete element to be removed from next ANSI standard.
J—Does not affect program execution in whichever compiler that allows element.
K—Element allows an explicit scope terminator in COBOL II.

Compiler Options Differences Between COBOL Versions

COBOL option	Features	Section references
AWO/NOAWO	E	8.6.1
BATCH/NOBATCH	A	
BUF	C(BUFSIZE)	
BUFSIZE	B(BUF)	
CDECK/NOCDECK	A	
CLIST/NOCLIST	B(OFFSET)	4.1
CMPR2/NOCMPR2	E	7.1
COMPILE/NOCOMPILE	C(NOSYNTAX, NOCSYNTAX, NOSUPMAP)	12.2.1
COUNT/NOCOUNT	A	4, 4.7.5
CSYNTAX/NOCSYNTAX	B(NOCOMPILE(S))	
DATA(24)/DATA(31)	D	6.2.2
DBCS/NODBCS	E	8.6.5
DBCSXREF	E	
DMAP/NODMAP	B(MAP)	
ENDJOB/NOENDJOB	A	
EXIT/NOEXIT	E	
FASTSRT/NOFASTSRT	D	4.6
FDECK/NOFDECK	A	
FDUMP/NOFDUMP	C(SYMDUMP)	12.4.2
FLAG(x,y)/NOFLAG	C(FLAGW, FLAGE)	4.2
FLAGE	B(FLAG(S,y))	4.2
FLAGW	B(FLAG(W,y))	4.2
FLAGMIG/NOFLAGMIG	C(MIGR)	7.1
FLAGSAA/NOFLAGSAA	E	8.6.3
FLAGSTD/NOFLAGSTD	E	
FLOW/NOFLOW	A	4, 4.7.4
LANGLVL(1/2)	A	
LANGUAGE=(EN,UE)	E	8.6.4
LCOL1/LCOL2	A	
LINECOUNT(60)	C(LINECNT=60)	
LINECNT=60	B(LINECOUNT)	
LIST/NOLIST	C(PMAP)	4.1, 12.3.1
LOAD/NOLOAD	B(OBJECT)	
LSTONLY/LSTCOMP/NOLST	A	4
LVL=(A/B/C/D)/NOLVL	A	
L120/L132	A	
MAP/NOMAP	C(DMAP)	12.3.2
MIGR/NOMIGR	B(FLAGMIG)	7.1
NAME	B(NAME(ALIAS))	
NAME(ALIAS/NOALIAS)	C(NAME)	
NOTRUNC	F(TRUNC(BIN))	8.6.2, 11.1.2, 12.5.1

A—The option was available in VS COBOL but is eliminated in COBOL II.

B—The VS COBOL option was renamed when implemented in COBOL II. The COBOL II name is indicated in parentheses.

C—The COBOL II option was renamed from VS COBOL. The VS COBOL name is indicated in parentheses.

COBOL option	Features	Section references
NUM/NONUM	B(NUMBER)	
NUMBER/NONUMBER	C(NUM)	12.3.4
NUMPROC(PFD/NOPFD)	D,G(PFDSGN)	4.5, 9.5, 11.1.2
NUMPROC(MIG)	E	4.5, 9.5, 11.1.2
OBJECT/NOOBJECT	C(LOAD)	12.2.2
OFFSET/NOOFFSET	C(CLIST)	4.1, 12.3.1
OSDECK	A	4, 6.3.2
OUTDD(SYSOUT)	C(SYST)	12.5.6
PFDSGN/NOPFDSGN	F(NUMPROC(PFD))	4.5, 9.5, 11.1.2
PMAP/NOPMAP	B(LIST)	4.1
RENT/NORENT	D	4.4, 6.2.2
SEQ/NOSEQ	B(SEQUENCE)	
SEQUENCE/NOSEQUENCE	C(SEQ)	12.3.5
SIZE=(MAX)	C(SIZE)	12.2.3
SPACE(1/2/3)	C(SPACE1)	
SPACE1/SPACE2/SPACE3	B(SPACE(1))	
SSRANGE/NOSSRANGE	D	4.3
STATE/NOSTATE	A	4
SUPMAP/NOSUPMAP	B(NOCOMPILE)	
SXREF/NOSXREF	B(XREF)	4.1, 12.3.3
SYMDMP/NOSYMDMP	B(FDUMP)	
SYNTAX/NOSYNTAX	B(NOCOMPILE)	
SYSDUMP/NOSYSDUMP	A	
SYST/SYS*x*	B(OUTDD(SYSOUT))	
TERM/NOTERM	B(TERMINAL)	
TERMINAL/NOTERMINAL	C(TERM)	
TRUNC	F(TRUNC(STD))	8.6.2, 11.1.2, 12.5.1
TRUNC(STD)	C(TRUNC),G(TRUNC)	8.6.2, 11.1.2, 12.5.1
TRUNC(OPT)	G(NOTRUNC)	8.6.2, 11.1.2, 12.5.1
TRUNC(BIN)	C(NOTRUNC)	8.6.2, 11.1.2, 12.5.1
VBREF/NOVBREF	C(VBREF/VBSUM)	
VBSUM	B(VBREF)	
WORD/NOWORD	D	
XREF/NOXREF	A,C(SXREF)	4.1, 12.3.3

D—The option is a new feature in Release 1 or 2 and still exists in Release 3.

E—The option is a new feature in Release 3.

F—The COBOL Release 2 option was renamed when implemented in Release 3. The COBOL II Release 3 name is indicated in parentheses.

G—The COBOL II Release 3 option was renamed from COBOL II Release 2. The COBOL II Release 2 name is indicated in parentheses.

Mutually Exclusive COBOL II
Compiler Options

Option specified	Options normally ignored	Options normally forced on
CMPR2	DBCS	NODBCS
	FLAGSAA	NOFLAGSAA
	FLAGSTD	NOFLAGSTD
DBCS	FLAGMIG	NOFLAGMIG
DYNAM	NORES	RES
FLAGSAA	FLAGMIG	NOFLAGMIG
FLAGSTD	DBCS	NODBCS
	FLAGMIG	NOFLAGMIG
	FLAGSAA	NOFLAGSAA
NOCMPR2	FLAGMIG	NOFLAGMIG
OFFSET	LIST	NOLIST
RENT	NORES	RES
TEST	FDUMP	NOFDUMP
	NOOBJECT	OBJECT
	NORES	RES
	OPTIMIZE	NOOPTIMIZE
WORD	FLAGSTD	NOFLAGSTD

Index

About the Author

Harvey Bookman's introduction to computers was in 1966 on the Monroebot XI, which he learned to code in machine language. This 2K machine with typewriter input and a paper tape punch for output needed over an hour to sort 200 numbers.

He began his professional career in computers using COBOL in the early 1970s. He has been an applications programmer, a technical representative supporting VM applications programmers, a software programmer coding PTFs for INTERCOMM (a competitive product to CICS), and he was headquarters manager for INTERCOMM worldwide technical support. Bookman has since done technical consulting and has designed and taught courses including "COBOL Efficient Coding Techniques" and "COBOL II for COBOL Programmers."

Bookman has had many technical articles published. He is a regular contributor to "Mainframe Journal" and has written for "Datamation," "Information Week," "Data Training," "Contingency Journal," and "Personnel Administrator." His articles include "COBOL II: Its Differences and Idiosyncrasies," "Why COBOL Efficiency Still Makes Sense," "COBOL Compiler Options: Understanding Your Choices," "What Programmers Don't Know (and Why They Don't Know It)," and "What You Should Know About the TGT."

Bookman currently programs on IBM mainframes and PCs. His expertise is in COBOL and Assembler language on both the 370 mainframe and the IBM PC. He has worked on machines where saving a few instructions or a few bytes of storage would make the difference between being able to execute a program or not. Having worked a great deal with software for more than 20 years, Bookman's insights into programming should be found quite interesting.

In 1979 Bookman formed Bookman Consulting, Inc. After forming the firm, he realized how difficult it was to find competent programmers to hire. He saw the need for a tool to verify potential employees' programming comprehension, for screening consultants, and for determining areas for improvement within a company's current data processing staff. Using expert system technology, he created the TECKCHEK programmer evaluator.

Bookman designed TECKCHEK and wrote all of the code in PC macro assembler language. This included designing the adaptive questioning algorithm, a complex marking program that weighs each response given, and the security routines (security being one of his specialty areas) to protect the questions from unauthorized individuals. He also wrote the TECKCHEK communications program, which uses a Hayes modem to transmit test results to the Bookman Marking Center.

TECKCHEK contains a series of tests that run on an IBM PC and are each administered individually. They are proficiency tests, using actual computer code, that measure requisite knowledge, comprehension of programming applications, depth of practical experience, and technical insight as well as determining categories of expertise and weakness within each subject. Tests exist for IBM's VS COBOL, COBOL II, DB2, SQL/DS, IMS, CICS, VSAM, JCL, 370 Assembler, PL/I, C, PC-DOS, PC Macro Assembler, and Computer Associates' IDMS. Bookman wrote the majority of questions for the COBOL, COBOL II, CICS, 370 Assembler, PC-DOS, and PC Macro Assembler tests. He edits all tests for accuracy, clarity, and consistency. (See the following page for details on how to receive more information about TECKCHEK.)

TECKCHEK™
THE REAL TEST

Have you ever been dissatisfied after a technical interview because you were not able to demonstrate your full technical ability? Have you ever wished for a more objective evaluation of your programming skills? With TECKCHEK, management can discover the full range of what a programmer actually knows.

TECKCHEK is an objective, online technical knowledge checker composed of an expert system driver and a wide array of proficiency tests. Each test is administered individually in approximately an hour. The tests use actual computer code to measure requisite knowledge, comprehension of programming applications, depth of experience, and technical insight as well as determining categories of expertise and weakness within each subject. TECKCHEK may be used for verifying a potential employee's programming comprehension and for screening consultants.

TECKCHEK is also a powerful training tool. It can be used to match programming skills to technical needs and to determine areas for improvement within the current data processing staff. If a training department administers TECKCHEK before and after a course, an immediate objective evaluation of the course is available for analysis. Future technical screenings will also help to chart a programmer's technical progress.

No two applicants ever see the same test. Each Self-Adjusting Response (SAR) leads the test taker to either a more difficult or an easier question depending on the correctness or the complexity of the previous answers. The expert system driver positions the test taker at that level of expertise at which he or she is most competent. A person with little knowledge will not be confronted with or confounded by questions of increasing difficulty, nor will a skilled individual be given the same battery of questions that could be found on an elementary test.

FOR MORE INFORMATION WRITE TO:

Bookman Consulting, Inc.
67 Wall Street
Suite 2411
New York, NY 10005

Please include the following:

Operating System
Number of Programmers in Company
Intended uses: Hiring, Screening Consultants, or Training
Applicable Tests: IBM COBOL, COBOL II, DB2, SQL/DS, IMS, IDMS, CICS, VSAM, JCL, 370 Assembler, PL/I, C, PC-DOS, PC Macro Assembler

OR CALL:

212 819-1955
718 435-5395